From
through <u>HIM</u> and
to <u>HIM</u>!

*Inspiration for Every
Day of the Year*

Rhode Jean-Aleger

Unless otherwise noted, all Scripture references are from the *New Revised Standard Version Bible*, copyright © 1989, Division of Christian Education of the National Council of the Churches of Christ in the United States of America. References marked NABRE are from the *New American Bible,* revised edition © 2010, 1991, 1986, 1970 Confraternity of Christian Doctrine, Inc., Washington, DC. References marked ESV are from the *The Holy Bible, English Standard Version*, copyright © 2001 by Crossway Bibles, a publishing ministry of Good News Publishers. References marked RSV are from The Revised Standard Version of the Bible, copyright © 1946, 1952, 1971, 1973 by the Division of Christian Education of the National Council of the Churches of Christ in the U.S.A. References marked NIV are from *The Holy Bible, New International Version*, copyright © 1973, 1978, 1984, 2011 by Biblica, Colorado Springs, Colorado. References marked NRSVUE are from the *New Revised Standard Version, Updated Edition*. Copyright © 2021 National Council of Churches of Christ in the United States of America. References marked NLT are from *The Holy Bible, New Living Translation*, copyright © 1996, 2004, 2007 by Tyndale House Foundation. Used by permission of Tyndale House Publishers, Inc., Carol Stream, Illinois. References marked NAB are from The New American Bible, copyright © 1970 by The Confraternity of Christian Doctrine, Washington, D.C. References marked ERV are from Easy-to-Read Version, copyright © 2006 by Bible League International. All rights reserved. Used by permission.

Published by:

McDougal & Associates
18896 Greenwell Springs Road
Greenwell Springs, LA 70739
www,ThePublishedWord.com

McDougal & Associates is dedicated to spreading the Gospel of the Lord Jesus Christ to as many people as possible in the shortest time possible.

ISBN: 978-1-950398-75-1

Printed on demand in the U.S., the U.K., Australia, and the UAE
For Worldwide Distribution

DEDICATION

To my mother, **Rhode Josette Jean,** and my late father, **Lucien Jean**, who passed the Christian faith on to me. This was the greatest gift I could have received from them.

Acknowledgments

First, I give thanks to my **God** for inspiring me to write this devotional book.

I am deeply grateful to my husband, **Vorbes**, who has supported me in all my ministries and through the production of this book. He provided the perfect setting to permit me to complete the work.

I thank my children, **Nathan, Neil, and Niah,** for their loving support, and my mom and sister, **Rhodeline,** for their prayers.

I express heartfelt and sincere gratitude to my friend, **Victoria Kutch,** who edited and commented on this book twice. Her contribution is beyond measure.

I also sincerely thank all those who have taken the time to read and comment on part or on the entire manuscript.

Lastly, thank you to the many people who have helped and encouraged me, especially my **Jax Prayer Club** and **Marian Servant Family**. Their teachings have helped me grow spiritually.

I thank God for all of you as I remember you in my prayers (see Philippians 1:3-6).

For FROM HIM AND THROUGH HIM AND TO HIM are all things. To him be the glory forever. Amen.
— Romans 11:36, NRSVUE

INTRODUCTION

"From Him and through Him and to Him" has become one of my life mottos, reminding me that everything comes from God and all must return to Him. Hence, I offer this book for the greater glory of God, the Creator of all things.

"Every good and perfect gift is from above" (James 1:17, NIV). This book has truly been a gift and a surprise from God. It seems like yesterday, but it was July 2015 when I started writing weekly spiritual thoughts (not reflections) to share with my family and friends. Although my father was a writer, I had no intention of following in his footsteps. However, God had a plan for me to turn this work into a daily devotional book and the Jax Prayer Club website. My story reminds me of the miracle at Cana, where the Lord turned water into wine (see John 2:1-11).

I sent my weekly thoughts to family and friends, some of whom suggested that I should turn this work into a book or website. I had never even considered that, but I now realize their words were a gentle nudge from the Lord. They continued to encourage me to write a daily devotional. As I was receiving greater clarity from the Lord through the Scriptures and at mass, I slowly rewrote my old thoughts, turning them into reflections.

Then God sent an extraordinary gift, Victoria Kutch, into my life through some mutual friends. Victoria has been a blessing every step of the way. She has been reviewing, commenting, and editing this entire work. God is faithful. He continues to send me help and inspire me.

The book publishing process has been tedious, and I've often wanted to skip some stages. Through it, though, God has been at work developing and transforming me. I've learned to trust Him more deeply and to allow His purpose to unfold with uncharacteristic patience.

I confidently write this to encourage you. God, who begins a good work within you, will bring it to completion (see Philippians 1:6). We must not be discouraged when we undertake work for God's glory. If you do not see immediate results, press on. God's work is never in vain. Even if you don't benefit directly from your good work, future generations may reap the fruits of your labor through the many blessings God will bestow on them.

To my readers, thank you for choosing this book. I pray that you find hope, joy, peace, and healing in this devotional. I hope that you receive many blessings and grace from the Lord. God cannot be outdone in generosity. If we sincerely ask, we will receive.

Please visit my website at www.jaxprayerclub.com or email me at jaxprayerclub@gmail.com.

May God bless you all!

Rhode Jean-Aleger
Jacksonville, Florida

Everlasting Promises!

Blessed be the Lord, the God of Israel, for he has visited and brought redemption to his people. Luke 1:68, NABRE

*You can read the full scripture at Luke 1:68-79.

In Luke 1:68-79, Zechariah praised God for His faithfulness in keeping His promises, for the gift of salvation, and for His mercy and peace. We live in a dark and broken world. Although the faces of terror, tragedy, death, illness, and disappointment are among us daily, the promises that God made long ago to our ancestors still apply today. God sent us a Savior, Jesus, who continues *"to shine on those who sit in darkness and death's shadow, to guide our feet into the path of peace"* (Luke 1:79, NABRE).

Jesus came to replace the darkness with light, transform and restore us, and make us perfect in God's sight. He has never failed to deliver what He promised. Therefore, let us start this New Year by thanking the Lord for His faithfulness, looking forward with hope, and trusting in His mercy for the days ahead. Let us pray to renew ourselves in the Lord, accept His guiding light, and surrender our all to Him because He is faithful. He will strengthen and protect us from the evil one (see 2 Thessalonians 3:3). Despite the terrors of life, we will lift our hands to Heaven to praise and thank the Lord. Blessed be the Lord, the God of Israel!

Action/Thought for Today: Pray using the praises of Zechariah in Luke 1:68-79.

Prayer: Lord Jesus, thank You for Your promises of salvation, deliverance, and peace. Jesus, we hope and trust in You. It is in Your name we pray. Amen!

BLESSING FOR LIFE'S JOURNEY!

The LORD bless you and keep you! The LORD let his face shine upon you, and be gracious to you! The LORD look upon you kindly and give you peace! So shall they invoke my name upon the Israelites, and I will bless them. Numbers 6:24-27, NABRE

We pray for blessings, and we need blessings, from God and others. Our life is incomplete without God's gift and favor. The blessing in Numbers 6:22-27 is for us too, for our families, friends, and the whole world. It implies that the Lord will keep us, be gracious and kind to us, smile on us, and give us peace. We need this in our life journey in this broken world. God has put this blessing at our disposal. So, all we have to do is claim it. He did not attach any condition to it. When we invoke His name, He blesses us (see Numbers 6:27).

The New Year allows us to renew ourselves in the Lord, claim His blessing and, in return, speak the same blessing over others. We ought to engrave this blessing in our hearts and say it daily, especially when discouraged, stuck, or lacking enthusiasm in life. As Christ's beloved children, we should not despair, but call on His name for His grace and blessing. To all of you reading this message today, I pray that God richly blesses you, and *"may he grant you your heart's desire and fulfill all your plans!"* (Psalm 20:4, ESV).

Action/Thought for Today: Speak words of blessing over your family and friends!

Prayer: Lord Jesus, thank You for Your everlasting love, mercy, and blessings. Give us the grace to always bless Your name and be a blessing to others. It is in Your name we pray. Amen!

January 3

New Year's Resolution!

So whoever is in Christ is a new creation: the old things have passed away; behold, new things have come.

2 Corinthians 5:17, NABRE

What is it about the New Year that prompts us to make changes in our lives? The New Year encourages us to re-evaluate life, reject the old ways, and adopt some new practices—perhaps making changes in our spiritual, social-economic, and family life. It is also common to attempt better lifestyle choices, such as rest, relaxation, exercise, and eating healthy food.

Many feel the need to change unhealthy or unproductive behaviors, but hold on to the old ways, and won't let go of their past failures, sins, habits, and shortcomings. Others may remain in the cycle of regret, unforgiveness, bitterness, revenge, etc., and keep living in the misery of their unfortunate situations, without attempting to surrender it all to God. Don't let the devil or your mindset hold you captive in your old ways. Submit to the Lord, resist the devil, and he will flee from you (see James 4:7).

As we renew ourselves in the Lord, let us give Him full permission to transform every area in our lives to His likeness. Let us pray for the grace and courage to adopt healthy new behaviors and live according to God's ways. If we commit to the Lord whatever we do, He will establish our plans (see Proverbs 16:3).

Thought/Action for Today: What changes do you want to make in the new year? Pray for the grace to do it.

Prayer: Lord Jesus, we commit ourselves and plans to You. Please help us with our New Year's resolutions. Jesus, we trust in You! It is in your name we pray. Amen!

SPIRITUAL RESOLUTION!

You were taught to put away your former way of life, your old self, corrupt and deluded by its lusts, and to be renewed in the spirit of your minds, and to clothe yourselves with the new self, created according to the likeness of God in true righteousness and holiness.

Ephesians 4:22-24

Having looked into the new year with great expectation, I planned some new spiritual resolutions. After a while, however, I forgot about my decision. I realized that my resolutions have sometimes not worked because I have not asked the Lord for His help. He said, *"Ask, and it will be given to you"* (Matthew 7:7, RSV). Furthermore, any resolution requires sacrifice and subtracting or adding something in life. Our human nature prefers to stay in our comfort zone, resist change, or give up if something seems difficult or impossible. How many of us plan to pray more, read the Scriptures, or do other spiritual reading in the New Year? Yet we stop because it requires extra effort to spend quality time with the Lord. Therefore, prayer is vital when making life changes.

Spiritual life requires that our actions, behaviors, and attitudes be focused on the Lord. We cannot choose to pray just when we feel like it or want something from God. Spiritual renewal involves taking time to pray, reading the Holy Scriptures, and asking the Lord to clothe us in righteousness, holiness, and with the strength and courage to persevere.

Action/Thought for Today: What spiritual resolution will you make in the New Year?

Prayer: O Lord, create a pure heart, and renew Your Spirit in me (see Psalm 51:10). I ask for the grace to get rid of my old self. Clothe me according to Your likeness. In Jesus' name I pray. Amen!

YOUR PRAYERS MATTER!

If my people, who are called by my name, will humble themselves and pray and seek my face and turn from their wicked ways, then I will hear from heaven, and I will forgive their sin and will heal their land. 2 Chronicles 7:14, NIV

Prayer matters in the new year, and every day, for prayer changes things. We live in a messy and challenging world; therefore, your urgent prayer is needed. The world needs your prayers to bring about the change God so desires for us. God has heard every cry of His people throughout history. From slavery in Egypt years ago to today's chaotic world, God will rescue us, for *"he has shown the mercy promised to our ancestors and has remembered his holy covenant"* (Luke 1:72).

Although God is the Miracle Worker, He needs you to intercede for the world and be part of his work of salvation. As we pray for the world, the Lord transforms us to make a difference and create a ripple effect. Our prayer can move God's hands to bring positive changes in our nation and the world. God is waiting for us to ask; therefore, let us act in prayer, for nothing is impossible for God.

Let us unite our voices in humble prayer for the world. May the Lord change hearts of stone to flesh, hatred to love, sorrow to joy, anxiety to peace, bitterness to acceptance, mercilessness to forgiveness, lies to truth, illness to health, and despair to hope. May the good and faithful Lord spare this world from all the devil's schemes. May the Lord have mercy on us and the whole world.

Action/Thought for Today: Pray for
the world today and every day.

Prayer: Lord Jesus, thank You for hearing our cry
for the world. It is in Your name we pray. Amen!

LOOKING FORWARD WITH HOPE!

Behold, God's dwelling is with the human race. He will dwell with them, and they will be his peoples, and God himself will always be with them. He will wipe every tear from their eyes, and there shall be no more death or mourning, wailing or pain, for the old order has passed away. The one who sat on the throne said, "Behold, I make all things new." Revelation 21:3-5, NABRE

Are you losing hope? Is anxiety taking over your life? Life is challenging, and many agree that, in recent years, the daily stress in our lives has increased. Jesus is aware of our suffering and pain. He knows our worries and fears. Do not be tempted to get discouraged or lose hope. As you look back at the past year, let the past be in the past. Focus on Jesus for a brighter tomorrow and expect Him to take care of you. He is able, and He is willing!

Even if your situation does not improve or change, know that Jesus is with you and forever present in your life. Jesus has the final word, and His promise for eternal life has never changed.

Amid our struggles, let us hold on to Jesus, as we remember that His light shines in the darkness, and He has overcome the darkness through His resurrection (see John 1:1-18).

One day, He will wipe every tear from our eyes and make all things new; therefore, let us resolve to look forward with the hope of Christ in the New Year. For *"those who hope in the LORD will renew their strength. They will soar on wings like eagles; they will run and not grow weary; they will walk and not be faint"* (Isaiah 40:31, NIV).

Action/Thought for Today: Pray for an increase in the virtue of hope in your life.

Prayer: Lord Jesus, be my Strength, Hope, and Light in this new year and forever. It is in Your name we pray. Amen!

BE RENEWED!

Remember not the events of the past, the things of long ago consider not; see I am doing something new! Now it springs forth, do you not perceive it? In the wilderness I make a way, in the wasteland, rivers. Isaiah 43:18-19, NABRE

Are you sick and tired of your sins? If you are, that's good, because the Lord is touching your heart to change your behavior. We all struggle with sins and bad habits. To some extent, we have the desire to do good, and we all can relate to this statement by the apostle Paul, *"I do not do the good I want, but the evil I do not want to do—this I keep on doing"* (Romans 7:19, NIV). Therefore, with God's grace and mercy, we must strive to firmly resolve to deny ourselves the things that prompt us to sin.

In this new year, let us renew ourselves in the Lord and strongly ask Him to deliver us from the habits and sins that keep us captive. Let us pray to continually acknowledge our sins, repent, and start anew every time we sin. As St. Basil put it, "There is still time for endurance, time for patience, time for healing, time for change. Have you slipped? Rise up. Have you sinned? Cease. Do not stand among sinners but leap aside."[1]

Action/Thought for Today: Let us examine ourselves in prayer. Take a particular sin in your life, and pray for the courage to give it up. Then, tackle the next sin. One by one, continue to do so daily, and the good Lord will help us overcome all sins.

Prayer: Lord Jesus, we can do all things through You. Give us the grace to examine ourselves and break free from past, repeated and all sins. Please help us abide in You. It is in Your name we pray. Amen!

JANUARY 8

OUR FATHER!

Our Father in heaven, hallowed be your name, your kingdom come, your will be done, on earth as it is in heaven. Give us today our daily bread. And forgive us our debts, as we also have forgiven our debtors. And lead us not into temptation, but deliver us from the evil one.   Matthew 6:9-13, NIV

What sustains you in your daily life? I hope your answer is prayer. Life is complicated, so God gave us prayer to communicate our needs to Him. Many can attest that our days are better when we pray. Even when things go wrong, we can move on with God's grace.

In my teenage to young adult years, I went through the motions of praying and attending church. It was not until I had my own family and a career that I realized that life is more challenging than expected, and cannot go through it alone. I need God in order to survive. Prayer became my sustenance. One who does not pray cannot fight life's battles.

Some say, "I don't know how to pray." If we can talk with people, we can talk with God. God is not looking for extravagant words but for a heartfelt and personal conversation between Him and His beloved daughters and sons. For instance, He gave His disciples a very simple prayer, beginning with *"Our Father."*

We can learn different ways of praying from books or other people. However, it is only with consistency and faithfulness that we can truly pray, and the words from the Spirit of God will flow within us, as *"the Spirit himself intercedes for us"* (Romans 8:26, NIV).

Action/Thought for Today: Let us make it
a habit to set time for daily prayer.

Prayer: Lord Jesus, teach us how to pray, as You taught the disciples the Lord's prayer. In your name we pray. Amen!

PRAYER IS GOD'S GIFT!

If you believe, you will receive whatever you ask for in prayer.
Matthew 21:22, NIV

Prayer is God's gift. "Prayer is the raising of one's mind and heart to God or the requesting of good things from God." "But when we pray, do we speak from the height of our pride and will, or 'out of the depths' of a humble and contrite heart? He who humbles himself will be exalted; humility is the foundation of prayer. Only when we humbly acknowledge that 'we do not know how to pray as we ought' are we ready to receive freely the gift of prayer."[2]

It is of utmost importance that we spend time with the Lord in humble prayer. Do not neglect your prayer time. Do not rush your prayer. If possible, plan your prayer time for the next day. Prepare your breakfast and outfit, etc., and those of your family in advance to allocate enough time to be with the Lord in the morning. As you deepen your prayer life, you will grow closer to Christ and receive many graces and spiritual gifts. Be sure to share with others the instructions and thoughts given to you in prayer. By doing so, you are helping them to pray better and love God more.

Action/Thoughts for Today: Are you in the habit of neglecting prayer time? How can you improve your prayer life? Ask the Lord for His help.

Prayer: Lord Jesus, thank You for the gift of prayer. We pray for those who do not pray. Open their hearts to meet You in prayer. In Your name we pray. Amen!

THE ESSENCE OF LIFE!

I pray that the eyes of your heart may be enlightened in order that you may know the hope to which he has called you, the riches of his glorious inheritance in his holy people. Ephesians 1:18, NIV

Prayer is the essence of life. It is the magnifying glass that brings our lives into spiritual focus. It helps us see ourselves more clearly—both our strengths and shortcomings. Through prayer, God reveals His glory and works, and we experience His beauty and majesty. It is also through prayer that our daily path is illuminated, and we can see God's actions in our lives.

Life makes more sense when we pray. Therefore, our prayer life is of the utmost importance. It is where we meet God, the Source of our lives. Although we may not have the right words to pray and worship the Lord, our senses can connect us deeply to Him. Our ears hear the whisper of His gentle voice, saying, "My child, I love you." Our eyes contemplate and reflect on the beauty of His works. Our noses smell the fragrance of God through His works in creation. Our hands raise to Heaven in praise and thanksgiving and to touch the wounds of others. We taste the goodness and sweetness of the Lord in all.

Let us rejoice in prayer! Let it be our daily priority, alive in our hearts.

Action/Thought for Today: Are you rejoicing in prayer?

Prayer: Lord Jesus, allow us to meet You more deeply in prayer. In Your name I pray. Amen!

PRAISE FOR LIVING WATER!

You would have asked him, and he would have given you living water.   John 4:10, RSV

Are you thirsty for God's living water? Lord, my thirst for You is great; I am continuously searching for You. How can my soul find rest unless You fill me with the water of Your salvation? *"Then I will go to the altar of God, to God, my joy and my delight"* (Psalm 43:4, NIV), to satisfy my thirst.

Lord, accept our prayers and allow us to come to the fountain of Your living water. Through the living water, cleanse us from our sins, wash away our iniquities, and draw us to the Father's heart. Lord, we immerse ourselves in the fountain of Your mercy and grace. Fill our spiritual cups beyond measure. Help us experience peace in our daily lives, grow spiritually, receive guidance from You, find help in time of need, and be filled with Your Holy Spirit. O, how marvelous you are, for giving us *"a spring of water welling up to eternal life"* (John 4:14, RSV)! My Lord, my God, from the depth of my heart, I declare Your majesty and goodness, and I praise Your holy name for giving us living water.

Action/Thought for Today: Let us sing a song of praise to the Lord for giving us His living water.

Prayer: Lord Jesus, we do not always have the right words to praise You. Teach us how to adore, glorify, and worship You. In your name I pray. Amen!

MY MEDITATING PRAYER!

Let the words of my mouth be acceptable, the thoughts of my heart before you, Lord, my rock and my redeemer.

Psalm 19:15, NABRE

As I sit with the Lord in the stillness, He blesses me with a meditating prayer. He guides me to reflect on what should be essential in my life. I hope you are as blessed by this prayer as I am:

Father, I do not ask for money, riches, honor, or recognition in this world. In Your goodness and mercy, grant me:

- A heart that loves You and is dedicated to You only.
- A mind fixed on You alone.
- A soul and spirit abiding in You only.
- Hands that praise and work for You only.
- Feet that run to You only.

Father, I am not perfect; permit my works to be perfected by You. I am not holy; may Your holiness shine through me. Please help me to know, love, and serve You as I should. *"I will bless You as long as I live, and in Your name, I will lift up my hands"* (Psalm 63:4, NIV).

Action/Thought for Today: Open your heart wider so that the Lord can pray within you. Ask Him to help you.

Prayer: Thank You, Lord Jesus, for blessing me with Your Spirit-filled words. I praise and adore You. It is in your name I pray. Amen!

JESUS ALWAYS PRAYED!

The report about him spread all the more, and great crowds assembled to listen to him and to be cured of their ailments, but he would withdraw to deserted places to pray. Luke 5:15-16, NABRE

In the busyness of our personal or ministry life, sometimes we may forget to pray and call on the Lord for guidance and direction. Jesus, the Son of God, always prayed before ministering to others and before every important decision. The Bible gives us many examples of Jesus praying:

- Before feeding the five thousand, He thanked His Father (see Matthew 14:19, Mark 6:41, and Luke 9:16).
- In the Garden of Gethsemane, before His passion, He said to His disciples, *"Sit here, while I go over there and pray"* (Matthew 26:36, RSV).
- Before He broke bread with His disciples, He prayed (see Luke 24:30).
- Before healing the sick, He prayed (see Mark 7:34-35).
- Before choosing His disciples, He prayed (see Luke 6:12-13).
- As He hung on the cross, He prayed: *"Father, forgive them; for they know not what they do"* (Luke 23:34, RSV).
- As He was dying, He prayed: *"Father, into your hands, I commit my spirit"* (Luke 23:46, RSV).

Jesus taught us the importance of prayer. We must remember to pray so that God can refill us with His power and grace, strengthen us in His works, and renew us spiritually.

Action/Thought for Today: Ask the Lord for the grace to pray in all circumstances.

Prayer: Lord Jesus, help us to make time to pray and praise You without ceasing. In Your name we pray. Amen!

LIVE IN HIS NAME!

He indeed died for all, so that those who live might no longer live for themselves but for him who for their sake died and was raised. 2 Corinthians 5:15, NABRE

Many think that prayer only consists of reading the Bible, saying a few vocal prayers of petition or thanksgiving, and meditating on God's words. Prayer is also when we:

- Let God live in us.
- Have faith in His name.
- Hope in His name.
- Love in His name.
- Make disciples in His name.
- Minister to others in His name.
- Serve in His name.
- Suffer in His name.
- Trust in His name.
- Work in His name.

We are not separated by time and place from the Lord. He is always with us. If we do all things in His name, we are praying without ceasing. This is a prayer of the heart, more profound than words can express. When we do all in His name, our lives become a prayer of adoration, praise, and thanksgiving. As we do all in His name, we recognize that God is our Creator, and we are His creatures. Therefore, let Christ live in us, as He died for us.

Action/Thought for Today: How can you do all in God's name?

Prayer: Lord Jesus, help me live my life for You. Teach me to do all things in Your name. I want to live for You, my Lord and my God! In Your name I pray. Amen!

IN JESUS' NAME, I PRAY!

The name of the LORD is a strong tower; the righteous man runs into it and is safe. Proverbs 18:10, ESV

Do you know the power in the name of Jesus? When you have a problem, concern, or exciting news, whom do you call first? I tend to call my family, when, in reality, I should be calling on the name of the Lord first. For the Lord said: *"Because he knows my name, I will set him on high. He will call upon me, and I will answer, I will be with him in distress, I will deliver him and give him honor"* (Psalm 91:15, NABRE). In everything, call upon the name of the Lord, and He will rescue and deliver you. The name of Jesus is a source of love, peace, joy, strength, deliverance, mercy, healing, and many more graces.

The Lord is not confined to place or time; He is near to all those who call His holy name. In John 14:13-14 (ESV), Jesus promised us, *"Whatever you ask in my name, this I will do, that the Father may be glorified in the Son. If you ask me anything in my name, I will do it."* Therefore, let us be bold and call on the name of Jesus with confidence for our every need. Jesus assures us that He will save those who call on Him: *"There is salvation in no one else, for there is no other name under heaven given among mortals by which we must be saved"* (Acts 4:12).

Action/Thought for Today: If you hear someone call the name of Jesus in vain, take a minute to bless His name and ask the Lord to forgive that person.

Prayer: Lord, so often I do not recognize the power of Your name. I go through trials without calling You, when all I need to say is, "Jesus." Lord Jesus, give me the grace to call You in everything and for everything, for You are my God. In Your precious name I pray. Amen!

January 16

Why Worry About Tomorrow?

Therefore do not worry about tomorrow, for tomorrow will worry about itself. Each day has enough trouble of its own.

Matthew 6:34, NIV

Financial concerns and instability can take a toll on our lives. If you are anxious about your financial situation, bring this problem to the Lord. God knows what you need, but He wants you to come to Him for help. He said, *"Ask, and it will be given"* (Matthew 7:7). Therefore, go to God in prayer, trust in Him, and He will bless you beyond measure.

In return for God's blessings in your life, try to be a blessing to someone else. The Lord said: *"Give, and it will be given to you. A good measure, pressed down, shaken together, and running over will be put into your lap; for the measure you give will be measured you get back"* (Luke 6:38). Never worry when you invest in others, give freely and wholeheartedly for you are serving God in His people. The Lord reminded us, *"Whatever you did for one of the least of these brothers and sisters of mine, you did it for me"* (Matthew 25:40, NIV).

Action/Thought for Today: Try to be a blessing to someone today.

Prayer: Lord, thank You for being my All-in-All. Thank You for being a good Father and for providing for me. Lord, please show me those I must help with the gifts You have given me. I praise You and thank You. In Jesus' name I pray. Amen!

The Lord Is My Hope!

But those who hope in the Lord will renew their strength. They will soar on wings like eagles; they will run and not grow weary, they will walk and not be faint. Isaiah 40:31, NIV

Many people are sad, depressed, and worried due to life's uncertainties. As a result, they fall into hopelessness. Some have stopped hoping in the Lord, and others are struggling to keep a spirit of hope. They have forgotten that the Lord is our Hope and Salvation.

As Christians, we should try not to worry when the world seems to crumble around us; we need to believe in the Lord's plan for us. I know this is easier said than done, but the Scriptures remind us: *"Do not be anxious about anything, but in everything by prayer and supplication with thanksgiving, let your request be made known to God. And the peace of God, which surpasses all understanding, will guard your hearts and your minds in Christ Jesus"* (Philippians 4:6-7, ESV).

For me, keeping my hope in God is accomplished through steadfast prayer and reminding myself that "God is God, and He is good." He is in control of it all, and I must trust Him. When things do not go my way, hope helps me move on to the next phase. Hope in God gives me the strength to fight temptation and sin and renew myself in the Lord when I fall short. Hope also gives me the courage to face my weaknesses and limitations because I know that I can accomplish great things with God's help.

Action/Thought for Today: Encourage someone who is sad or depressed today.

Prayer: *"May the God of hope fill you with all joy and peace in believing, so that you may abound in hope by the power of the Holy Spirit"* (Romans 15:13). Lord Jesus, thank You for the hope we have in You. Thank You for the hope that comes from the gift of salvation. In Your name we pray. Amen!

HOPE, THE ANCHOR OF THE SOUL!

Rejoice in hope, endure in affliction, persevere in prayer.
Romans 12:12, NABRE

All Christians should rejoice in the hope of sharing the glory of God. Likewise, we should also *"boast in our suffering, knowing that suffering produces endurance, and endurance produces character, and character produces hope, and hope does not disappoint us"* (Romans 5:2-5). Jesus endured affliction for our sake, with the hope of the resurrection. Therefore, there is hope that our suffering will end one day, even if not in this life.

If we are suffering in this world, we should try to rejoice in hope because our current problems will be seen as nothing compared to the glory that is to come (see Romans 8:18). Let's hold on to hope, for it is the anchor of our soul (see Hebrews 6:19). Hope encourages us to stay connected with the Lord, to endure trials and to remain cheerful and hopeful in difficult times. Also, steadfast prayers are required to help us be patient, trustful, and confident in God's providence.

Action/Thought for Today: Are you afraid of or tired of suffering? Pray fervently for the grace to endure affliction.

Prayer: Lord Jesus, give us the grace and courage to rejoice in You. Give us the grace to suffer and rise with You in glory. I am rejoicing in hope alone because I am Your beloved child, and Your plan is perfect for me. I praise, adore, and love You, my sweet Jesus. In Your holy name I pray. Amen!

GOD ALONE IS MY HOPE!

For God alone, my soul waits in silence, for my hope is from Him. He alone is my rock and my salvation, my fortress; I shall not be shaken. On God rests my deliverance and my honor; my mighty rock, my refuge is in God. Psalm 62:5-7, NRSVUE

Many of us have all or most of life's necessities and yet feel a void. Some fill that emptiness by overworking, overspending, using illicit drugs or alcohol. Others hide behind their hobbies, job, or work title, or search for money, power, glory, honor, or popularity. After acquiring worldly possessions and fame, many are still unhappy and discouraged, and hustle for more. The missing piece of the puzzle in their life is God.

Once God becomes a part of our life, and as His Spirit lives in us, worldly riches and possessions are no longer a priority, and we are more willing to surrender all to God. We become more obedient, loving, and compassionate. The Spirit of God becomes more evident in our lives as we live in freedom and harmony with God and others. Faith, hope, joy, love, and peace in the Lord increase in us. Let us place our hope in God alone and not in the riches of this world.

Action/Thought for Today: Are you living in God's freedom? Are you putting your hope in God alone?

Prayer: Lord Jesus, without You, I am nothing. Let me trust in You alone. Increase my love for You and others. Help me live in Your freedom. In Your name I pray. Amen!

MAKE THE BEST OF LIFE!

For surely, I know the plans I have for you, says the Lord, plans for your welfare and not for harm, to give you a future with hope.
Jeremiah 29:11

I have seen this scripture on many graduation cards and programs, at significant accomplishment and celebration events, and even on home decor. Some people use it as their life scripture, holding on to God's hope for a better future. When we read this scripture, we may not think about life's unfortunate circumstances or painful events. However, Jeremiah wrote these words in a letter sent to the people of Jerusalem while they were in exile in Babylon. This letter further told the people in exile that God wanted them to: *"Build houses and live in them; plant gardens and eat their fruits. Take wives and have sons and daughters; find wives for your sons and give your daughters to husbands, so that they may bear sons and daughters. Increase there; do not decrease"* (Jeremiah 29:5-6, NABRE).

One might assume that exile was not good; where was the future of hope that God had promised? Because the people from Jerusalem would be in exile for seventy years, God wanted them to make the best of their situation. As humans, we tend to be upset, devastated, or discouraged when things do not go according to our plans. As hard as this truth may be, know that God's plan is perfect; His ways and thoughts are nothing like ours (see Isaiah 55:8). We can be comforted knowing that God has a plan for us regardless of the problems we are facing today. Therefore, let us pray to make the best of life despite any setbacks. We should trust in God, search for Him, call on Him, and pray for the grace to submit to His will. Friends, may God bless you with a future of hope.

Action/Thought for Today: Are you making the best of your present life's situation? Ask the Lord to help you accept His plan.

Prayer: Lord, fill us with Your hope so that we can accept Your plan for us. Please give us the grace to make the best of our life's situations. May Your will be done. In Your name we pray. Amen!

HOPE AND FAITH IN ACTION!

Blessed are those who trust in the LORD, whose trust is the LORD.   Jeremiah 17:7

My mom told me a story a long time ago, and it has always stayed with me. There was a lady in my native land who was poor and had no work. She had many children. One day, she had nothing to feed her children. She put a pot of water on her stove and added salt to it. Then she prayed and cried to the Lord, expecting God to send her some provisions. As the water was boiling, she heard a knock at her door, and someone brought her food to prepare for her family. The Lord heard and rescued her (see Psalm 34:17). He is the God of hope.

To me, this story is hope and faith in action. Although everyone's story will not have this same ending, we should take comfort that those who hope in the Lord shall have no fear in difficult moments. We must submit to God's will and remain steadfast in prayers. When one walks with God and depends on Him for everything, He will help and bless them. Those who hope and trust in the Lord shall taste and see His goodness (see Psalm 34:8). The Lord gives joy to those who confide in Him, for *"joyful are those who have the God of Israel as their helper, whose hope is in the LORD their God"* (Psalm 146:5, NLT).

Action/Thought for Today: Show your faith and hope in action and help someone who needs hope.

Prayer: *"Let your steadfast love, O LORD, be upon us, even as we hope in you"* (Psalm 33:22). Lord, please increase our hope and faith in You. We thank and praise You. In Jesus' name I pray. Amen!

CONSIDER THE WILDFLOWERS!

Consider how the wild flowers grow. They do not labor or spin.
Yet I tell you, not even Solomon in all his splendor was dressed
like one of these. If that is how God clothes the grass of the field,
which is here today, and tomorrow is thrown into the fire, how
much more will he clothe you—you of little faith! And do not set
your heart on what you will eat or drink; do not worry about it.
For the pagan world runs after all such things, and your Father
knows that you need them. Luke 12:27-30, NIV

In times of uncertainty, trials, and tribulations, God does not abandon us. He is always with us. He has a plan and blessings in store for us. When things are difficult or unbearable, it is crucial to focus on the Lord and double our prayer, for worrying will not change anything. *"Can any of you by worrying add a single hour to your span of life?"* (Luke 12:25). Then, why do you worry about life (see Luke 12:26)?

Therefore, be at peace, believe in God's promises and plans, expecting your lives to be fully transformed, free of fear, worry, and anxiety. Let us strive to allow ourselves to be seen by God, loved, set free, and healed. The Lord is gazing at us with His eyes of mercy, love, hope, and encouragement, and He is ready to give us a new life in Him, a life full of promise.

Action/Thought for Today: Share your hope with someone. Pray for the Lord to direct you to someone who needs hope.

Prayer: Lord Jesus, thank You for hearing our prayers. Thank You for the plan You have for us. Please give us the grace to trust and hope in You. We praise and adore You, Lord. It is in Your name we pray. Amen!

THE PROMISE OF TOMORROW!

What then shall we say to this? If God is for us, who can be against us? He who did not spare his own Son but handed him over for all of us, how will he not also give us everything else along with him? Romans 8:31-32, RSV

It is natural for us to worry about our finances, health situation, or other life issues. We try to plan or save for "rainy days" because we don't know what tomorrow holds. There is nothing wrong with preparing for the future, but we must be mindful that tomorrow's promise comes from God alone. Sometimes we feel anxious to face the future, but faith in God will reassure us. Trust and depend on the Father's care, for the Lord will always provide (see Genesis 22:14).

If you have God, you have everything. His grace is sufficient for you, for His power is made perfect in weakness (see 2 Corinthian 12:9). Through His grace, worries and fears will vanish, even when life is difficult and unfair. Through His grace of humility, you will learn to live according to His plan and be content. With His amazing grace, you will experience expected and unexpected blessings and favors. Through His powerful grace, chains will be broken, roadblocks will be removed, and you can live your life to the fullest potential. Furthermore, you will experience joy and peace beyond understanding, regardless of your circumstances.

Action/Thought for Today: When you are worried, say a short prayer, call on the name of Jesus, and ask Him to give you peace. He will bless you with peace.

Prayer: Lord, in time of desolation or joy, help me to trust in Your providential care for me. Please give me the grace to depend on You. Thank You, Lord, for Your blessing, favor, and mercy! In Jesus' name I pray. Amen!

WHAT IS FAITH?

It is not easy to describe faith because it is not visible. The Scriptures tell us: *"Faith is the realization of what is hoped for and evidence of things not seen"* (Hebrews 11:1, NABRE). *Webster's* online dictionary states: "The faith of the gospel is that emotion of the mind which is called trust or confidence exercised toward the moral character of God, and particularly of the Savior.—Dr. T. Dwight."[3] In both definitions, we see that faith is trust and hope in God. It is to believe in God's plan, even if it is not seen or understood. It is to surrender to God's providence. Faith is a choice to believe in God and His love, and to accept His gift of salvation. *"Without faith, it is impossible to please Him, for anyone who approaches God must believe that he exists and that he rewards those who earnestly seek him"* (Hebrews 11:6, NABRE). Let's reflect on the unshakable faith of some of our forefathers:

By faith, Noah, warned by God about events as yet unseen, respected the warning and built an ark to save his household.   Hebrews 11:7

By faith Abraham, when put to the test, offered up Isaac. He who had received the promise was ready to offer up his only son, of whom he had been told, "it is through Isaac that descendants shall be named for you."   Hebrews 11:17-18

By faith the people passed through the Red Sea as if it were dry land, but when the Egyptians attempted to do so, they were drowned.
                                                             Hebrews 11:29

Action/Thought for Today: Do you have faith?

Prayer: Lord Jesus, increase our faith. Give us an unshakable faith. In your name we pray. Amen!

LORD, INCREASE MY LITTLE FAITH!

The apostles said to the Lord, "Increase our faith!" And the Lord said, "If you had faith the size of a mustard seed, you would say to this mulberry tree, 'Be uprooted and planted in the sea,' and it would obey you." Luke 17:5-6, NABRE

I have heard many great testimonies where the impossible became possible, and it all stemmed from someone's faith. Those testimonies have helped increase my own faith in the Lord. The Lord tells us in the Scriptures that we can accomplish a great deal if we have faith, even if our faith is as small as a mustard seed. Whether our faith is minimal or extraordinary, God will honor it and develop it more deeply. When we take the first step, God, in His goodness, does the rest. In Mark 6:5, we see where Jesus did not do many miracles in His hometown, except for laying His hands on a few sick people and curing them, because of their lack of faith.

Faith can help us fight fear, break the chains in our lives, and move toward God's plans for us. Faith can pick one up when all else fails. Faith will help us live in the most challenging moments because nothing is impossible with the help of God. *"This is the victory that conquers the world, our faith"* (1 John 5:4, NIV). Therefore, we must pray for an increase in faith and for the grace to share our testimonies of faith.

Action/Thought for Today: Share your faith's testimony/journey with someone today. Ask the Lord for the grace to share from your heart.

Prayer: Lord Jesus, so many times I want to share my testimony with others, but I hold back because I fear rejection or criticism. Lord, forgive me for those times and give me the grace to share my faith testimony when it is needed. Lord, increase my little faith in You. In Your name, I pray. Amen!

GOD IS FAITHFUL!

Know therefore the LORD your God is God, the faithful God who keeps covenant and steadfast love with those who love him and keep his commandments, to a thousand generations.

Deuteronomy 7:9-10, RSV

A few years ago, I was part of a small group of people who started a ministry. Everyone was enthusiastic, and it went well for a couple of months. The ministry required time however, and many dropped out due to time constraints and other reasons. I was very disappointed and unsure of what to do, but God gave me the grace to persevere. When I felt that the work was too much and I felt weak, God reminded me: *"My grace is sufficient for you, for my power is made perfect in weakness"* (2 Corinthian 12:9, NIV). When I was in despair, He strengthened me and filled my heart with joy and peace. God sent me help when I felt helpless. He did not forsake me. *"God is faithful"* (1 Corinthian 1:9, ESV). By Him, I was *"called into the fellowship of his Son, Christ our Lord"* (1 Corinthians 1:9, ESV).

When you have uncertainties, know that God is with you and will continue to help you. Even if you do not see immediate relief, persevere, ask Him for His help, and remain steadfast in prayer. He will not abandon you. He always keeps His promises. Let us be trustworthy and an imitator of Christ.

Action/Thought for Today: Are you as faithful to God as He is to you? *"Examine yourselves to see whether you are living in the faith. Test yourselves"* (2 Corinthians 13:5).

Prayer: Lord Jesus, we pray for the grace to be faithful to You and to be like You. Thank You, Lord, for Your faithfulness. We pray in the holy name of Jesus. Amen!

GOD HAS CALLED YOU!

Today, if you hear his voice, do not harden your hearts as you did in the rebellion.
Hebrews 3:15, NIV

Suppose an angel of the Lord came to you and said: "The Lord wants you to build a church" or "the Lord wants you to evangelize every corner of the world," what would be your answer? "Me? Lord, are You sure You have the right person?" Or "Lord, I don't know how to speak." Or "Lord, I can't leave my family behind." Or "Lord, people will think that I'm mentally ill." Or would you say, *"I am the servant of the Lord, let it be done to me according to your word"* (Luke 1:38, ESV). That's what Mary said when the angel Gabriel told her she would conceive and bear a son she was to name Jesus (see Luke 1:26-38).

In order to answer Yes to the Lord without hesitation, we must pray to have faith in His plan. It is faith that helps us surrender to the Lord and serve Him beyond our human imagination and strength. We must remember that God's plan is always perfect, and if He calls us, He will not leave or forsake us. In addition, He will give us the grace and the courage to accomplish the tasks that He wants us to do. Always remember: *"The one who calls you is faithful, and he will do it"* (1 Thessalonians 5:24, NIV).

Action/Thought for Today: Is God calling you to serve Him? What is blocking you from obeying?

Prayer: Lord Jesus, You have called me by name. Here I am. I welcome You in my heart, soul, and spirit. I offer You my heart, time, service, talent, and tithe. Grant me the grace to use them for Your work of salvation and greater glory. Thank You for coming to save me. I praise, adore, and glorify You. In Jesus' name I pray. Amen!

THE SHIELD OF FAITH!

Take the shield of faith, with which you will be able to quench all the flaming arrows of the evil one. Ephesian 6:16

The Covid-19 Pandemic made us more aware of our surroundings as we maintained the social distancing as required by State and Federal mandates. Face masks and wearing gloves are required as the new normal, along with all other precautionary measures, to protect ourselves and our family.

Other than a face mask and gloves, do we wear the shield of faith? Are we covering ourselves with God's armor of protection and prayer? While the physical barrier is essential, the shield of faith is more important, for it protects us against the schemes of the enemy. We cannot go on in this life without the protection of God. The apostle Paul tells us to put on the whole armor of God that we may be able to stand against the devil's schemes.

A soldier gets the correct training and equipment before a battle. Likewise, a Christian must be prepared through prayer, fasting, and God's words to repel the forces of the enemies. Through God's grace and wisdom, let us abide in Him and wear His whole armor. In our walk of faith, let us strive to support and empower each other to have more confidence in the Lord.

Action/Thought for Today: Pray and meditate on Ephesian 6:10-20.

Prayer: Lord, give us the grace to take up Your whole armor. Fill us with Your wisdom and truth to stand against the enemy. We thank and praise You. In Jesus' name we pray. Amen!

LIVE BY FAITH, NOT BY SIGHT!

For we live by faith, not by sight. We are confident, I say, and would prefer to be away from the body and at home with the Lord. So we make our goal to please him, whether we are at home in the body or away from it. 2 Corinthian 5:7-19, NIV

In all walks of life, we ought to choose to live by faith – a way that is pleasing to the Lord—while we are waiting to be home with Him. Those who live by faith die to the world to live in Christ and He in us. They speak with the voice of Jesus. They love with the heart of Jesus. They see with the eyes of Jesus. They serve with the hands of Jesus and do all for His glory.

The world may have different expectations or standards, but those who live by faith trust in the Lord over the world's beliefs, follow His commandments, accept His teaching, and choose righteousness over sin. They believe that *"God exists and that He rewards those who seek him"* (Hebrews 11:6). To live by faith, we must make every attempt to hope for eternal life, reject worldly passions and sins, meditate on the things from above, and pray for guidance from the Lord in all our ways.

Action/Thought for Today: Am I living by faith or by sight? Do I care more about the things of this world or God?

Prayer: Lord, help us to live by faith, not by sight. Please give us the grace to fix our minds on You alone, for You are our hope. Thank You for Your faithfulness. We love, adore, and praise You! In Jesus' name we pray. Amen!

Well Done, Good and Faithful Servant!

Well done, good and faithful servant! You have been faithful with a few things; I will put you in charge of many things. Come and share your master's happiness. Matthew 25:21, NIV

In the Parable of the Talents (Matthew 25:14-30), a master entrusted five talents to one servant, two to another, and one to another, before leaving for a journey. After a long time, the master returned and settled the accounts with them. The one with the five talents earned five more talents, the one with the two earned two more, and the master said to both of them, *"Well done, good and faithful servant"* (Matthew 25:23, ESV). The one with the one talent hid it in the ground and did not invest it. When he told his master that He had earned no interest, the master then said, *"You wicked, lazy servant"* (Matthew 25:26, NABRE)! After he harshly reprimanded the servant, he caste him into darkness (see Matthew 25:26-30).

This parable is teaching us to be faithful with the gifts and talents that God has given us. When you use a gift that God has given you, He blesses you with much more, so that you can do more for His glory. *"For to all those who have, more will be given, and they will have an abundance, but from those who have nothing, even what they have will be taken away"* (Matthew 25:29, NRSVUE). Let us pray for the grace to use our gifts fully and hope that we hear these words from the Lord on the last day: *"Well done, good and faithful servant!"*

Action/Thought for Today: Have you been using your God-given gifts to the best of your ability?

Prayer: Father God, please give us the grace to use our talents and gifts for Your glory. In Jesus' name we pray. Amen!

WHO ARE THE POOR IN SPIRIT?

Jesus said: "Blessed are the poor in spirit, for theirs is the kingdom of heaven." Matthew 5:3, NIV

Poor in spirit does not refer to financial poverty; it implies spiritual poverty. It refers to the humble, the spiritually wounded and broken who recognize their sins and rely only on God to help them. To be poor in spirit, we must renounce self-reliance, self-confidence, and self-righteousness and detach ourselves from worldly possessions, riches, fame, and power.

We become poor in spirit when we give our all to God and accept His way and will in our lives. When we depend on the Lord to fill our nothingness, He provides us with strength and confidence and makes us righteous. We become poor in spirit by acknowledging the need for God's mercy and accepting that only the Lord can heal, forgive, and make us whole.

Recognizing that God is our All-in-All will help us experience His love and know Him better. In return, He promises to reward the poor in spirit with happiness. They will inherit the Kingdom of God, and the Lord will further bless them with many graces. God affirms, in Isaiah 66:2, that He will look upon the humble and contrite in spirit who tremble at His words. Jesus continues to invite us to follow in His footsteps and be more like Him.

Action/Thought for Today: Pray for the grace to be poor in spirit and acknowledge the need for God in your life.

Prayer: Lord Jesus, deliver me from self-reliance, self-confidence, and self-righteousness. Please help me to always depend on You. Give me the grace to offer You my entire being as I am, and sustain in me a willing spirit (see Psalm 51:12), for You will accept my broken spirit and contrite heart. (see Psalm 51:17). In Your name I pray. Amen!

THERE WILL BE JOY AFTER SORROW!

Jesus said: "Blessed are those who mourn, for they will be comforted."   Matthew 5:4

As I meditate on this scripture, I think of Jesus' sorrowful passion, His agony in Gethsemane (see Matthew 26:36-39), knowing what was awaiting Him in Jerusalem, His betrayal by Judas (see Matthew 26:48-50), His scourging, the carrying of His cross, and finally, His crucifixion (see Matthew 27:27-37). I imagine Jesus' mother at the foot of the cross. I imagine the disciples' bitter sorrow and tears, and their uncertainties because they had lost their Master. Through His resurrection, Jesus turned their grief into joy and gave them peace.

Eighteen years ago, after my father's death, I felt as if the tree that held all of us had been cut down. I felt like a lost branch in the air, disconnected from everyone and everything. Jesus consoled and healed my heart, as well as my family's. Although at first I had not felt the Lord, He was my Comforter every step of the way. For those who are mourning or suffering, Jesus understands your pain. He is near to your heart (see Philippians 4:5). He is reaching out to you for a hug. He will heal your heart, and He promises to console you. There will be joy after the sorrow, and the joy of the Lord will last forever (see John 16:22). Be patient, and allow Jesus to heal, console, and love you.

Action/Thought for Today: Sit quietly for two to five minutes or longer and let Jesus love and heal you.

Prayer: Lord Jesus, so many are broken-hearted and suffering. Please help them feel Your tender love and console their hearts. In Jesus' name I pray. Amen!

WHAT A BLESSING FOR THE MEEK!

Blessed are the meek, for they will inherit the earth.

Matthew 5:5

The meek people I know are like a blessing from above. It is a joy to be around them. They reflect kindness, peace, gentleness, and freedom. As noted in 1 Peter 3:4, *"Let your adornment be the inner self with the lasting beauty of a gentle and quiet spirit, which is very precious in God's sight."* Meek people are true imitators of Christ, for they are gentle and humble of heart, like Christ (see Matthew 11:29). They serve God and others with charity and kindness. They neither self-inflate nor have an inferiority complex; they live in God's freedom and are not defined by the world's power.

Because we live in a power-driven world, some think meekness is a sign of weakness. To the contrary, meekness is strength under control because the Spirit of God empowers the meek. One may think the powerful will inherit the earth. To the contrary, Jesus said the meek will inherit the earth (see Matthew 5.5). Let us pray for the grace to allow God to work on our inner character and to be molded in His image. Finally, *"Let your gentleness be known to everyone"* (Philippians 4:5), and be an example to those around you.

Action/Thought for Today: What action should you take in your life to be meek and gentle like Christ?

Prayer: Lord Jesus, it is hard to be meek and gentle, but I desire both. Please mold me and help me to be gentle and humble of heart. Let me raise my voice only to praise You. Let me fight only the sins and evils in my life. Let me speak only with gentleness and love. In Your name I pray. Amen!

HUNGRY AND THIRSTY FOR RIGHTEOUSNESS?

Blessed are those who hunger and thirst for righteousness, for they will be filled. Matthew 5:6

Have you ever been on a prolonged fast, perhaps for a spiritual or medical reason? After many hours you strongly crave food and drink. Regardless, you should desire righteousness even more than food and drink.

To me, hunger and thirst for righteousness is a deep and constant longing for God's things—His words and commands. Jesus said, *"One does not live by bread alone, but by every word that comes from the mouth of God"* (Matthew 4:4). Therefore, we must aim to be filled with God's words, meditate on His precepts, and fix our eyes on His ways (see Psalm 119:15).

People who have a thirst and hunger for righteousness strive to live godly lives, commit to a serious prayer life, and observe God's statutes. With their whole being—attitude, actions, way of life—they continually cry out to the Lord. *"With my whole heart, I seek you"* (Psalm 119:10). They do not conform to the world. Instead, they dedicate their lives to God. We cannot become righteous on our own, but God's grace is sufficient for us (see 2 Corinthian 12:9). Therefore, let us pray for the grace to *"pursue righteousness, godliness, faith, love, endurance, and gentleness"* (1 Timothy 6:11).

Action/Thought for Today: Are you hungry and thirsty for righteousness? If so, pursue it with all your heart.

Prayer: Lord Jesus, make me hungry and thirsty for righteousness, give me the grace to seek You with my whole heart, and help me walk in righteousness. In Your name I pray. Amen!

NOT A ONE-WAY STREET!

Blessed are the merciful, for they will receive mercy. Matthew 5:7

Mercy is undeserved grace. Without a doubt, now is a time to cry out to the Lord for mercy – *"Have mercy on me, O God, according to your steadfast love; according to your abundant mercy blot out my transgressions"* (Psalm 51:1). In a world so broken and with people so deeply wounded, we all need mercy and forgiveness like never before. We need to accept God's mercy, which is available to every soul. He loves us, and He faithfully continues to show us His mercy. He does not abandon us despite our sins, wickedness, and wretchedness. God knows our deficits and that we cannot avoid sin, so He continuously heals our wounds, forgives our wrongdoings, restores us, and makes us whole again.

We also need others' mercy to pick us up, forgive us, help us heal, console us, and walk in faith with us. Mercy is not a one-way street. As we receive mercy from God and others, we also must be merciful to others in deeds and words, and the Lord will bless us.

Let us hope and pray for a world where everyone is striving to be merciful to each other, a world where the hungry are fed, the naked are clothed, the immigrants are welcomed, the sick and marginalized are protected, and enemies forgive each other. This world would then be the face and heart of mercy, the face and heart of Jesus.

Action/Thought for Today: Ask the Lord for an opportunity to be merciful today. If you succeed, praise the Lord. If you fail, ask Him to help you and try again until you reach your goal.

Prayer: Lord Jesus, You ask us to be merciful.
Without Your help, it is impossible. Please teach us
to be merciful. In Your name I pray. Amen!

CREATE A PURE HEART IN ME!

Blessed are the pure in heart, for they will see God. Matthew 5:8

The world and its technological advancements are moving quickly. Many feel that they must try to keep up, leaving them no time to pray and worship the Lord. Many have lost their way to God, for their hearts are attached to the world. Fear not! We can still have a pure heart, for God is always in control, and if we draw near to Him, He will draw near to us (see James 4:8). God desires a pure heart within us—a clean and honest heart without hypocrisy and blame, and with a good conscience. He wants us to reflect His image in words and deeds.

What does it take to have a pure heart in our world? We must accept God to the fullest in our lives. It involves prayer and partnering with God for our purification, not standing in His way. Only by God's power can a soul reach purity of heart. Jesus Christ has already paid the price for our hearts to be pure and blameless before His Father. It is up to us to accept this precious gift, for *"he who loves purity of heart, and whose speech is gracious, will have the king as his friend"* (Proverbs 22:11, ESV).

Action/Thought for Today: Are you willing to let go of the world's demands in order to have a pure heart? Ask the Lord for help.

Prayer: Lord Jesus, I long to see You. I ask You to create a pure heart in me. Please make my heart pure like Yours. In Your name I pray. Amen!

CALLED TO BE PEACEMAKERS!

Blessed are the peacemakers, for they will be called children of God.   Matthew 5:9

World Peace Day is celebrated annually. Why do we have a special Peace Day? Do you feel and see peace in the world, your community, and life? Are you at peace with God, others, and yourself? Many countries in the world are fighting, some within their borders, and some with other countries. Many people suffer from anxiety and depression. Many hold a grudge against others and are unable to forgive. Some are suffering from injustice in the workplace and their communities and discord in their family. These people may look at peace, but inside they are *not* at peace. But Jesus can bring peace to our lives through prayer. He can bless us with a peace beyond understanding, for He clearly said: *"Peace I leave with you; my peace I give to you"* (John 14:27).

"Blessed are the peacemakers." Jesus referred to the makers of peace, for we must *"pursue peace with everyone"* (Hebrews 12:14). Peace requires that we let go of grudges and resentment and speak with kindness and gentleness to avoid quarrels. Let us pray to cultivate peace by loving one another, showing respect, accepting apologies, and forgiving one another. Finally, *"Let the peace of Christ rule in your hearts, to which indeed you were called in the one body. And be thankful"* (Colossians 3:15).

Action/Thought for Today: Are you at peace with God, others, and yourself? Are you able to apologize and ask for forgiveness?

Prayer: My Lord, fill us with the Spirit of Your peace, love, and joy. Teach us and help us maintain a peaceful heart in all circumstances. Thank You for Your peace that surpasses all understanding. In Your name we pray. Amen!

HAVE YOU BEEN PERSECUTED?

Blessed are those who are persecuted for righteousness' sake, for theirs is the kingdom of heaven. Matthew 5:10

Have others persecuted you because you are serving Christ? Have you been reviled because you refuse to be politically correct or diplomatic when it applies to God's teaching on social justice and His commandments? Have you been put down because you have chosen what is just and right? Don't be discouraged. Jesus also suffered persecution because He was direct in His teaching and encounters with others. He spoke to the most profound areas of people's hearts, pierced the soul and spirit, and discerned their thoughts and intentions. Many did not like Jesus' teaching because He was not politically correct; He spoke the hard truth. The disciples also suffered persecution for proclaiming the name of Jesus and His message.

To this day, some Christians still suffer for the sake of the Kingdom of God. Therefore, do not be afraid; gird your loins and fight for what is righteous, just, holy, and pure. Let us look forward to the Kingdom. Take courage and be still, knowing that the Lord your God will fight for you (see Exodus 14:14).

Action/Thought for Today: Are you willing to accept persecution for the sake of the Kingdom of God?

Prayer: Lord Jesus, keep us from what is popular in this world. Help us to thirst for holiness and to stand for what is right and just. Please give us the strength and courage to fight for righteousness amid persecution. May all the people on Earth praise You! In Jesus' name I pray. Amen!

GOD'S EXPRESSION OF LOVE!

Yours, O LORD, are the greatness, the power, the glory, the victory, and the majesty; for all that is in the heavens and on the earth is yours; yours is the kingdom O LORD, and you are exalted as head above all.   1 Chronicles 29:11

As I walk through my neighborhood, I reflect on God's creation. I am in awe as I contemplate the incredible work of His hands. I am confident that God's creation is an expression of His love. The beauty of the sun and the moon reminds me of the light of God and how we must be a light for others. The sunrise and sunset help me contemplate the beauty of God. The fresh air tells me that I need God for every breath that I take, and without Him, I am nothing. The gentle breeze assures me of God's peace that surpasses all understanding. The still water of a pond calls me to be still and know that God is God (see Psalm 46:10). The rain showers us and the land with God's many blessings. The singing of a bird tells me that God whispers, "I love you," and I must strive to respond with praise and gratitude.

God gave us dominion over all the things on this Earth so that humankind can enjoy life. He wants our joy to be complete and overflowing (see John 15:11). We must not take His creation for granted. We should take care of God's creation and all His living creatures. As I meditate on the sweetness and goodness of God, I praise and sing with the psalmist, *"The heavens are telling the glory of God, and the firmament proclaims his handiwork"* (Psalm 19:1).

Action/Thought for Today: Try to see God's love in nature.

Prayer: Lord, our God, I bless and praise Your name. Thank You for loving me beyond measure and for giving me dominion over Your creation. Give me the grace to care for Your creation. In Jesus' name I pray. Amen!

WHERE DO YOU SEE GOD'S LOVE?

And so we know and rely on the love God has for us. God is love.
Whoever lives in love lives in God, and God in them.

1 John 4:16, NIV

Jesus Christ has never failed to show His love for us. Throughout sacred Scriptures, we see His love in His public ministry. His death and resurrection were offered for the salvation of all humankind. Through prayers and meditation, He gives us peace, hope, and shows us His mercy. Through a simple gesture from a family member, a conversation with a friend, a kindness from a coworker, and through the many favors and blessings He has bestowed on us, God shows us His love.

We also see His love in nature—the beauty and fragrance of a plant, the sunrise and sunset, the rain, the quiet breeze, and the warm sea. To see the love of Christ in others and in all things, we must establish a personal relationship with Him. We must accept to be guided by His spirit and live in Him and He in us. Open the eyes of your heart to see God's love in everything!

Action/Thought for Today: Take a moment to reflect on how and where God has revealed His love for you.

Prayer: Lord Jesus, thank You for Your love and mercy. Give us the grace to love You and one another. We praise and thank You. It is in Your name that we pray. Amen!

THE GAZE OF LOVE!

For I am the Lord your God, the Holy one of Israel, Your savior. I give Egypt as your ransom, Ethiopia and Seba in exchange for you. Because you are precious in my sight, and honored, and I love you, I give people in return for you, nations in exchange for your life. Do not fear, for I am with you. Isaiah 43:3-5

The Lord gazes on us with love, mercy, encouragement, hope, and goodness. He does not tire of looking at us because we are precious in His sight, and He loves us (see Isaiah 43:4). We must allow God to see us, to set us free, and heal us from illness, shame, guilt, fear, worry, and sin. God wants to take away our humiliation, suffering, sorrow, and loneliness. Do not be afraid to give them all to Him, for He cares for us. God wants to provide us with a new life in Him, a life full of promise, for He has a plan for all of us.

I invite all to look at Jesus on the cross with love, hope, and faith, and expect Him to transform our lives. I encourage all to be still in His presence and receive His inner peace. Let us be Jesus' intimate friend and listen to the whisper of His voice. He calls each one of us by name.

Action/Thought for Today: Touch someone today with the gaze of love, like Jesus did and does.

Prayer: Lord Jesus, we pray for the grace to accept Your mercy. Thank You for redeeming us and for calling us by name. Thank You for the promise of a future of hope. I praise and thank You. In Your name I pray. Amen!

PERFECT LOVE!

Beloved, since God loves us so much, we also ought to love one another. No one has ever seen God; if we love one another, God lives in us, and his love is perfected in us. 1 John 4:11-12

We do not see God with our physical eyes; therefore, it is vital to be Christ for others and to see Him in others. During my first year in the School of Spiritual Direction, I asked the Lord for a profound experience with Him. The Lord showed His deep love and kindness for me through my classmates, who were total strangers at that time. *"Perfect love casts out fear"* (1 John 4:18). Their love was perfect and powerful; it cast out my fears and anxieties. When I was down, their compassion and love picked me up and gave me joy. When evil thoughts tried to enter my mind—I would not be successful in the program—their words of encouragement and love resounded in my mind, giving me peace.

This experience inspires me to reflect on the beauty of God's creation and the work of His hands. It remains with me and opens my eyes to see God in every individual and encourage the people I encounter daily. *"Therefore encourage one another and build each other up"* (1 Thessalonians 5:11), all for the glory of God.

Action/Thought for Today: Take a minute to pause and reflect. Do others see Christ in you? Do you see Christ in others?

Prayer: Lord, for every time I failed to show love, encouragement, and support to my family, friends, and neighbors, please forgive me. Help me love You deeply, as well as my neighbors. Open my eyes and my heart to see others as You see them. I praise and thank You. In Your name I pray. Amen!

FAITH, HOPE, AND LOVE!

And now faith, hope, and love abide, these three, and the greatest of these is love.   1 Corinthians 13:13

Francis Fernandez-Carvajal, in his book, *Through Wind and Waves,* has said, "People who are truly united to God through the theological virtues of faith, hope, and love also perfected themselves humanly. They are refined in their relationships with others, loyal, affable, well-mannered, generous, sincere, precisely because they have placed all their affections in God."[4] Right now, the world needs men and women who are willing to open their hearts to love without limit, people who are eager to bring the light of Christ to others. The world needs people who have hope and faith in God's purposes and promises and who will be an example to others. Parents must teach their children to display the virtues of faith, hope, and love, and live like Christ. Are you willing to be one who will guide others to Him?

Action/Thought for Today: Bring the light of Christ to someone by living the virtues of faith, hope, and love.

Prayer: Lord Jesus, please grant us the virtues of faith, hope, and love. Give us the grace to be an example to those around us and to be more united with You in all walks of life—in church, family, and professional life. We thank You and praise You, O Lord. In Your holy name we pray. Amen!

A POWERFUL LANGUAGE!

Because your steadfast love is better than life, my lips will praise you. So I will bless you as long as I live; I will lift up my hands and call on your name. Psalm 63:3-4

Love is an extraordinary language. It is universal and needs no special education. It was first spoken by God when He created us, and He wants us to emulate His love language. We can communicate love in many ways and do not need to have the same dialect. We can speak it with a kind gesture, a smile, or a tender gaze. We do not need to know someone to express a gentle, loving, and encouraging message.

- Love brings us together in unity.
- Love forgives us and others.
- Love heals us.
- Love helps us serve wholeheartedly.
- Love encourages and lifts us in good and bad times.
- Love humbles us like Jesus on the cross.
- Love makes us free and whole.
- The simplest expression of love can bring out the best in us.

We must cultivate love so it can be part of us. Give everything for love, do everything in love, and suffer because of love as Jesus did for us. I pray that we can let our love language guide us in all things.

Action/Thought for Today: Pray to speak
the love language fluently and always.

Prayer: Heavenly Father, teach us how to speak Your love language in all circumstances. Help us be a blessing to others through Your love. It is in Jesus' name I pray. Amen!

WHAT IS LOVE?

Love is patient; love is kind; love is not envious or boastful or arrogant or rude. It does not insist on its own way; it is not irritable or resentful; it does not rejoice in wrongdoing, but rejoices in the truth. It bears all things, believes all things, hopes all things, endures all things. Love never ends. 1 Corinthians 13:4-8

I grew up in a culture where people didn't simply say "I love you"; they showed their selfless love in the actions of the heart and the many sacrifices they made for others. We must be a reflection of love in the way we live and treat others. 1 Corinthian 13:4-8 teaches us how to live daily with family, at work, and in the community.

"*God is love*" (1 John 4:16), and He commanded us to love Him first, then our neighbors as ourselves (see Mark 12:30-31). Love requires sacrifice to put others first, just as Jesus laid down His life for us (see John 15:13). Love requires that we act with patience, kindness, humility, truthfulness, justice, and mercy. Love is one of the greatest commandments, and we ought to strive to respect God's teaching. As we look deeply into the mirror of our hearts, do we see God's love within us?

Action/Thought for Today: In the scripture above, first place Jesus' name where it says "*love*" and read the scripture aloud. Then repeat the same scripture, placing your name where it says "*love.*" Examine yourself to see if you reflect the characteristics of love as described by the apostle Paul. If not, pray for the grace to love more.

Prayer: Lord Jesus, I don't know how to love, but I can do all things with Your grace. Bless me with the sincere gift of love, to love You above all things and love my neighbor like myself. I pray in Your name. Amen!

Maintain Constant Love!

Above all, maintain constant love for one another, for love covers a multitude of sins. Be hospitable to one another without complaining. Like good stewards of the manifold grace of God, serve one another with whatever gift each of you have received.

1 Peter 4:8-10

We all know people who irritate, frustrate, or upset us due to their behaviors and actions. Yet, God has called us to love everyone regardless of their shortcomings. As humans, we all have weaknesses and defects. Therefore, let us strive to see others' goodness instead of their flaws. Let us love the unlovable, show kindness to the unkind, and be considerate to those who are inconsiderate. The more we show love to others and speak blessings over them the more love we will receive in return. We are weak, but if we ask God to love like Him, He surely will give us this grace. Let us reflect on this quote from St. Therese of Lisieux: "I know now that true charity consists in bearing all of our neighbors' defects—not being surprised at their weakness, but edified at their smallest virtues."[5]

Action/Thought for Today: Today, be kind to those who do not deserve your kindness.

Prayer: Lord Jesus, give me the grace to remember that I am not perfect. Give me the desire to love like You, and teach me to love unconditionally. Lord, teach me to endure my neighbor's defects without complaining. I praise and love You, my Lord and Savior. In Your name I pray. Amen!

WHY MUST WE LOVE?

For God so loved the world that he gave his only Son, so that everyone who believes in him may not perish but may have eternal life. John 3:16

Love is not just a warm fuzzy feeling. Love is putting God and others above ourselves and loving our neighbors as ourselves. We must love because it is a commandment, not a choice. The first commandment is: *"You shall love the Lord your God with all your heart, and with all your soul, and with all your mind, and with all your strength. The second is this, you shall love your neighbor as yourself. There is no commandment greater than these"* (Mark 12:30-31).

We must love because God loved us first. God the Father gave us the ultimate example of love when He sent His only Son to lay down His life to save us. God's love is beyond measure, beyond understanding. Even in our wickedness and faults, God loves us blindly.

The Lord shows us multiple examples of love in the Scriptures and our daily lives: He comes to us in the Eucharist (see John 6:53) and prayers. He washed the disciples' feet (see John 13:1-17). He heals, cleanses, and forgives us (see Mark 2:1-11). *"God is love"* (1 John 4:16).

The apostle Paul reminded us: **"If we speak in human and angelic tongues but do not have love, we are a clashing cymbal. And if we have the gift of prophecy and comprehend all mysteries and knowledge; if we have faith to move mountains but do not have love, we are nothing"** (1 Corinthians 13:1-7, My Paraphrase). Therefore, let us love first, then exercise our faith and do good deeds.

Action/Thought for Today: Examine yourself. Do you sincerely love the Lord and your neighbor as yourself?

Prayer: Lord, without You, we cannot love. Please help us love more and more every day. In Your name we pray. Amen!

ONE MAN'S RIGHTEOUSNESS!

The LORD saw that the wickedness of humankind was great in the earth, and that every inclination of the thoughts of their heart was only evil continually. And the Lord was sorry that he had made humankind on the earth, and it grieved him to his heart. So, the LORD said, "I will blot out from the earth the human beings I have created—people together with animals and creeping things and birds of the air, for I am sorry that I made them." But Noah found favor in the sight of the LORD. Genesis 6:5-8

After the fall of Adam and Eve, God could have erased the human race from the Earth. Our sins and rebellion cause a wound in His heart, but He showed mercy, and Noah found favor in His eyes, and mercy became forgiveness. Noah's righteousness changed God's mind about destroying the Earth. Today, when there is so much sin, injustice, violence, and wickedness in the world, we need to be a Noah of our time. We must work in collaboration with the Lord, helping the world change from evil to good, receiving forgiveness from God for others and ourselves.

Beloved friends, we cannot just continue watching the world fall apart; we must work together and fervently pray for all to meet Jesus. He needs all of us to help Him in the salvation of this world. St. Augustine said, "He who created us without our help will not save us without our consent."[6]

Action/Thought for Today: Do you want to walk with God like Noah? Pray for that grace. Also, pray for an end to wickedness in the Earth.

Prayer: Lord, forgive me and the world for our sins. Please create in us a pure and clean heart and renew the face of the Earth. I praise and thank You for Your mercy and kindness. In Jesus' name I pray. Amen!

FEBRUARY 18

A GIFT FROM GOD!

*If we confess our sins, he who is faithful and just will forgive us
our sins and cleanse us from all unrighteousness.* 1 John 1:9

Forgiveness is an extraordinary gift from God. We receive
healing through the forgiveness of sins. It is human nature to
fail and sin, but God wants to purify us from all sins. God continues to love us despite our failures and shortcomings.

If we acknowledge our sins, repent, and go to the heart of the
Father for healing, God will forgive us. Even when we reject the
Lord due to our sins and are unfaithful, God is faithful to us
because He cannot deny Himself (see 2 Timothy 2:13).

True conversion can and should occur daily and at every moment in our lives. We must acknowledge that we are weak and
need God's grace for a change of heart. We should try to live
with determination and make every effort not to sin but to
live a life in Christ. Therefore, let's humble ourselves in prayer,
kneeling at Jesus' feet, asking for forgiveness, making a firm decision to repent, and being grateful for His love and mercy.

Action/Thought for Today: Examine yourself.
Ask the Lord to forgive your sins.

Prayer: Lord Jesus, thank You for loving me so much, for
forgiving my sins, and for dying for me. Jesus, I praise
You and adore You. In Jesus' name I pray. Amen!

BE MERCIFUL!

Whenever you stand praying, forgive, if you have anything against anyone; so that your Father in heaven may also forgive you your trespasses. Mark 11:25

God is always willing to bless us. Sometimes, however, our hardness of heart and lack of good will toward others block us from receiving His forgiveness and blessing. Our prayers are more effective when we forgive those who trespass against us. Our ministries prosper when we are willing to let go of our grudges. Our lives improve in every area when we are free of resentment and bitterness.

To receive God's mercy, we must forgive and be merciful to one another. This is a vital message in the Gospel, for Jesus said: *"Blessed are the merciful, for they will receive mercy"* (Matthew 5:7). Forgiveness heals, gives hope to others, and helps us to not repay evil with evil, but to do good to our enemies (see Romans 12:20-21). It is key to holiness and salvation.

Action/Thought for Today: Show mercy
and love to someone today.

Prayer: Lord Jesus, please give me the grace to forgive.
I cannot do this on my own. Please help me to show
mercy to others. Show me, Lord, whom I need to
forgive, and help me put compassion into action. Jesus,
I praise and adore You. In Your name I pray. Amen!

SEVENTY-SEVEN TIMES!

Then Peter approaching asked him, "Lord, if my brother sins against me, how often must I forgive him? As many as seven times?" Jesus answered, "I say to you, not seven times but seventy-seven times." Matthew 18:21-22, NABRE

When someone offends me, if I remain patient and pray, God always lifts my burden and heals my heart. In return, I can forgive easily. When I take the matter into my own hands, I usually become bitter, sad, and take longer to forgive. Unforgiveness and resentment are spiritual poisons that hurt you more than the person you hold in your heart: *"For I see that you are in the gall of bitterness and the chains of wickedness"* (Act 8:23). Unforgiveness and revenge take God's job, for He said: *"Beloved, never avenge yourselves, but leave room for the wrath of God; for it is written, "Vengeance is mine, I will repay, says the Lord"* (Romans 12:19).

When we forgive, we are freeing and being kind to ourselves. Let God be God so that He can act freely in us and for us. Forgiveness lightens our hearts as well as setting the other person free. Let's be encouraged and practice mercy and charity, not seven times but seventy-seven times.

Action/Thought for Today: Let's forgive someone today. Ask the Lord to show you who needs your forgiveness.

Prayer: Lord, give us the grace to forgive and remind us always of Your mercy. Speak to us, Lord, and break the hardness of our hearts. Create in us tender, compassionate, and loving hearts. In Jesus' name we pray. Amen!

ACCEPTING GOD'S FORGIVENESS!

The LORD is merciful and gracious, slow to anger and abounding in steadfast love. He will not always accuse, nor will he keep his anger forever. He does not deal with us according to our sins, nor repay us according to our iniquities. Psalm 103:8-10

Many understand that Jesus died to save us and give us eternal life, yet some have great difficulty accepting and welcoming God's forgiveness and mercy. We may ask God to forgive us for the same sin repeatedly, or we may feel that He does not forgive or forget our sins. Forgiving ourselves from past sins and mistakes may be challenging, and we may dwell in shame or regret. That is because we do not trust in God's forgiveness.

Complete trust in God gives us access to His mercy. It also helps us forgive ourselves. The more we trust God, the more we please Him and are blessed by Him. Through almsgiving, prayer, and fasting, let's make a firm decision to trust in God's love and mercy.

Action/Thought for Today: Ask the Lord to help you forgive yourself for past mistakes, sins, or shortcomings.

Prayer: Lord Jesus, we put our trust in You. Please help us accept and welcome Your forgiveness and mercy. In Your name we pray. Amen!

REPENTANCE IS NECESSARY!

Remember therefore from where you have fallen; repent and do the works you did at first. If not, I will come to you and remove your lampstand from its place, unless you repent. Revelation 2:5, ESV

How would you feel if someone asked you for forgiveness and then commited the same offense against you again? Repentance is necessary to move beyond the injury. If someone does not acknowledge his/her fault, there is no guarantee that this person will not repeat the same wrongdoing. Therefore, each of us should try to recognize our transgressions, ask for forgiveness, and decide not to injure again. Repentance opens the heart to love again and to live with others in harmony, sympathy, compassion, and humility (see 1 Peter 3:8-17).

Reconciliation is possible with sincere remorse. This is true in our relationship with both God and man. Repentance is possible when we accept correction for our wrongdoing. If we must correct someone, let us pray to act with kindness, love, and mercy. Reprimanding someone may be very hard, but the Holy Spirit can guide us to be kind and lead our enemies to a change of heart. *"Correcting his opponents with gentleness. God may perhaps grant them repentance leading to a knowledge of the truth"* (2 Timothy 2:24, ESV).

Action/Thought for Today: What step would you take to correct someone with love and kindness?

Prayer: My Jesus, my Savior, give us the grace to be united, to live in peace, to grow perfect in love with all. Create in us a pure heart and renew Your spirit within us (Psalm 51:10). In Your name we pray. Amen!

A TRUE TEST OF LOVE!

Blessed those whose way is blameless, who walk by the law of the Lord. Psalm 119:1, NABRE

Do you know that enemies can bring us closer to Christ? Our enemies can help us follow the law of the Lord, which is to love without limit. They allow us to intentionally love and forgive others because that is what God requires of us. Loving our enemies is the true test and meaning of love, for it is easier to love your friends than your enemies. *"If you love those who love you, what reward will you get? Are not even tax collectors doing that?"* (Matthew 5:46, NIV). The Lord further instructed us to love our enemies, do good to them, and lend them without expecting anything back (see Luke 6:35).

Our enemies teach us to die to ourselves and put others first, as Christ did. They allow us to experience freedom in Christ as we stop being resentful, hateful, and bitter. We cannot do this without God's grace. Therefore, let us ask the Lord for His help. Let us pray for our enemies and ask the Lord to give us a loving and forgiving heart. Let us try to be kind and considerate to those who have offended us, and let God do the rest.

Action/Thought for Today: Pray for your enemies. Bless those who persecute you.

Prayer: Lord Jesus, bless me with a forgiving heart so that I may show love and mercy toward my enemies. In Your name I pray. Amen!

GONE ASTRAY!

I have gone astray like a lost sheep, seek out your servant, for I do not forget your commandments.　　　　Psalm 119:176, NRSVUE

Crying out like the psalmist, I have gone away from the Lord so many times, lost in my doubts, shame, sins, and regrets. I have disobeyed the Lord's laws. Yet, I know the Lord's commandments. I let my weaknesses challenge my courage to do the right thing, when I could have asked the Lord for help but did not. I make resolutions to avoid past sins, yet I stumble from time to time and fall into the same traps. I believe in the Lord's promises, yet I sometimes doubt His forgiveness. Only Jesus can constantly keep me steadfast in the heart of His Father.

I ask that you seek me out, my Lord. *"Let my cry come before you, O Lord; give me understanding according to your word"* (Psalm 119:169, NRSVUE), so I may learn Your commandments (see Psalm 119:73) and obey them.

Today, let us give the Lord permission to seek us out if we run away from Him. If we ask the Lord to bring us home, He will do it, but we must work collaboratively with Him. His faithfulness endures from generation to generation (see Psalm 119:90).

Action/Thought for Today: Meditate on and pray Psalm 119.

> **Prayer:** Father in Heaven, I hope in You. Help me
> observe Your commandments. Father, do not let
> me go astray. I ask You to seek the depth of my
> heart. It is in Jesus' name that I pray. Amen!

SEEK THE LORD ONLY!

But strive first for the kingdom of God and his righteousness, and all these will be given to you as well. So do not worry about tomorrow, for tomorrow will bring worries of its own. Today's trouble is enough for today. Matthew 6:33-34

There are many things in life to desire or seek, but the Lord is asking us to seek Him first and in all things. With Him, we are complete and lack nothing. Often, we forget to seek God in the details of our lives. We may not remember to ask God for direction before an important project or decision. Some are so consumed by their worries and troubles that they fail to seek the Lord in their suffering, assuming they can solve their problems or count on other people to help them. Remember, *"Do not put your trust in princes, in mortals, in whom there is no help"* (Psalm 146:3).

When we seek God only, He always provides what we need. Our problems may still exist, but know that God is close to us, He cares for us, we can cast all our anxieties on Him (see 1 Peter 5:7) and confide in Him. When we seek Him first, He further blesses us with our heart's desire or what we need the most. Our prayer should be for the grace to pursue the Lord in all things. Therefore, let us commit our all to the Lord, and He will establish our plans (see Proverb 16:3).

Action/Thought for Today: What are you seeking in this world? Pray for the grace to seek God only.

Prayer: Lord, You are the Way, the Truth, and the Life. Give us the grace and wisdom to seek You before all other things. Honor and glory be to You only! In Your name we pray. Amen!

WHAT IS YOUR TREASURE?

For where your treasure is, there your heart will be also.

Matthew 6:21

What is your treasure? To some, treasures are comfort, riches, pleasures, honor, power, prestige, and glory—all temporary. Others value success, education, talents, and physical fitness/beauty, etc. These things should not define who we are, for they do not last forever.

The Lord demands a heart that is undivided and reserved for Him alone, one that is not occupied by the world's affairs. When our heart is dedicated to God only, the need for comfort, power, honor, and riches, etc., becomes unimportant. Instead, we devote ourselves to prayer, to service, and to being more kind, gentle, humble, generous, and compassionate. Let us remember not to store up treasures on Earth where a thief can steal them, but keep all our treasures in Heaven, where life is everlasting (see Matthew 6:19-20).

Let us also remember God's promise, *"I love those who love me, and those who seek me diligently find me. Riches and honor are with me, enduring wealth, and prosperity. My fruit is better than gold, even fine gold, and my yield than choice silver. I walk in the way of righteousness, along the path of justice, endowing with wealth those who love me, and filling their treasuries"* (Proverb 8:17-21).

Action/Thought for Today: Where is your
heart? Is it fixed on God or the world?

Prayer: Lord Jesus, I am not asking for riches, power, or
glory. I am asking to serve You and others all the days
of my life. Lord, keep my heart fixed on You alone, for
You are my Treasure! In Your name I pray. Amen!

Where Is God's Kingdom?

The coming of the kingdom of God is not something that can be observed, nor will people say, "Here it is," or "There it is," because the kingdom of God is in your midst. Luke 17:20-21, NIV

Do you believe that God's Kingdom is within you and among us? He is in our hearts when it is free of clutter and when we surrender our all to Him. How do you feel, knowing that God's Kingdom is in your midst? Do you look at the world differently, knowing that God is within you?

Jesus calls us to Himself as He said, *"Repent, for the kingdom of heaven is at hand [he is near]"* (Matthew 3:2, ESV). Jesus asks us to change our old ways to experience His Kingdom in our daily lives and everything we do. He invites us to seek His Kingdom, where we are now, by letting go of our hurts and past sins, focusing solely on Him for mercy and grace. Jesus wants us to live our best life in Him by striving to eliminate worldly attachments that prevent us from loving Him with all hearts. He wants us to see Him in all things. He is ready to make His home in our hearts and renew our relationship with Him. Let us accept His invitation and pray for the grace to give it all to God.

Action/Thought for Today: Take a few minutes in silence and search for the Lord in your heart.

Prayer: Father, thank You for promising us Your Kingdom. Lord, thank You for living in us and among us. We praise and bless You! It is in Your name we pray. Amen!

TWO LOVES!

You shall love the LORD your God with all your heart and with all your soul and with all your might.   Deuteronomy 6:5, ESV

This world is flooded with pleasures, distractions, and many other things that distract us from the Lord. Don't let worldly things separate you from God. Don't be blinded by things that look or feel good. For instance, if a piece of music sounds good but has vulgarity in it, reject it. If a food tastes good but leads to gluttony, fast from it.

I echo St. Augustine, "There are two loves, the love of God and the love of the world. If the love of the world takes possession of you, there is no way for the love of God to enter into you. Let the love of the world take the second place, and let the love of God dwell in you. Let the better love take over."[7] For *"No one can serve two masters, for either he will hate the one and love the other, or he will be devoted to the one and despise the other"* (Matthew 6:24, ESV). Therefore, always seek first the things of God. Ask Him for the grace to reject the things of this world. If we ask Him with honesty, rest assured that He will free us from the bondage of the things of this world.

Action/Thought for Today: Which love are you choosing? Ask the Lord to help you choose Him.

Prayer: Lord Jesus, draw me closer to You and keep me in Your heart. Help me place You above all things. I pray in Your holy name. Amen!

Rework Us!

Can I not do with you, O house of Israel, just as this potter has done? says the LORD. Just like the clay in the potter's hand, so are you in my hand, O house of Israel.   Jeremiah 18:6, NRSVUE

Are you broken, hurt, or desolate? Are you suffering from loss, or are you isolated from the world? Friends, do not despair, for no child of God is broken beyond repair. Know that the Lord can repair our brokenness and turn us into unimaginable and beautiful children of His Kingdom.

Do not let your situation define you. You are not a coward, nor desperate, nor hopeless. Like clay in the hands of God, let Him reshape you, heal you, and make you whole again. The Lord does not need glue to repair you. He can *"rework us into another vessel, as seem[s] good to Him"* (Jeremiah 18:4, NRSVUE). All He needs is our collaboration to breathe fresh air into our future. Lift your hands, shout the sound of victory, and expect God's healing and miracles in your life. Then, be still, and let our powerful God recreate you for the best.

Action/Thought for Today: Take a few minutes and prayerfully reflect on Jeremiah 18:6. Surrender yourself to God and ask Him to have His way with you.

Prayer: Heavenly Father, thank You for Your hope, love, and peace. Thank You for redefining our hearts, minds, and thoughts to align with Yours. Thank You for blessing us with a new life in You. In Jesus' name I pray. Amen!

TIPS FOR A PRAYERFUL LIFE!

Pray in the Spirit on all occasions with all kinds of prayer and requests. With this in mind, be alert and always keep on praying for all the Lord's people. Ephesians 6:18, NIV

St. Teresa said, "Prayer is nothing else but an intimate sharing between friends; it means taking time frequently to be alone with Him whom we know loves us."[8] Although our lives are busy, we can raise our eyes to Heaven from time to time, for at least a second. Here are some tips that I have learned from friends and family over the years:

- If your day is chaotic, say a short prayer such as "Jesus, I need You now."
- If you see a car accident or ambulance, say a one-minute prayer for those involved.
- Pray before a meal, even for a minute.
- Pray for the people in the car in front of or behind you or for a random person on the street.
- Pray or sing a song of praise while driving or cleaning the house.
- Say a quick prayer at work for your clients and coworkers.
- Thank the Lord every time you swipe your bank card to pay for something.
- Thank God for safety when your family comes home from school, work, or travel.

If you can lift your heart to the Lord often, you will remain in a prayerful spirit at all times.

Action/Thought for Today: Try to say many short prayers during your day.

Prayer: Lord Jesus, teach me how to communicate with You throughout my day. In Your name I pray. Amen!

DISTRACTION IN PRAYER!

I am saying this for your own good, not to restrict you, but that you may live in a right way in undivided devotion to the Lord.

1 Corinthians 7:35, NIV

Are you distracted in prayer? If so, you are not alone in this struggle. At times, our prayers unite us to the Lord. At other times, we seem to be drifting away from Him. When you are distracted in prayer, strive to return to the Lord once you realize that you are not focusing on Him as often as necessary.

First, to decrease distraction in prayer, start your prayer by asking the Lord to help you *"set your minds on things that are above, not on things that are on earth"* (Colossians 3:2, ESV).

Second, pray about your distractions. For instance, if your mind wanders to your family while praying, pray for them. If you are thinking about your work, say a prayer for your coworkers or work situation. If you are thinking about food, then thank God for your daily bread. I learned these lessons from a priest, and they have been vital in my prayer life. They help bring my every wandering thought to the Lord. It is better to say a short fervent prayer than a long prayer full of distraction.

Third, if you are paying attention to someone other than God during church services, close your eyes while opening your heart to the Lord. Let us pray for the grace to focus on God at all times.

Action/Thought for Today: Make a plan to help you be less distracted in prayer.

Prayer: Lord Jesus, I am often distracted in prayer. Please help me set my heart and mind on You alone. In Your name I pray. Amen!

SHUT THE DOOR AND PRAY!

But when you pray, go into your room and shut the door and pray to your Father who is in secret.   Matthew 6:6, ESV

A prayer life will encounter some roadblocks, and distraction is one of them. Distractions in prayer are thoughts that prevent us from fully turning our hearts and minds to God. Voluntary distraction occurs when we allow our minds to shift to the things of this world during prayer or church services. Involuntary distraction is when we have no control over our lack of focus during prayer, and this could be due to illness, life's problems, or the evil one distracting us. We must recognize the stumbling block that causes the lack of concentration in prayer and take action against it.

When I say short one-second prayers throughout the day, there is not enough time for me to be distracted because it is just a glance at the Lord. However, to spend quality with the Lord, I must shut out the world, for noise is my pitfall. It is challenging for me to concentrate on prayer in a noisy place. For that reason, I try to pray as much as possible in the early morning when everyone at home is still sleeping and there is less noise from pedestrian and street traffic.

Action/Thought for Today: What is your pitfall in prayer? Ask the Lord to help you discern it and for the grace to pray without distractions.

Prayer: Lord Jesus, please help me keep my gaze directly on You only. Keep me steadfast in prayer. In Your name I pray. Amen!

NOT A MATTER OF EATING AND DRINKING!

For the kingdom of God is not a matter of eating and drinking, but of righteousness, peace and joy in the Holy Spirit.

Roman 14:17, NIV

Sometimes we may think comfort and luxury are most important in life. The apostle Paul told us, in Roman 14:17, that life is not only about eating and drinking. I add, it is also not about sleeping, resting, making money, or being merry. The essential thing is to love, know, and serve the Lord with our whole hearts and minds. It is also to live with righteousness, bringing joy and peace to others in our daily encounters.

We ought to be more concerned about our spiritual well-being than our physical state, which is temporary. Seeking the Kingdom of God and His righteousness should matter to all Christians, for all we have is Jesus. Death is inevitable, and this world is not our home. God's Kingdom is everlasting! Our priority must be our relationship with God; therefore, seek Him only!

Action/Thought for Today: Today, from time to time, say this short prayer: "Lord, I commit myself to You."

Prayer: Lord Jesus, let my prayer be an offering of myself to You. May it be done to me according to Your will. Please teach me to commit myself to You, live righteously, and bring joy and peace to all. Thank You, Father, for Your kindness, grace, and mercy. In Your name I pray. Amen!

GOD CARES ABOUT THE LITTLE THINGS!

Simon's mother-in-law lay sick with a fever. They immediately told him about her. He approached, grasped her hand, and helped her up. Then the fever left her and she waited on them.

Mark 1:30-31, NABRE

Do you include Jesus in the minute details of your life—the small desires, accomplishments, problems, worries, or illnesses? A fever, headache, or cold are normal parts of life, and, usually, those illnesses require very little to no intervention. Often, we do not involve Jesus in the small problems of our lives, thinking that we can take care of them by ourselves.

The disciples did not see fever as a mild ailment. They told Jesus about Simon's mother-in-law's fever, and He healed her immediately. The disciples' action is an example for us to include Jesus in all the details of our lives. He wants us to put Him in everything. No problem is too small for Jesus. He wants to know about it all. All minor to major issues belong to Jesus.

Jesus even cares about our hair. Indeed, the very hairs of our heads are numbered (see Luke 12:7). He knows when we sit or stand (see Psalm 139:2). Nothing is too small or too big for Him. Therefore, let us confide all to Jesus as we pray in all circumstances.

Action/Thought for Today: Do you include Jesus in every small detail of your life?

Prayer: Lord Jesus, sometimes I forget to include You in the small details of my life. I am so sorry for those times. Please help me remember to put You at the center of my life. In Your name I pray. Amen!

A ROUTINE FAST!

The days will come when the bridegroom is taken away from them, and then they will fast.   Matthew 9:15 9, NAB

Has fasting become routine for you? We can lose the value of prayer and fasting if it becomes routine and less meaningful. If this is happening to you, don't despair and don't stop fasting. Just adjust. Add abstinence beyond your usual degree of fasting. You may add an extra hour to your standard time or fifteen more minutes of prayer. Consider refraining from social media and entertainment on your fast day. When I feel that my fast is less meaningful, I offer it as intercessory prayer for others. This helps me focus on the Lord and adds meaning to my fast.

Fasting has many benefits. It is the best way to defeat the devil. Jesus defeated the devil while fasting forty days and nights in the desert (see Matthew 4:1-11). According to St. Francis de Sales, "Even if we do not fast to any great extent, Satan is the more afraid of those who, he is aware, know how to fast."[9] Fasting changes us to be more like Christ. It purifies the heart, submits the flesh to discipline and self-control, corrects weaknesses, and strengthens virtues. Fasting brings us closer to the Father's heart as we rely on Him to fill us during the period of abstinence. Therefore, let us not neglect to add fasting to our spiritual life.

Action/Thought for Today: Add an extra abstinence/sacrifice to your usual fast.

Prayer: Lord Jesus, You fasted and prayed for forty days and nights. Teach us how to pray and fast like You. It is in Your name we pray. Amen!

FAST FROM IDOLS AND SIN!

Finally, beloved, whatever is true, whatever is honorable, whatever is just, whatever is pure, whatever is pleasing, whatever is commendable, if there is any excellence and if there is anything worthy of praise, think about these things. Philippians 4:8

Fasting has more meaning, importance, and value when we change our former way of life and move away from sin. In addition to the abstinence of food and drink, let us ask the Holy Spirit to assist us with detachment from idols and sins that prevent us from experiencing the glory of God and knowing His purpose for us. Therefore, let us:

- Fast from pride, arrogance, and selfishness (we must get rid of "it's about me, myself, and I").
- Fast from lust, controlling, overspending, greed, gluttony, bitterness, resentment, judging others, gossiping, lying, and perverted speech. God hates evils (see Psalm 5:1-12).
- Fast from idols such as power, money, wealth, success, and failure, etc.
- Fast from whatever keeps us away from the Lord, such as social media, entertainment, worries, fears, etc.

I know that a spiritual fast can be challenging. No matter how devoted we are to our fast, temptations to fall into sin will come our way. Therefore, let us *"pray without ceasing"* (1 Thessalonians 5:17, NAB) for God's divine grace and mercy to help us resist temptations.

Action/Thought for Today: Examine yourself and ask the Lord to help you detach from all idols and sins in your life.

Prayer: Lord, please forgive our sins. Help us detach from idols and sins and renew ourselves in You. In Your name we pray. Amen!

THE DIVINE PHYSICIAN!

Jesus answered them, "It is not the healthy who need a doctor,
but the sick."   Luke 5:31, NIV

Who among us does not need a doctor? Some may feel that they don't need a doctor, either physically or spiritually. They don't believe that they need God's salvation. Many, aware of their defilement, agree that a doctor is essential in their life.

Jesus came to heal and save ALL OF US, for we all have sinned, but only those who recognize their illnesses will be saved. For instance, a woman who was bleeding for twelve years knew that she was sick. In search of healing, she touched the fringe of Jesus' cloak. Instantly she was healed (see Matthew 9:20-21), and Jesus said to her, *"Daughter, your faith has made you well"* (Matthew 9:22).

We all need Jesus, the Divine Physician, to heal us in every area of our lives. We continually need His mercy to restore us from our sins. We need His living water to purify our minds, spirits, and hearts and make us blameless and upright before Him. *"Good and upright is the LORD; therefore, he instructs sinners in the way"* (Psalm 25:8).

When Jesus heals us, He also transforms us to change others. Our healing affects others as we become role models to those around us and bring change to their lives. Therefore, let us pray to accept the healing that Jesus offers.

Action/Thought for Today: What areas in
your life need healing right now?

Prayer: Lord Jesus, I need Your healing today and every
moment of my life. In Your name I pray. Amen!

JESUS CAME FOR SINNERS!

I have not come to call the righteous, but sinners to repentance.
Luke 5:35, NIV

Jesus did not come for the righteous; He came to seek and save the lost (see Luke 19:10). Jesus called sinners to new life every day. He stayed at the house of Zacchaeus, a chief tax-collector who defrauded others (see Luke 19:1-10). Jesus asked the Samaritan woman, who had five husbands, to give him a drink (see John 4:1-30). He called Matthew, a tax collector, to follow him (see Matthew 9:9-13). He called Paul, a persecutor of Christians, to evangelize (see Acts 9:1-19).

Jesus did not judge or speak ill about the people He met. He does not alienate others because of their way of life, but He heals, transforms, and restores every sinner who comes to repentance.

We are all sinners in need of help to become better. When you see someone involved in sin, do you judge them, stay away from them, or talk ill about them? Or do you become like Jesus to them, calling them to a new life in a gentle way? As the apostle Paul stated, we must meet others where they are and help them to live under the law of God: *"To those outside the law I became like one outside the law—though I am not outside God's law but within the law of Christ—to win over those outside the law. To the weak, I became weak, to win over the weak. I have become all things to all, to save at least some"* (1 Corinthians 9:21-22, NAB).

Action/Thought for Today: Do you help others
to a new life in Christ or judge them?

Prayer: Lord Jesus, teach me to meet others where they are. Teach us to live within Your law. In Your name I pray. Amen!

IT IS FINISHED!

When Jesus had received the vinegar, he said, "It is finished"; and he bowed his head and gave up his spirit. John 19:30, RSV

Indeed, Lord, it is finished. You have completed Your Father's work of salvation. My Lord, You have been obedient and accepted a cruel death for the sake of humanity. You paid the price for us in full. Indeed, Your work on Earth is finished, but You continue to be with us in our daily trials and tribulations. You continue to send us Your Spirit to intercede for us in our weakness (see Romans 8:26).

Do you see Jesus' crowns of thorns when you look upon the cross? Do you recall His bruised body and pierced side gushing blood and water? Do you see His pierced hands and feet? Do you see your sins and shame upon the cross? What I see is this:

My Lord humbled Himself to the point of death to save you and me. My Savior stretched out His arms to me, asking to become one with me. My God's eyes are full of compassion, love, and mercy, letting me know that my sins are washed away by His precious blood. Death is not victorious because Christ died for us to gain eternal life. Jesus looks past my sins and does not give up on me, but sees a beloved child of God.

I pray and hope that we all find meaning in the sacrifice Jesus made for us on the cross.

Action/Thought for Today: Whenever you see a cross, please take a minute to reflect on the ultimate sacrifice the Lord has made for you.

Prayer: Lord Jesus, thank You for dying for me. Please help me understand more and more the sacrifice You made for me on the cross. In Your name I pray. Amen!

REPETITION, REPETITION, REPETITION!

Jesus said to him [Thomas], "I am the way, and the truth, and the life; no one comes to the Father, except through me." John 14:6

Every year, during Holy Week, we hear the reading of Jesus' passion, crucifixion, and resurrection. But why do we read and re-read the narrative story of the events leading to Jesus' death and resurrection? The Church wants us to remember God's love, His great mercy, and the gift of salvation offered to humanity. Those words ought to transform us every time we hear them, for they are the testimony of our faith and expression of the ultimate sacrifice Jesus made for the forgiveness of our sins.

Every time we read Jesus' story, He reveals more deeply the truth of His identity and how we should live. We must always keep God's words in our hearts. *"When you walk, they will guide you; when you sleep, they will watch over you; when you awake, they will speak to you"* (Proverbs 6:22, NIV). The next time you hear Jesus' remarkable stories of salvation, will you let them pierce your heart and renew you again? Will you ponder His immeasurable love and mercy for you and be grateful? Will you let them positively affect your relationship with Him and others? Let us not hear the repetitions of these holy stories in vain, but *"come to the knowledge of the truth. For there is one God; there is also one mediator between God and humankind, Christ Jesus, himself human, who gave himself a ransom for all"* (1 Timothy 2:4-6).

Action/Thought for Today: Reflect on these questions.

Prayer: Lord Jesus, please transform me through Your words and deepen my relationship with You. Holy Spirit, help me live by them. It is in Your name I pray. Amen!

WORKS OF MERCY!

For I was hungry and you gave me food, I was thirsty and you gave me drink, a stranger and you welcomed me, naked and you clothed me, ill and you cared for me, in prison and you visited me. Matthew 25:35-36, NABRE

* For the full scripture, read Matthew 25:32-36

We live in a society that encourages us to care for ourselves and forget about others. Jesus tells us otherwise. He wants us to care for all. The Lord has mercy on us and fills us with many blessings, so He wants us to be merciful to our neighbors as well. The Lord reminds us in scripture, *"Whatever you did for one of these least brothers of mine; you did for me"* (Matthew 25:40, NABRE). Do you only think of yourself, your family, and friends?

The Catholic Church encourages the faithful to perform Works of Mercy. Mercy is revealed in words, deeds, and the desire to do good for others. The Corporal Works of Mercy are: feeding the hungry, giving drink to the thirsty, clothing the naked, welcoming strangers, visiting the sick, visiting those in prison, and burying the dead (see Matthew 25:32-36). These works of mercy must not come from the hands only, but, most importantly, from the heart, meaning it must be done with love and compassion. Therefore, *"let your love be genuine"* (Romans 12:9), and let your works of mercy be sincere.

Action/Thought for Today: Pray about those to whom you can bring mercy and love today. What can you do to relieve the suffering of others?

Prayer: Lord Jesus, open my eyes and heart to see the suffering of others. Please show me whom I must help and give me the desire to do Your work. In Your name I pray. Amen!

NOT EVERYONE!

Not everyone who says to me, "Lord, Lord," will enter the kingdom of heaven, but only the one who does the will of my Father in heaven.   Matthew 7:21

Someone once said to me, regarding ministry work: "It is not doing these things that will make God love you." Yes, God indeed loves, me no matter what. I cannot buy His love because He loved me first (see 1 John 4:10). However, as a disciple of Christ, I must follow in His footsteps.

Jesus healed the sick (such as the leper in Mark 1:40-45). While I may not have the power to touch and cure someone, I can show compassion by praying and visiting the sick. Jesus fed the five thousand in the multiplication of the loaves of bread and fish (see Matthew 14:13-21). While I cannot feed five thousand, I can provide for one person. Jesus transforms others miraculously. Perhaps I can be an example to those around me so that I can change their lives for the better.

Therefore, let us be an imitator of Christ. *"Whoever says, 'I abide in him', ought to walk just as He walked"* (1 John 2:6). Every time we positively touch someone we are changing the world, one person at a time. I echo Mother Teresa: "I alone cannot change the world, but I can cast a stone across the water to create many ripples."[10]

Thought/Action for Today: Visit, call,
and pray for the sick and dying.

Prayer: Lord Jesus, thank You for first loving me.
Please give me the grace to serve those who are
in need. Help me bring Your love in words and
deeds to all. In Your name I pray. Amen!

WHAT ARE YOU LOOKING FOR?

Jesus turned and saw them [the disciples] following, he said to them, "What are you looking for?" John 1:38

* For the full scripture reference, see John 1:35-42.

It is satisfying to find that for which we are looking or searching in life. I believe that the disciples had been looking for their Master. When John announced, *"Look, here is the Lamb of God"* (John 1:36), the disciples followed Jesus. Seeing the desire of their hearts to listen to His teachings, He then asked them, *"What are you looking for?"* This question is an invitation for us too, to follow and be with the Lord, respond to His voice, and become imitators of Christ.

We are incomplete human beings who are continuously searching for something. Some search for the riches, titles, and pleasure of this world, only to discover that these things cannot replace God. Others seek God in their lives. We should not seek God only when we are in trouble or need something. We should do so just because He is God. We must recognize Him as our Lord and Savior. We must let God find us, and in return, find Him in our day-to-day life. Our search will be complete when we see Jesus face to face at the end of our life journey. In the meantime, let us increasingly seek to know and be with Him.

Action/Thought for Today: Let us reflect and pose this question to ourselves, "What are we looking for?"

Prayer: Lord Jesus, help us find You in our day-to-day life. In Your name we pray. Amen!

FREE FROM ALL BONDAGES!

The God of our ancestors raised Jesus, whom you had killed by hanging him on a tree. God exalted him at his right hand as Leader and Savior that he might give repentance to Israel and forgiveness of sins.   Acts 5:30-31

God has raised Jesus from the dead and placed Him at His right hand to be our Leader, Savior, and Deliverer. Through Christ's resurrection, we are free from all bondage. However, we must take responsibility and be willing to live a life of freedom in Him. Our deliverance comes from trusting and believing in the Lord, repenting for our sins, and asking the Lord to create in us a pure heart (see Psalm 51:10). Our deliverance comes through prayer and fasting, resisting temptation and renouncing the works of the devil. Our deliverance comes by forgiving others as the Lord has commanded us (see Matthew 6:14-15).

Remember: *"Be alert and of sober mind. Your enemy, the devil, prowls around like a roaring lion looking for someone to devour. Resist him, standing firm in the faith, because you know that the family of believers throughout the world is undergoing the same kind of sufferings. And the God of all grace, who called you to his eternal glory in Christ, after you have suffered a little while, will himself restore you and make you strong, firm and steadfast"* (1 Peter 5:8-10, NIV).

Action/Thought for Today: What deliverance do you want from the Lord at this time in your life?

Prayer: Father, thank You for the gift of salvation. Please give us the grace to believe and trust You. Send forth Your Spirit and create in us a pure heart. Help us walk in Your path. I praise and thank You, Lord. Amen!

SINS, BARRIERS TO GOD'S GRACE!

Rather, your iniquities have been barriers between you and your God, and your sins have hidden his face from you. Isaiah 59:2

Sin puts barriers between God and us. Adam and Eve were afraid because they had sinned, so they hid from God's presence (see Genesis 3:8-10). It is the same with us. When we sin, our spiritual life weakens because we turn away from the Lord. Our sins block us from being in full communion with Him. Therefore, we must fast, pray, and receive the Sacrament frequently (if you belong to a Sacramental Church) , so that the Lord will help us overcome sin in our lives.

In prayer one day, the Lord told me to stop complaining about a particular person who had hurt me. It was only in prayer that I was able to recognize my wrongdoing. I then asked the Lord to help me change my behavior. In prayer, the Lord allows us to see our sins. He corrects us by drawing them before our eyes (see Psalm 50:21) and gives us the grace to turn our minds, souls, and hearts to Him. If we recognize our faults and repent when we fall, the Lord will forgive us and help us stay in His grace.

Action/Thought for Today: Do an examination of conscience at the end of the day. Ask the Lord to forgive your sins.

Prayer: *"Have mercy on me, O God, according to your steadfast love; according to your abundant mercy blot out my transgressions. Wash me throughout from my iniquity and cleanse me from my sin. … Create in me a clean heart, O God, and put a new and right spirit within me"* (Psalm 51:1-2 and 10). In Jesus' name I pray. Amen!

AM I MY BROTHER'S KEEPER?

Then the LORD said to Cain, "Where is your brother, Abel?" He said, "I do not know; am I my brother's keeper?" Genesis 4:9

* For the full scripture reference, see Genesis 4:1-16.

Yes, indeed, we are our brothers' and sisters' keepers. Sometimes I wish this statement were not true, for I struggle with some people in life. But, regardless of our relationship, we are still their keeper, and there is no escape from this fact.

Our lives depend on each other for better or worse. What we do, think, or say influences the lives of others. If we gossip about others to someone, we cause that person to sin as well. If we hurt others and they become bitter or resentful, we bear some responsibility for their reaction. Although we cannot control others' responses to hurt and pain, we are still the cause of the problem.

If we bring joy and peace to others, their lives and attitude may change for the better because of us. Therefore, we must do whatever is in our power to help everyone live their best life ever. We can do this by being considerate, encouraging, and loving. Jesus showed us how to love by placing us first and agreeing to die for our salvation. He knows that our eternal lives depend on Him. Let us follow Jesus and make an effort to be the best brothers' and sisters' keepers we can be.

Action/Thought for Today: How can you be the best brother's or sister's keeper?

Prayer: Lord Jesus, give us the grace to embrace each other with affection, love, and respect, for we are family in Christ. Please unite and solidify us in prayer. In Your name we pray. Amen!

AMBASSADORS FOR CHRIST!

So we are ambassadors for Christ as if God were appealing through us. We implore you on behalf of Christ, be reconciled to God. 2 Corinthian 5:20, NABRE

According to *Merriam-Webster's* online dictionary, an ambassador is "an official envoy, especially a diplomatic agent of the highest rank accredited to a foreign government or sovereign as the resident representative of his or her own government."[11] Since our homes are in Heaven, God has chosen us to be His ambassadors in this world. He wants us to represent Him and inform this world of His laws, His commands, and that *"whoever believes in Him shall not perish but have eternal life"* (John 3:16, NIV). Jesus wants us to proclaim His Good News to those who do not know Him or refuse to accept Him. He desires that His ambassadors inform others of His forgiveness, goodness, love, and mercy for all. Jesus is looking forward to enjoying eternity with us all.

Ambassadors often experience difficulties living in different countries, yet they must be able to accomplish the mission of their homeland. We must follow the same path in our works for Christ. Since we are from Christ, many will accept us, but others may reject us. We may suffer hardship or persecution like the disciples to proclaim the message of salvation. Regardless of what others do, we must share Jesus' ministry.

Action/Thought for Today: Are you willing to be an ambassador for Christ? In what way can you be His ambassador?

Prayer: Lord Jesus, help me be an ambassador for Your Kingdom. In Your name I pray. Amen!

WHAT CAN I DO FOR YOU, LORD?

Jesus asked him [a blind man], "What do you want me to do for you?" He said, "Lord, let me see again."   Luke 18:41

* For the full scripture, see Luke 18:35-43.

Jesus asked, *"What do you want me to do for you?"* The blind man asked for healing, and Jesus restored his sight (see verse 43). Jesus is also willing to grant us our hearts' desires and fulfill our plans and petitions (see Psalm 20:4-5). Have you ever taken the time to ask Him, "What can I do for You, Lord?" If we take the time to ask and listen to Him, He will tell us.

One day, I asked the Lord that question. I was expecting a significant assignment from Him, but His answer surprised me. He gently spoke to my heart, "Be kind today." I reflected, "Am I not kind?" I didn't understand the Lord's request, but the All-Knowing God, who knows my every unspoken word and thought (see Psalm 139), was asking me to imitate Him. That very day, a few people stepped on my toes. My first reaction was to fight back. Then the Lord reminded me of what He had asked of me: "Be kind today." With God's grace, I accepted my little trials without speaking, and I learned to be a bit more kind and patient through this experience. When God asks us for something, He also supplies us with the grace necessary to follow His commands. Therefore, let us not be afraid to ask, "What can I do for You today, Lord?"

> **Action/Thought for Today:** Open your heart to
> listen as you ask, "What can I do for You, Lord?

Prayer: Lord Jesus, give me the grace to follow Your precepts and imitate Your characteristics. In Your name I pray. Amen!

BLESSED IS THE MAN!

Blessed is the man who does not walk in the counsel of the wicked. Nor stand in the way of sinners, nor sit in company with scoffers. Rather, the law of the LORD is his joy; and on his law he meditates day and night. Psalm 1:1-2, NABRE

We choose the path we walk—good or evil. We cannot do both. Psalm 1 gives us a profound message, advising us to avoid the path of the wicked and the evildoers, for it will lead to ruin (see Psalm 1:6). In contrast, the Lord will bless the just with His joy and the gift of life.

At a retreat I attended, a man asked this question: "Suppose your neighbor abused your children. Would you take revenge?" The retreat leader told him to pray and forgive. The man then asked, "What if the abuser tried again?" One person suggested more prayers, calling law enforcement, and moving out of the area, but the man insisted that the best response would be to take revenge to protect his family from future dangers. It is a parent's duty to protect their children, and every abuser should be held accountable, but this must be done from a place of love and forgiveness. As Christians, we should do what is possible to help the offender turn away from evil and walk the path to repentance and reconciliation with God.

In the face of injustice and mistreatment, it is very easy to walk in the counsel of the wicked. Therefore, we must be very cautious. If we take an eye for an eye, we, in turn, become wicked. Therefore, God's grace is needed to avoid the path of wickedness. Let us not rely on our understanding, but on God's grace for guidance.

Action/Thought for Today: Are you walking in the path of the wicked or with God? If you are not walking with God, ask for His grace. He wants to help.

Prayer: Lord Jesus, help me walk in Your counsel and meditate day and night on Your laws. In Your name I pray. Amen!

DO YOU HAVE EYES AND EARS?

Jesus said to them [the disciples], "Are your hearts hardened? Do you have eyes and fail to see? Do you have ears and fail to hear?"

Mark 8:17-18

* For the full scripture, see Mark 8:14-21.

I reflect on this scripture, saying "Lord, sometimes I neither hear nor see You." Many times, we choose to hear the message of the Gospel only when it is convenient for us. If Christ's message does not fit our circumstances, we tend to give a deaf ear instead of trying to change to God's ways. Some even stop going to church or reading the Bible because God's words pierce to the core and *"judge the thoughts and attitudes of the hearts"* (Hebrews 4:12, NIV). So, *"Today, if you hear His voice, do not harden your hearts"* (Hebrews 3:15, NIV). Therefore, when the Word of God rebukes or corrects us, let us ask Him for forgiveness and the grace to accept His teachings.

Do you see Christ in your world? Many pray and desire to see Christ in their lives. He gives us multiple opportunities to see Him daily. Jesus is the Person to whom you are unkind at home, at work, and in church. The face of Jesus is in the poor, the homeless, and the marginalized. It is the face of Jesus in the foreigners whom you are rejecting. He is everywhere in everyone. When we see others, think of Jesus and see Jesus. Let us pray to show gentleness, kindness, love, and mercy to all.

Action/Thought for Today: Are you open to listening to God's voice? Do you see Christ in others?

Prayer: Lord Jesus, please bless my ears to hear Your message of love and mercy. Give me loving eyes to see You in others. In Your name I pray. Amen!

WHO IS JESUS CHRIST TO ME?

He [Jesus] said to them, "Who do you say that I am?"

Matthew 16:15

* For the full scripture reference, see Matthew 16:13-20.

When Jesus asked this question, Simon Peter replied, *"You are the Messiah, the Son of the living of God"* (Matthew 16:16). Although we know from the Bible and others who Jesus is, we must pause and look deeply into our hearts, "Who is Jesus Christ to me?" The response to this question is vital to a Christian. Our faith, actions, and way of life depend on our beliefs.

The disciples followed Jesus with all their hearts because they believed in Him and had established a personal relationship with Him. It is the same for us. If we do not believe in Christ, why should we follow or trust Him? If we do not know Christ, why should we adhere to His commands and teachings?

For me, Jesus Christ is my Savior, the One who has given His life for the salvation of my soul. In a nutshell, Jesus is my Everything, my All-in-All. This gives me great confidence, knowing that He loves me, and I can count on Him for everything. Now it's your turn. "Who is Jesus to you?"

Action/Thought for Today: Reflect on the above scripture and ask the Lord for the grace to answer this question correctly.

Prayer: Lord Jesus, I know and believe that You are the Christ, the Son of the living God, my Savior. Thank You for dying on the cross to save me. I praise You all the days of my life. In Your name I pray. Amen!

ALMSGIVING!

You received without payment; give without payment.
                                    Matthew 10:8, ESV

Jesus calls us to give. Our donations are vital for maintaining our places of worship and helping the poor and the less fortunate. Whatever we have is from God. We cannot deny others the gift that God has given us. *"Give, and it will be given to you"* (Luke 6:38). There is a lot of joy in almsgiving:

- **The joy of encouragement:** Barnabas sold his field and gave the disciple the money (see Acts 4:36-37).
- **The joy of freedom:** Jesus told the rich young man, *"Go, sell everything you have and give to the poor, and you will have treasure in heaven; then come, follow me"* (Mark 10:21, NIV).
- **The joy of love:** *"We must support the weak, remembering the words of the Lord Jesus, for he himself said, 'it is more blessed to give than to receive'"* (Acts 20:35).
- **The joy of obedience:** *"Each of you should give what you have decided in your heart to give, not reluctantly or under compulsion, for God loves a cheerful giver"* (2 Corinthians 9:7, NIV).
- **The joy of repentance:** Zacchaeus gave half of his belongings to the poor (see Luke 19:8).

Therefore, let us give without counting the cost, and the Lord will bless us abundantly.

Action/Thought for Today: Make an effort this week to give to those in need.

Prayer: Lord Jesus, teach me how to give without counting the cost. Open my hands to give all to You for Your greater glory. In Your name I pray. Amen!

The Son of Man Is the Sign!

This generation is an evil generation; it asks for a sign, but no sign will be given to it except the sign of Jonah. For just as Jonah became a sign to the people of Nineveh, so the Son of Man will be to this generation. Luke 11:29-30

Have you ever asked the Lord for signs? We are people who want to know our destinies. Some search for signs in horoscopes and palm readings, etc., which are wrong places. Others look in the Bible or through prayers. God often speaks to us, but sometimes we miss hearing Him because we are seeking a big supernatural sign.

One day I asked God for a sign about something. He stayed silent. Later that day, I found an article entitled "Trust in the Slow Work of God." While I did not get the expected sign from the Lord, this article spoke to me. I knew that I needed to pray, wait, and trust in God. A few months later, God revealed His plan for me. He wants me to live by faith and not to depend on a sign.

Jesus wants us to fix our gaze on Him instead of looking for a sign as an answer in life. Jesus' death and resurrection are substantial signs for us. Therefore, we must have faith in Him and stop seeking signs. Be patient and believe that what God is doing in us will work out for our good.

Action/Thought for Today: Pray for an increase of faith and trust in the Lord.

Prayer: Lord Jesus, please grant me the grace not to ever look for a sign as an answer in my life, but to trust in You. In Your name I pray. Amen!

THE WORD OF GOD!

I will meditate on your precepts and fix my eyes on your ways. I will delight in your statutes; I will not forget your words.

Psalm 119:15-16

Today, there are many books about life coaching, motivation, and better living. These may help those who use them, but the ultimate answers and guidance are in the Bible. There we find the Word of God, which is never outdated or changed because *"Jesus Christ is the same yesterday and today and tomorrow"* (Hebrews 13:8).

God knows that we need a guide in life, so He gave us the Bible as an anchor for Christian living. Through the Bible, God speaks, comforts, corrects, strengthens, leads, and directs us. Through meditating on His words, we will know the Lord more deeply, know ourselves better, recognize our faults, obtain a more profound conversion, and be more like Christ. God's words sustain us in times of trouble and give us peace.

When my life is difficult, I read the Psalms. In them, I experience God's kindness, love, mercy, and presence. Through reflection on the Word of God, I receive direction which gives me hope. Therefore, it is of utmost importance that we take time to meditate daily on His Word.

Action/Thought for Today: Try to pray with the Holy Scriptures daily, even for five to ten minutes.

Prayer: Lord Jesus, *"Let the words of my mouth and the meditation of my heart be acceptable to you, O LORD, my rock and my Redeemer"* (Psalm 19:14). Lord, thank You for Your words which sustain me daily. In Your name I pray. Amen!

HAVE YOU RECOGNIZED JESUS?

Jesus himself came up and walked along with them; but they were kept from recognizing him.　　　Luke 24:15-16, NIV

* For the full reference, see Luke 24:13-35.

Have you missed walking with Jesus? Have you seen Him and not recognized him? I am sure I have missed Him many times. A few years ago, I was rushing home after a long day at work. As I stopped for gas, a lady walked up to my car and asked me for my shawl. I quickly responded, "I cannot give it to you," but I did give her some food. As I drove away, I felt guilty and thought to myself that I should have given her my shawl.

The next day, while at the homeless ministry, a random lady approached me and said, "Can I have the shawl in your trunk?" This time, without hesitation, I gave it to her. The lady thanked me and left immediately. She did not even wait for food. Looking amazed, the priest who was there asked me what happened. I replayed the scene for him, but I was puzzled. How did that woman know I had a shawl in my trunk? The priest told me, "The Lord gave you another chance to serve Him." Just like the disciples, my heart was burning within me (see Luke 24:32) as I encountered Jesus more deeply. This experience has taught me to open my eyes and heart more to the Lord and others in need, and I have become more receptive to the Lord's action in my life.

Sometimes we are so focused on ourselves that we miss Jesus standing next to us or walking with us. He is always with us, even if we don't feel His presence. He is among the people we encounter daily. When we pause and reflect, we can see and feel Jesus in others. This requires prayer, living in the Word of God, and making the effort to see Christ in others.

Action/Thought for Today: Have you missed walking with Jesus?

Prayer: Lord Jesus, open my eyes so I can see You more in others. Open my heart to be more like You. I praise and thank You! In Your name I pray. Amen!

WALKING WITH JESUS!

And He [Jesus] said to them, "What are you discussing with each other while you walk along?" Luke 24:17

* For the full scripture reference, see Luke 24:13-35.

Walking on the road to Emmaus, the disciples were talking about Jesus and the things that had happened leading up to His death and resurrection. Suddenly Jesus appeared to them, then walked and conversed with them.

Do you talk about Jesus on your walk with your friends? Do you talk about Him in your day-to-day living, at home, at work, in school, when you meet a stranger? I had the opportunity to visit Emmaus when I was on a pilgrimage in Israel. I remember the Scriptures coming alive as we walked and talked about Jesus. Although we did not physically see Jesus, we knew that He was present in our conversation. There was a sense of joy and serenity as we talked about Him.

Sometimes, in our conversation with others about Jesus, He brings clarity to unanswered prayers and direction and guidance on our faith's journey. He reveals Himself to us more and more as we speak *about* Him and *to* Him. Also, as we share our faith and Christian life with others, it encourages others, gives them hope, and strengthens them in their walk with God. I pray and hope that our conversation is centered around Jesus in our daily lives.

Action/Thought for Today: Is your conversation centered on Jesus?

Prayer: Lord Jesus, sometimes, I want to talk about You, but I am afraid of what others may think or say. Help me direct all my conversations toward You for Your greater glory. In Your name I pray. Amen!

CARRY YOUR CROSS WITH JESUS!

We are afflicted in every way, but not crushed; perplexed, but not driven to despair; persecuted, but not forsaken; struck down, but not destroyed; always carrying in the body the death of Jesus, so that the life of Jesus may also be made visible in our bodies. 2 Corinthians 4:8-10

Jesus accepted His passion and crucifixion without complaining and did not give up on us. How many of us fall in life and then refuse to get up? How many are losing hope or despair because of life's misfortunes? Jesus demands that we become like Him, *"carrying in the body the death of Jesus"* (2 Corinthians 4:10). No matter how often we fall, we must get up, shake off the dust from us, start over, and move on.

We must pray for the determination and courage not to let the setbacks of life bring us down. Sometimes our losses, regrets, disappointments, or shame stop us from living a purposeful and hopeful life. Jesus looked at Calvary with hope, knowing the result would be the salvation of humankind. As His followers, we should see our setbacks as an opportunity for improvement and a better life in Christ. We must pray not to dwell in the past, but to let God heal us from past hurts and bless us with wisdom for a brighter future.

As my friend, Dr. Johanne Belizaire-Francois said, "Today is more than yesterday and less than tomorrow."[12] Yes, we must improve each day. With Christ as our Guide and Strength, let us never be discouraged. Let us continue to move forward in life despite any setbacks.

Action/Thought for Today: Are setbacks
stopping you from living a purposeful life?

Prayer: Lord Jesus, give us the courage and
strength to get up every time we fall. We thank
You, Lord. In Your name I pray. Amen!

LOVE CARRIES MY CROSS!

And when they had mocked him, they stripped him of the cloak, dressed him in his own clothes, and led him off to crucify him.
Matthew 27:31, NABRE

Although the cross was heavy with my sins, Jesus did not complain as He carried it. He was bruised, weak, and in tremendous pain, yet, out of love for me, He continued to move on without speaking or murmuring. He was pushed and mocked, but He did not fight back for my sake. A crown of thorns was placed on His head to save me (see John 19:2). He was crucified because He loved me enough to sacrifice Himself and die to save me.

The price that Jesus paid for me was enormous, yet He does not regard my sins. No matter how much I sin, He always forgives me when I come to Him in prayer. He protects me from all dangers. He washes away my sins with His precious blood.

Jesus did all this for you and me, not because of what we have done, but because He loves us. Even if you or I were the only person on this Earth, He would have still died for the one, for we are all precious in His sight (see Isaiah 43:4). God the Father has given us the gift of Jesus: *"For God so loved the world that he gave His only Son, so that everyone who believes in Him may not perish but have eternal life"* (John 3:16).

Action/Thought for Today: Say a prayer of gratitude to the Lord for dying for your sins.

Prayer: Lord Jesus, thank You for carrying my cross and loving me enough to die for me. I praise and love You, my Lord and God. In Your name I pray. Amen!

HIS SIDE PIERCED FOR US!

But when they came to Jesus and saw that he was already dead, they did not break his legs. Instead, one of the soldiers pierced his side with a spear, and at once blood and water came out.

John 19:33-34

As I meditate on the pierced side of Jesus and His blood shed for me, I unite my bleeding wounds to Jesus' pierced side. I want to cover my wounds, but the Lord says to me, "Keep your wounds exposed so that I can heal them." I feel relieved knowing that God is with me, and He will heal these wounds from many years.

How many of you have spiritual and emotional wounds that have been covered with a bandage for years? How many of you have put on thick skin to cope with your wounds? If you are suffering from deep hurts or pain, it is time to uncover your wounds and unite your suffering with the Lord. God sees our hurts, concerns, pains, and desires and knows our deepest secrets. He understands what it is to have a wound, and He wants to heal us all. The precious blood and water that gushed forth from Jesus' side were poured out for all of us, to cleanse us from all defilement. Therefore, let us not be afraid to ask the Lord to heal our wounds with His precious blood.

Action/Thought for Today: Unite your wounds
with the Lord's and permit Him to heal you.

Prayer: Lord Jesus, thank You for healing my wounds.
I praise and thank You. In Your name I pray. Amen!

WATCH AND PRAY!

Watch and pray that you may not undergo the test.

Matthew 26:41, NABRE

* For the full scripture, see Matthew 26:36-46.

In the garden of Gethsemane, Jesus was sorrowful. His passion and death were imminent. Although He was filled with anxiety and fear, He wanted to accomplish the will of His Father. So, Jesus turned to His Father in prayer and asked the disciples to *"watch and pray"* with Him. When He returned, He found the disciples asleep. He said to Peter, *"So you could not keep watch with me for one hour?"* (Matthew 26:40, NABRE).

As Christ's disciples, Jesus instructs us to watch so that we do not enter into temptations and to spiritually unite our hearts and minds to Him. Jesus invites all of us to be more available to Him, dedicated to a life of prayer and discipleship. We must pray for assistance from the Father as Jesus did in the Garden of Gethsemane.

Prayer is discipleship's pathway. It prepares us for God's mission. Without prayer, the disciples could not have accomplished the task that the Lord entrusted to them (see Mark 9:29). God helps us turn our prayers into actions, such as healing the sick, preaching the Gospel, and serving the poor, etc. Therefore, do not fall asleep, make yourselves more available to God, and *"watch and pray"* with Him.

Action/Thought for Today: How can you make yourself more available for the Lord?

Prayer: My Jesus, give us the grace to be Your disciples. Strengthen us so that we can always watch and pray with You and those in need. In Your name we pray. Amen!

PROCLAIMING THE GOOD NEWS!

So then the Lord Jesus, after he had spoken to them [His disciples], was taken up into heaven and sat down at the right hand of God. And they went out and proclaimed the good news everywhere, while the Lord worked with them and confirmed the message by the signs that accompanied it. Mark 16:19-20

The Catechism of the Catholic Church states, "We firmly believe, and hence we hope that, just as Christ is truly risen from the dead and lives forever, so after death the righteous will live forever with the risen Christ and he will raise them up on the last day."[13] Christians wake up! Let the resurrection of the Lord strengthen us. Let us not be afraid to proclaim the Good News of the Lord to every corner of the world. Let us bring light to those living in darkness and bind the wounds of the afflicted. Let us set free those in bondage. Let us transform one life at a time with a touch of God's love, as we proclaim to the world that Jesus is the Resurrection and the Life. The ones who believe in Christ will live, even though they die; and whoever lives by believing in Him will never die. Do you believe this? (see John 11:25-26). As we proclaim the Gospel, Jesus will strengthen and bless us with all spiritual gifts and blessings to enable us to do His work.

Action/Thought for Today: What message do you want to give to the world today?

Prayer: Lord Jesus, give us the grace to proclaim the Good News everywhere. Lord, send forth Your spirit and renew the face of the Earth. We praise and adore You, Lord Jesus! In Your name we pray. Amen!

HOSANNA IN THE HIGHEST HEAVEN!

Those who went ahead and those who followed shouted, "Hosanna!" "Blessed is he who comes in the name of the Lord!" "Blessed is the coming kingdom of our father David!" "Hosanna in the highest heaven!"　　　　　　Mark 11:9-10, NIV

* For the full scripture reference, see Mark 11:1-10 and John 12:12-16.

Each year, on Palm Sunday, we commemorate Jesus' glorious entrance into Jerusalem. He was riding a colt, and the people took palm branches to meet Him. Less than a week later, on what we now call Good Friday, the same people who exalted Jesus turned their back on Him and cried out to Pilate, "*Crucify Him!*" (Matthew 15:6-15). Jesus has proven His love for us by accepting a cruel death. Still today, we continue to betray our dear Savior. How?

- When we refuse to stand against discrimination, prejudice, poverty, sins, social injustice, and violence.
- When we do not help the least of His people.
- When we conform to the world, but not His ways.
- When we believe that His grace is not enough for us and we rely on worldly things to satisfy us.

Let us pray never to turn our backs on Jesus, but to echo the Psalmist, "*How can I repay the LORD for all the great good done for me?*" (Psalm 116:12, NABRE).

Action/Thought for Today: Do something nice for the Lord today.

Prayer: Lord Jesus, I exalt and glorify You, for You are my Lord and my God. In Your holy name I pray. Amen!

APRIL 3

I Do Not Know the Man!

Then Peter remembered the word that Jesus had spoken: "Before the cock crows you will deny me three times." He went out and began to weep bitterly. Matthew 26:75, NABRE

*For the full scripture, see Matthew 26:69-75.

We do not have to say, *"I do not know the man"* (Matthew 26:74 NABRE), like Peter did to deny Christ. Often, we deny Jesus by our actions, deeds, and way of living that are not in accord with His teachings. We deny Him when we are too busy with the world's affairs and forget to let Him be first in our lives. We deny Him when we refuse to abandon our net and follow Him as the disciples did (see Matthew 4:20). Furthermore, we deny Jesus when we do not serve our hungry, thirsty, naked, or homeless neighbors.

Our concerns must be like those of Jesus in His public ministry, directed toward the underprivileged, sick, and homeless. The Lord makes it clear in the Gospel: *"Whatever you did for one of the least of these brothers and sisters of mine, you did for me"* (Matthew 25:40 NIV). Therefore, let us make Jesus the center of our lives by loving Him above all. Let us abide in Him always, follow His footsteps, and respect His commandments. Pray for the grace to never deny Jesus, regardless of the circumstances.

Action/Thought for Today: Have you ever denied Jesus by not serving the poor or the underprivileged? If so, ask the Lord to help you.

Prayer: Lord Jesus, give us the grace to never deny You. Give us the grace to serve and follow You always. Lead and guide us in Your ways only. We praise and thank You, Lord. In Your name we pray. Amen!

THIRSTY FOR YOU!

After this, aware that everything was now finished, in order that the scripture might be fulfilled, Jesus said, "I thirst."

John 19:28, NABRE

Jesus said on the cross, *"I thirst."* Today He is thirsty for you to come to Him in your weakness, with your sins, shortcomings, and struggles, and in all your affairs. He died for all, and He is thirsty for all humanity. Jesus still calls today, *"Let anyone who is thirsty come to me, and let the one who believes in me drink"* (John 7:37-38). He is ready to give us living water, which will become in us a spring of water welling up to eternal life (see John 4:14). Are we ready to accept His offer?

As Jesus gives us His fountain of living water, He also wants us to quench our neighbor's thirst. He said, *"For I was hungry, and you gave me no food, I was thirsty, and you gave me no drink, a stranger, and you gave me no welcome, naked, and you gave me no clothing, ill and in prison, and you did not care for me. Then they will answer and say, 'Lord, when did we see you hungry or thirsty or a stranger or naked or ill or in prison, and not minister to your needs?' He will answer them, 'Amen, I say to you, what you did not do for one of these least ones, you did not do for me"* (Matthew 25:42-45, NABRE). Let's pray for the grace and courage to satisfy Jesus' thirst in our love for Him and our neighbor.

Action/Thought for Today: Are you thirsty for Jesus?

Prayer: Lord Jesus, thank You for dying for me and giving the precious gift of salvation. Thank You for Your kindness and mercy toward me, a poor sinner. Grant me the grace to always satisfy Your thirst in all that I do. Lord, I praise and adore You. In Your name I pray. Amen!

DO YOU REALIZE WHAT I HAVE DONE FOR YOU?

"Do you realize what I have done for you? You call me "teacher" and "master," and rightly so, for indeed I am. If I, therefore, the master and teacher, have washed your feet, you ought to wash one another's feet. John 13:12-14, NABRE

*For the full scripture, see John 13:1-20.

In washing the disciples' feet, Jesus, the Master of the Universe, illustrated for us the characteristics of greatness, humility, service, and love. Jesus taught all of us to let go of our pride and become humble servants like Him. He clearly said in Matthew 20:28 (NABRE), *"The son of man did not come to be served but to serve, and to give his life as a ransom for many."* Jesus showed us that the greater you are, the more is expected of you, and the more you must humbly serve and sacrifice for others.

When Jesus washed the disciples' feet, He said to them (and also to us), *"I have given you an example, that you should do just as I have done to you"* (John 13:15, ESV). As Christians, we must follow Jesus' footsteps in our daily encounters with others through humble service, love, and compassion. Have you washed someone's feet lately with love, kindness, compassion, a word of encouragement, or a smile? Or have you missed the opportunity to serve those in need? What is stopping you from washing your neighbor's feet?

Action/Thought for Today: Reflect on these questions and ask the Lord to give you the grace to follow in His footsteps.

Prayer: Lord Jesus, we are sometimes so busy in this world's affairs that we do not see the suffering and needs of others. Give us the grace to wash one another's feet and teach us to be humble servants. We praise, adore, and glorify You. In Your name we pray. Amen!

BY HIS STRIPES!

But He was wounded for our transgressions, crushed for our iniquities; upon him was the punishment that made us whole, and by his bruises we are healed.   Isaiah 53:5

In this ever-changing society, many are tempted to live a life without Christ. Others are lukewarm in their faith or lack confidence in the Lord. We cannot live without Christ. Do not let your spiritual life falter. Pray and meditate on the Lord's passion and ask Him for help.

God the Father knew that we were going to betray His only Son. Yet He sent Him (see John 3:16) to the world in human likeness to save us because He loves us (see Philippians 2:7). We scourged Jesus, ridiculed Him, placed a crown of thorns on His head, gave Him a heavy cross, and crucified Him (see John 19). Jesus accepted this suffering to save us.

We must never forget Jesus' ultimate sacrifice and the price He paid for our salvation. We must ask Him to deliver us from selfishness and help us to be more like Him. We must let Him enter our lives and turn us into His image in the way we love and live. We must live by His Word and accept His invitation to unite with Him. We must let Hims gaze on us with His merciful eyes as we call out, *"Father, into your hands I commend my spirit"* (Luke 23:46). Let Him be our God, and let us be His people.

Action/Thought for Today: Take a little time to reflect on God's love and mercy for you.

Prayer: Lord Jesus, through Your death and resurrection, bring hope to the hopeless, faith to the faithless, love to the unlovable, and joy to the depressed. In Your name we pray. Amen!

SEEK THE THINGS ABOVE!

So if you have been raised with Christ, seek the things that are above, where Christ is, seated at the right hand of God. Set your minds on things that are above, not on the things that are on earth, for you have died, and your life is hidden with Christ in God.   Colossians 3:1-3

Through Christ's resurrection, God has called us to live in the fullness of His life. He has urged us to seek what is above and put away whatever is earthly. Christians are not immune to being unjust, unloving, unfair, untruthful, and unfaithful. Therefore, we must be prayerful and watchful, to live in Christ, to be guided by the Spirit of God, and to do what is right. *"He [the Lord] has shown you, O mortal, what is good. And what does the LORD require of you? To act justly and to love mercy and to walk humbly with your God"* (Micah 6:8, NIV).

Although we are still living in the flesh, we must pray to live by faith and in harmony with the Spirit of Christ. We must make every effort to maintain peace and unity in our society (see Ephesians 4:3). We must defend the oppressed, weak, and orphaned (see Psalm 82:3). We must speak the truth (see Ephesians 4:25). We are required to love well (see Romans 12:10), serve, forgive others (see Matthew 6:14-15), and accept forgiveness. Then, we can say like the apostle Paul, *"I have been crucified with Christ; and it is no longer I who live, but it is Christ who lives in me"* (Galatians 2:19-20).

Action/Thought for Today: What are you seeking in life, the things from above or the things on Earth?

Prayer: Lord, my heart is willing, but my flesh is weak. Give me the grace to act justly, love mercy, and walk humbly with You (see Micah 6:8). In Your name I pray. Amen!

IMPERISHABLE CROWNS!

I am coming soon; hold fast to what you have, so that no one may seize your crown. Revelation 3:11

Jesus wore the crown of thorns for us to save us (see Matthew 27:29). He has prepared many imperishable crowns for His faithful people:

- We may suffer hardship and persecution, but if we stay strong in the Lord, we will win the crown of life. *"Blessed is the one who perseveres under trial because, having stood the test, that person will receive the crown of life that the Lord has promised to those who love him"* (James 1:12 NIV).

- If we remain righteous, despite the ups and downs of life, God will bless us with the crown of righteousness. *"I have fought the good fight, I have finished the race, I have kept the faith. Now there is in store for me the crown of righteousness, which the Lord, the righteous Judge, will award to me on that day"* (2 Timothy 4:8 NIV).

- If we tend to God's people and are good examples to them, God will give us the unfading crown of glory (see 1 Peter 5:1-4).

- On the last day, God will wipe away our tears (see Revelation 21:4) and give us the crown of rejoicing (see 1 Thessalonians 2:19).

Let us follow the law of the Lord no matter the circumstances. For no eye has seen what God has prepared for those who love Him (see 1 Corinthians 2:9).

Action/Thought for Today: Pray fervently to win the race.

Prayer: Lord Jesus, help me to run and win the race of life so that I may be with You for eternity. In Your name I pray. Amen!

APRIL 9

THE CHRISTIAN LIFE IS A RACE!

This one thing I do: forgetting what lies behind and straining forward to what lies ahead, I press on toward the goal for the prizce of the heavenly call of God in Christ Jesus. Philippians 3:13-14

* For the full scripture reference, see Philippians 3:12-21.

When my sons were in high school, they were involved in Cross Country and Track and Field. These sports required a lot of preparation and discipline. They practiced daily, ate healthily and rested before each race. Their teams never took anything for granted; they focused on achieving their goals. As they ran, they never looked back but always forward, toward their goals.

The apostle Paul described spiritual life as a race. He said he was not looking to the past but pressing forward toward the finish line to accomplish his calling through Christ Jesus. We are in a spiritual race together and our goal must be to win it. God calls us to this race to receive the gift of eternal life. He asks us to work out our salvation with fear and trembling, and He promises to work in us for His purpose.

Let us make it our mission to focus on our spiritual goals, regardless of our past sins, mistakes, and shortcomings. Let us not look back, discouraged, living with regret or shame. Instead, let us continually work toward eternal life, fighting against temptation and sin with the help of God's grace. He calls us to be in fellowship with Him and to recruit disciples for this spiritual race. Let us strive to remain in the race through steadfast prayer and living according to God's will.

Action/Thought for Today: What are your plans to press on with the race?

Prayer: Lord Jesus, take my hand and journey with me in my spiritual life. I need You, Lord. In Your name I pray. Amen!

LIFE MUST BE A PRAYER!

Then Jesus told them a parable about their need to pray always and not to lose heart. Luke 18:1

We are called to *"pray without ceasing"* (1 Thessalonians 5:17) because the Christian life must BE a prayer. To pray continually does not mean we must be in prayer all the time. It implies that we must have a prayerful and peaceful attitude throughout our day. It means that everything we do must be a prayer, for without prayer, we have no life, we are nothing, and we accomplish nothing.

God loves us so much that He gave us prayer as a means of communicating with Him. Prayer helps us maintain and nourish our relationship with God. When we pray, our knowledge of God, love for Him, and service to His people increase more and more. In prayer, we can discern and accept God's will, which transforms us to live a life in Christ.

When we pray, the Lord Himself prays for us, with us, and within us. Romans 8:26 tells us, *"the Spirit helps us in our weakness; for we do not know how to pray as we ought, but that very Spirit intercedes with sighs too deep for words. And God, who searches the heart, knows what is in the mind of the Spirit because the Spirit intercedes for the saints according to the will of God."* Therefore, let us ask the Spirit for help in our daily prayer and at all times as we journey with Jesus.

Action/Thought for Today: From time to time, raise your hearts to God, and say a small prayer, such as "Lord, I trust in You," or "Lord, have mercy on me and the world."

Prayer: Lord Jesus, we lift our hearts and souls to You. Help us to pray without ceasing. In Your name we pray. Amen!

THE CHRISTIAN LIFE IS A BATTLE!

Do not be afraid of them; the LORD your God himself will fight for you.   Deuteronomy 3:22, NIV

The Christian life is a battle, one that is worth fighting. It is a battle between God and Satan. The Spirit of God always encourages us to do the right thing. On the contrary, the evil one wants to lead us down to the path of destruction. This battle is constant, and as long as we live, we will face adversities. Some of us do not think we are battling Satan because he is unseen. The apostle Paul told us that we are not fighting with blood and flesh but with the spiritual forces of evil (see Ephesians 6:10-17). These are some examples of our daily battles:

- Temptation that comes when we pray, fast, or try to do good is a battle. When tempted in the desert, Jesus did not comply with Satan's demands. He fought the temptation and was victorious (see Matthew 4:1-11).
- Distraction in prayer is a battle. We must bring our hearts back to the Lord as soon as we realize that we are distracted.
- Sinning is a battle of the soul, but as we repent and choose what is right and acceptable to God, we are victorious in the Lord.
- Lies, disharmony, unhappiness, impurity, vulgarity, anxiety, depression, etc., are all the enemy's tactics to discourage us. Through prayer, we can discern the truth and way of God.
- Pride, greed, lust, selfishness, and unforgiveness are also enemies of our soul. We must fight to uproot these sins in our lives.

God did not promise that we would be free from troubles; He promised that He would help us carry our crosses. As we struggle to follow God in this battle, let us not lose hope and heart. Let us remind ourselves that we need God's grace and ceaseless prayer to sustain us with courage, freedom, joy, and peace and help us to persevere in this battle.

Action/Thought for Today: What is your plan to win the spiritual battle of life?

Prayer: Lord Jesus, thank You for sustaining us in spiritual battle. Help us, Lord. We need Your help. In Your name we pray. Amen!

THE RULE OF LIFE!

This Book of the Law shall not depart from your mouth, but you shall meditate on it day and night, so that you may be careful to do according to all that is written in it. For then you will make your way prosperous, and then you will have good success. Joshua 1:8, ESV

Life has rules, for work, home, community, traffic, etc. Some religious communities live by a Rule of Life centered on Christ's way of life. Do you have a spiritual Rule of Life, such as daily prayer, regular church attendance, and daily scripture and other spiritual reading? Do you adhere to certain principles or a motto such as "treat others as you would like to be treated" (see Matthew 7:12) or *"love your neighbor as yourself"* (Leviticus 19:18)?

I was introduced to a Rule of Life by a Christian Association whose rues are as follows. The first is obedience to God and authority (see John 14:15). The second, they strive to live a life of holiness, which God asks of us, *"You shall be holy to me, for I, the LORD, am holy"* (Leviticus 20:26). The third, they aspire to be humble servants. God wants us to walk humbly with Him (see Micah 6:8). These Rules of Life keep me mindful in my walk with Christ and encourage me to be more like Him in my day-to-day living.

Fr. Jeffrey Kirby, in his book, *Lord, Teach Us to Pray*, has said: "It is very important that the rule of life is an act of discipleship. We want to be with the Lord, hear him, and do what he tells us in our daily lives, and the Rule of Life is a means to deepening this relationship."[14] It is well worth it for Christians to create a rule of life, to have a motto, etc. It helps us to put God at the center of our lives, strengthen our relationship with Him, seek to do His will, and live His call. It reminds us that we are in His presence at all times.

Action/Thought for Today: What is your rule of life or motto?

Prayer: Lord Jesus, help me to live for You and be more like You. In Your name I pray. Amen!

RULES FOR THE NEW LIFE!

All bitterness, fury, anger, shouting, and reviling must be removed from you, along with all malice. [And] be kind to one another, compassionate, forgiving one another as God has forgiven you in Christ.   Ephesians 4:31-32, NABRE

* For the full scripture reference, see Ephesians 4:25-32.

In this scripture, the apostle Paul taught us what Christian life, behaviors, and attitude should be. It is a call to a morally good life in Christ and applies to all. Society may encourage us to live a different kind of life. If we are kind and meek, we are perceived as weak. If our language is full of grace, we are seen as religious fools. If we do not lie or steal, we are considered naïve. And a "little white lie" is considered okay for some. Instead of fighting for what is right and just, we quarrel with others to justify our beliefs, etc.

Can you imagine if we lived according to the teaching of the apostle Paul? We would not need the court system to settle disputes or deal with constant pain and hurts from others. Instead, we would live in love, peace and harmony, reflecting God's likeness. Therefore, we must observe Paul's tenets in how we live. Let us pray for the grace to display good judgment, appropriate conduct, and discipline.

Action/Thought for Today: Read the scripture above one more time, examining your actions and attitudes, to see if you are reflecting God's likeness.

Prayer: Lord Jesus, help me renounce bitterness, anger, shouting, foul language, lies, and reviling. Please give me the grace to let go of my former way of life and help me be kind, compassionate, and forgiving. In Your name I pray. Amen!

THE CHRISTIAN'S MINISTRY!

He [Jesus] came home. Again, the crowd gathered, making it impossible for them even to eat. When his relatives heard of this they set out to seize him, for they said, "He is out of his mind."

Mark 3:20-21, NABRE

The self-preservation culture dictates that one should stay healthy, protect oneself from harm, and take care of oneself first. In this Gospel message, Jesus and the disciples were not thinking about protecting themselves. They could not even eat as they ministered to the crowd. Jesus surrendered everything to serve those around Him.

Christian ministry may not require us to forgo eating, but it does call us to let go of time, hobbies, and entertainment, and to fully devote ourselves to the service of the Lord. People may think that we are "out of our minds" as we sacrifice ourselves in God's work. We, too, may be faced with loved ones' opposition, contradiction, or mockery because we have abandoned our lives to God. No matter what others say or how difficult it is to serve, refuse to give in to discouragement. Know that Christian ministry is a high and honorable calling from the Lord. *"Therefore, my beloved, be steadfast, immovable, always excelling in the work of the Lord, because you know that in the Lord your labor is not in vain"* (1 Corinthian 15:58).

Action/Thought for Today: Are you afraid to take a risk for the Lord because of what others may think of you or say?

Prayer: Lord Jesus, give me the grace and courage to serve You with zeal despite opposition, mockery, and contradiction. Lord, bless and strengthen all those who have devoted themselves to Your service. In Your name I pray. Amen!

Open the Door of Your Heart!

But God, who is rich in mercy, out of the great love with which he loves us even when we were dead through our trespasses, made us alive together with Christ—by grace you have been saved.

Ephesians 2:4-5

The Lord's mercy endures forever because He loves us so much. Christ saves us through His death and resurrection, not because we deserve it, but because He is a merciful God, full of compassion and love. He is ready to forgive us whenever we fail, just like the Samaritan woman (see John 4:4-42). He is prepared to welcome us home no matter what sins we have committed, without judging, just like the prodigal son (see Luke 15:11-32). He is ready to heal us, just like the woman who was bleeding for twelve years (see Luke 8: 43-48). We see in the sacred Scriptures that the Lord's mercy has no limit or boundary. Therefore, let's open our hearts and receive His mercy and forgiveness. The Lord is saying to us, *"Behold, I stand at the door and knock. If anyone hears my voice and opens the door, I will come in to him and eat with him, and he with me"* (Revelation 3:20, ESV).

Action/Thought for Today: Will you open the door of your heart to receive God's mercy?

Prayer: Lord Jesus, give us the grace to accept Your mercy and love and to be merciful and loving to others. Give us the grace to be just like You, rich in kindness and slow to anger at all times. *"O give thanks to the Lord, for he is good; for his steadfast love endures forever"* (1 Chronicles 16:34). In Your name we pray. Amen!

April 16

Be Merciful!

Blessed be the God and Father of our Lord Jesus Christ, the Father of mercies and the God of all consolation, who consoles us in all our afflictions, so that we may be able to console those who are in any affliction with the consolation with which we ourselves are consoled by God. 2 Corinthians 1:3-4

Joseph is a great example of love, forgiveness, and mercy. His brothers conspired to kill him and threw him into a pit. Then they decided, instead, to sell him into slavery for twenty pieces of silver (see Genesis 37). Still, Joseph rose to a position of great power in Egypt, in charge of food distribution during the seven years of famine. When his brothers came to Egypt from Canaan to buy food, Joseph, whom his brothers did not recognize, could have exacted revenge and refused to give or sell them grain. Instead of consigning them to death, he saved their lives by giving them the food they needed to survive (see Genesis 42). This is mercy. Let us pray to be merciful and forgiving like Joseph. Our heart is limited, but God's grace is sufficient and abundant. If we ask God for His help, He will undoubtedly increase our ability to love and forgive more.

Action/Thought for Today: Decide to forgive someone who has offended you. Ask the Lord to help you recall who most needs your forgiveness.

Prayer: Lord Jesus, please give me the grace to show mercy, kindness, and forgiveness to all who have offended me. Lord, please increase my ability to love and forgive. In Your name I pray. Amen!

CRY UNTO THE LORD FOR MERCY!

When the righteous cry for help, the LORD hears, and rescues them from all their troubles.   Psalm 34:17

We are living in an upside-down world filled with uncertainties, so we must call upon the Lord to come to our aid. Just as a child calls "Daddy! Daddy!" for attention, we need to cry continually, *"Abba, Father!"* (Galatians 4:6), to ask God to come and repair the broken vessel of this world. We are broken due to our sinful nature. It is only through Christ that we can become whole again and have freedom in this life.

It is now time to WAKE UP and PRAY! We cannot wait for tomorrow, for tomorrow is not guaranteed. Today is the day to examine ourselves (see 2 Corinthians 13:5-9), ask for forgiveness, and return with faith to the Father's heart. More than ever, it is time to submit to God's will. He will deliver His people who cry unto Him, just as He delivered the *"Israelites out of bondage after forty years"* (Exodus 3:9-12).

Action/Thought for Today: Make an act of trust. Offer all your uncertainties and problems to our loving Lord.

Prayer: Lord Jesus, I am crying out to You for mercy, just like the Psalmist: *"Will you forget me forever? How long will you hide your face from me?"* (Psalm 13:1). Lord, accept the prayer of Your people. In Your kindness, mercy, and compassion, come in haste to save us and the world. In Your name I pray. Amen!

FATHER, FORGIVE US!

For we do not have a high priest who is unable to sympathize with our weakness, but we have one who in every respect has been tested as we are, yet without sin. Let us therefore approach the throne of grace with boldness so that we might receive mercy and find grace to help in time of need. Hebrews 4:15-16

Some people feel that they are too broken to go to the Lord. Know that Jesus loves us as we are and will never stop loving us. He loves us, regardless of what sins we have committed and what wounds or illnesses we bear. Despite our messy lives, troubles, and shortcomings, Jesus is near to us and is gazing at us with mercy. On the cross, Jesus said to the Father, as he looked at us with compassion, *"Father, forgive them, for they know not what they do"* (Luke 23:34). Therefore, we should never despair or be afraid to go to the Lord. He always wants to receive us with unconditional love and mercy. Jesus said, *"No one has greater love than this, to lay down one's life for one's friends"* (John 15:13). He called us "friends" not because we loved Him first, but because He loved us first.

Action/Thought for Today: What sin is keeping you away from the Lord? Examine your conscience and ask the Lord to forgive your sins.

Prayer: Lord Jesus, we thank and praise You for Your unconditional love and mercy. Give us the grace to accept Your mercy and love. In Your name I pray. Amen!

GOD'S MERCY IS FOR ALL!

For you, O LORD, are good and forgiving, abounding in steadfast love to all who call on you.   Psalm 86:5

Just as the Lord *"makes his sun rise on the evil and on the good, and sends rain on the righteous and on the unrighteous"* (Matthew 5:45), God's mercy does not discriminate. His mercy is impartial. It does not care about race, cultural background, language, religion, education level, socioeconomic status, or political affiliation. It is for everyone. God's mercy will never end (see Lamentation 3:22); it is from generation to generation for those who fear him (see Luke 1:50). God's mercy is new every morning (see Lamentations 3:23). It renews our strength because He wants to help us with our daily suffering and struggles. Let us open our hearts to let His mercy shine on us and bring us peace. *"The LORD is good to all, and his compassion is over all that he has made"* (Psalm 145:9). Blessed be God for His grace, compassion, and love that never fails us.

Action/Thought for Today: Pray for the grace to be merciful to others daily, just like God is merciful to us.

Prayer: Lord Jesus, thank You for Your unending mercy and steadfast love. Thank You for Your kindness toward us. I praise and thank You. Amen!

WE ARE GOD'S CHILDREN!

And because you are children, God has sent the spirit of his son into our hearts, crying "Abba! Father!" So you are no longer a slave but a child, and if a child then also an heir, through God.

Galatians 4:6-7

No sin is too great for God's mercy. Our sins may be many, but if we repent, God is always ready to forgive and create in us a pure heart and spirit. Jesus sees past our sins and wounds. He doesn't look at our brokenness. He sees in us a child of God. Jesus does not condemn us for our past actions, but delights in us, for we are the Father's creation. He is willing to set us free. He wants to make us new. He is ready to restore in us the joy of salvation. He calls us to Himself to be His people, heirs of the Father.

Because we are God's children (see 1 John 3:2), He will never reject us, for He cannot deny us. We must accept our identity as His beloved children, walk in His way, and be more like Him. Then, we will see Him as He is (see 1 John 3:2).

Action/Thought for Today: With prayer, decide today to make known your identity as a child of God everywhere you go and in all you do.

Prayer: Father in Heaven, we praise You, for we are *"fearfully and wonderfully made"* (Psalm 139:14.). Thank You because we are no longer slaves but children of the Most High God. Thank You for giving us Your freedom. In Jesus' name we pray. Amen!

MERCY AND FORGIVENESS!

As God's chosen ones, holy and beloved, clothe yourselves with compassion, kindness, humility, meekness, and patience. Bear with one another and, if anyone has a complaint against another, forgive each other; just as the Lord has forgiven you, so you also must forgive. Colossians 3:12-13

I am writing this during a challenging time of the Covid-19 Pandemic. For over forty days now, we have been under mandatory quarantine. Businesses are closed and we are obliged to stay at home and be more present in our family's life. For some, impatience, limitations, and weaknesses are exposed. Tempers, faults, and shortcomings are revealed. Those still going out to work and serving others may feel frightened, anxious, and frustrated. These moments of fear, frustration, and anger come at home, at work or in our community.

Should we run from it all? What should we do? Despite our current situation, we must show love and mercy to all, and also accept it. We must pray for God to open our eyes to see, and open our hearts to love, like Jesus. We must hope for a brighter tomorrow in the Lord and share this hope with others. We must embrace with charity those on our daily path. Let us not lose the opportunity to be like our merciful Heavenly Father.

Action/Thought for Today: Say a prayer of thanksgiving for your family, those in your community, and the workplace.

Prayer: Lord Jesus, clothe us with compassion, kindness, humility, meekness, and patience to bear with one another. In Your name we pray. Amen!

COME, HOLY SPIRIT, COME!

Repent, and be baptized every one of you, in the name of Jesus Christ so that your sins may be forgiven; and you will receive the gifts of the Holy Spirit. Acts 2:38

The world needs the Holy Spirit for a complete renovation of our hearts. We cannot bring about this renovation on our own, but the Spirit of God can complete the change and engender the repentance of sins. However, all of us should make an effort to let the Spirit of God guide and teach us, and detach us from worldly desires and sins. If we submit to the Holy Spirit, the renovation of hearts will change injustice into justice, hatred into love, unhappiness into the joy of the Lord, chaos into peace, impatience into patience, rudeness into kindness, malice into good will, faithlessness into faithfulness, self-indulgence into self-control.

Without the Holy Spirit, we cannot accept to bear the offenses of others and accept our daily crosses, as Jesus endured His cross for us. Without the Holy Spirit, we will not see the needs of those who are suffering. If each of us faithfully practices the fruits of the Holy Spirit (see Galatians 5:22-23) for a day, it could start a continuous ripple effect to change many lives. We can then fully live as sons and daughters of God and walk hand and hand with others as God intended us to live. Let's fight together to open our hearts to accept the baptism of the Holy Spirit to transform our inner being.

Action/Thought for Today: Which fruit of the Spirit is most difficult for you to embrace? Ask God for the grace to embrace and practice this fruit.

Prayer: Come, Holy Spirit, come! Give us the grace to love genuinely and treat others with respect. Renew our minds and hearts. Restore our broken world and hearts. Give us a spirit of forgiveness, kindness, gentleness, and peace. Come, Holy Spirit, come! In Jesus' name we pray. Amen!

PLANTED IN THE HOUSE OF THE LORD!

Planted in the house of the LORD, they will flourish in the courts of our God. They will still bear fruit in old age, they will stay fresh and green. Psalm 92:13-14, NIV

One day I received beautiful artwork from my coworkers with this quote: "Bloom where you are planted" (Author unknown). I sensed that the Lord was speaking to me through these words, and it led me to reflect. Am I planted in the house of the Lord and blooming love, hope, and faith?

If one plants the seed of love, one will bear the flower of friendship; if hope, then patience to wait for the Lord; if faith, then perseverance in life; if the fear of the Lord, then humility and wisdom; if tolerance, then kindness and gentleness. These plants must be watered with prayers, meditation, and the Word of God to bloom in our hearts. It is of utmost importance that our attitudes reflect the fruits and gifts of the Holy Spirit (see Galatians 5:22-23) everywhere and to all. If you see someone with a lack of love, faith, or hope, pray for them and show them God's love through kindness and gentleness. If someone lacks humility, be humble before them. If someone is sad, depressed, or lacks hope and faith, encourage them with God's words. Let us be a reflection of God's goodness and mercy. Thus, we will bloom where God places us and remain in the House of the Lord.

Action/Thought for Today: Are you planted in the house of the Lord? Are you sharing your love, hope, and faith with others?

Prayer: Lord Jesus, help us bear good fruit and teach us to live a life of love, hope, and faith. In Your name we pray. Amen!

GUIDED BY THE SPIRIT OF GOD!

*For this reason, make every effort to add to your faith goodness;
and to goodness, knowledge; and to knowledge, self-control; and
to self-control, perseverance; and to perseverance, godliness; and
to godliness, mutual affection; and to mutual affection, love.*

2 Peter 1:5-7, NIV

One day, while praying, I found myself reflecting on what it means to be guided by the Spirit of God. This reflection came to me by surprise. As the apostle Paul said, *"We do not know how to pray as we ought, but that very Spirit intercedes with sighs too deep for words"* (Romans 8:26).

People who are guided by the Spirit of God have an internal peace that surpasses all understanding (see Philippians 4:7). They do not fret over an injury, and they remain peaceful amid trials and chaos. They have an everlasting joy and a cheerful heart, even in difficult times. They never lose sight of the Lord and remain hopeful and faithful, no matter what life brings. They remain steadfast in prayer and meditate day and night on God's words. They observe His instructions and statutes. They love God and others with all their hearts. In adversity, they show patience. In all things, they accept God's will and show self-control—with food and drink, emotions, actions, and attitude, etc. They demonstrate goodness and kindness to everyone and in everything. The Spirit of God produces the fruit of the Spirit within these individuals (see Galatians 5:22-23).

Action/Thought for Today: What is the
Spirit of God doing in your life?

Prayer: Lord Jesus, lead and guide us with Your Spirit.
Please grant us the gifts of the Spirit through the knowledge
of our Lord and Savior. In Your name I pray. Amen!

KNOWLEDGE OF GOD'S SPIRIT!

Grace and peace be yours in abundance through the knowledge of God and of Jesus our Lord. His divine power has given us everything we need for a godly life through our knowledge of him who called us by his own glory and goodness. 2 Peter 1:2-3, NIV

Yesterday, we saw that one who is guided by the Spirit of God has an internal peace that surpasses all understanding (see Philippians 4:7). In contrast, if one is engaged in sinful behavior, the Spirit of God nibbles at one's conscience so that one moves toward God and changes the bad practice. That's why Christians feel guilty when they engage in sinful behaviors or have impure thoughts. Therefore, we must pay close attention to the movement of the Spirit of God within us. What is the Spirit of God telling me right now? We must pray for guidance and direction to live a godly life and not fall into sin. *"For all who are led by the Spirit of God are children of God"* (Romans 8:14). The Spirit provides us right counsel and judgment, courage and strength, hope, inspiration, consolation, and healing tears, to continue our faith journey with the Lord and others, and to always to do good.

> **Action/Thought for Today:** Reflect on how God's Spirit directs your daily life to stay away from sins.

> **Prayer:** Lord Jesus, thank You for Your Spirit who is always guiding us to do good. Give us the grace to understand the movement of Your Spirit within us and to follow Your leadership. We praise and thank You. In Your name we pray. Amen!

DOCILITY TO THE HOLY SPIRIT!

The LORD went in front of them in a pillar of cloud by day, to lead them along the way, and in a pillar of fire by night, to give them light, so that they might travel by day and by night. Neither the pillar of cloud by day nor the pillar of fire by night left its place in front of the people. Exodus 13:21-22

One breezy day, I noticed how the branches on a tree were blowing in the wind. They moved according to the direction of the wind without any objection. I thought to myself, "My life will be better if I can be docile to the Spirit of God, just as these branches are with the wind." I prayed with the Psalmist: *"Lead me in your truth, and teach me, for you are the God of my salvation; for you, I wait all day long"* (Psalm 25:5).

When we abandon ourselves to the Holy Spirit, He leads us with such gentleness that, at the beginning of the journey, we may not even realize it. However, little by little, the Spirit of God gives us the clarity to see His guidance in our lives. As we submit to the Holy Spirit, He guides and walks with us, just as He did the Israelites after they escaped from Egypt. The Spirit of God guided them by *"a pillar of cloud by day, and in a pillar of fire by night."* The Israelites followed the pillar and moved or stopped as to the pillar moved or stopped. That is how we should let the Holy Spirit lead and direct our path.

Action/Thought for Today: Pray for the grace to be docile to the Holy Spirit.

Prayer: Spirit of the living God, please teach me Your truth. Lead me in Your ways. Help me submit to Your holy will. In Your name I pray. Amen!

THE SPIRIT OF TRUTH!

For surely you have heard about him, and were taught in him, as truth is in Jesus. You were taught to put away your former way of life, your old self, corrupt and deluded by its lusts, and to be renewed in the spirit of your minds, and to clothe yourselves with the new self, created according to the likeness of God in true righteousness and holiness. Ephesians 4:21-24

The Word of the Lord is truthful, valid, and accurate. Do not look for truth in the world, for the world can be misleading and may lead to destruction. The devil always tries to turn people away from God. He is *"the father of lies"* (John 8:44) and the root of all evils. *"He ... does not stand in the truth because there is no truth in him"* (John 8:44). The devil wants us to stay silent amid injustice, violence, and cries for help. The devil leads one to applaud powerful men and women, to keep the status quo. He supports people's belief in power, money, and fame. He wants us to remain in darkness, alienated from God, and this deepens the hardness of our hearts so that we continue to be indifferent and cold to our brothers and sisters.

We must not conform to the world's truth but renew ourselves in God's way of life. The Spirit of Truth is Jesus, the only Truth. *"I am the way, and the truth, and the life; no one comes to the Father but through Me"* (John 14:6). The Spirit of God is embraced by spiritual men and women who are devoted to God and want to walk humbly with Him. They speak love and justice, listen to the poor and marginalized, and rescue the afflicted—despite the cost. Never neglect the Scriptures and prayer, for in them you will find the Lord—the Way, the Truth, and the Life.

Action/Thought for Today: Let us continue to pray for peace and God's truth throughout the world.

Prayer: Holy Spirit, sanctify us in Your truth. Please give us an eagerness to search for the truth and fill us with Your love as we seek it. In Jesus' name we pray. Amen!

THE SPIRIT OF GOD IS UPON ME!

The Spirit of the LORD God is upon me, because the LORD has anointed me; he has sent me to bring good news to the oppressed, to bind up the brokenhearted, to proclaim liberty to the captives, and release to the prisoners, to proclaim the year of the LORD's favor, and the day of vengeance of our God; to comfort all who mourn; to provide for those who mourn in Zion—to give them a garland instead of ashes, the oil of gladness instead of mourning, the mantle of praise instead of a faint spirit. Isaiah 61:1-3

Do you believe that the Spirit of God is also upon you as He was upon Jesus? After Jesus went up to Heaven, He sent God's Holy Spirit to the disciples so that they could continue His mighty work (see Acts 2). The apostle Peter reminded us that God said He will pour out His Spirit upon all flesh (see Acts 2:17). Through His Spirit, we shall prophesy, see visions, dream dreams (see Acts 2:17), and *"everyone who calls on the name of the Lord shall be saved"* (Acts 2:21).

The Spirit of God has anointed all of us to proclaim God's message to all, as noted in Isaiah 61. We ought to apply the above scripture to our lives and respond to it with faith. For those unsure of their life's purpose, Isaiah 61:1-3 defines multiple life missions in which we can all partake. Let us ask the Holy Spirit of God to lead us and help us set the world on fire as the disciples did.

Action/Thought for Today: Are you willing to set the world on fire for the Lord? Then submit yourself to the Spirit of God.

Prayer: Come, Holy Spirit! Come into my heart and help me set the world on fire for the Lord. In Jesus' name I pray. Amen!

RESPECT AND HONOR OTHERS!

Love one another with mutual affection; outdo one another in showing honor.   Romans 12:10

The French Poet, Jean La Fontaine, wrote a proverb: *"La raison du plus fort est toujours la meilleure,"* meaning "The reason of those best able to have their way is always the best."[15] Although influential people or leaders are not always right or have the best answer, this proverb still holds true. Many believe their words are final. The latter is true in church, family life, ministry, workplace, and community. Many in high positions mistreat others because of their rank. Some cannot admit their mistakes or say, "I was wrong," or "I am sorry."

Jesus gave us an explicit model of the characteristics of a great leader. He held a position of power on earth, and He still has humanity in His hands. Jesus is the Son of God, yet He *"humbled himself, and became obedient to the point of death—even death on a cross"* (Philippians 2:8). Although Jesus did not commit any crime, He accepted a violent death to save us. Our Lord did not exhibit His mighty power to the soldiers who abused and crucified Him. Let us pray to model Jesus. Great leaders are humble. They show integrity and respect to others, regardless of their position, and value the opinion of others. They model Jesus in all things.

Action/Thought for Today: Pray to have the heart of Jesus.

Prayer: Lord, give me the grace to accept that I am not always right. Help me to treat others with respect, regardless of my position in life. It is in Your name I pray. Amen!

PROTECT YOUR THOUGHTS!

Set your minds on things that are above, not on things that are on earth. Colossians 3:2

Do you have anxious, angry, or harmful thoughts? Are you obsessed by your work or family responsibilities? When unhealthy thoughts take over one's life, the soul is in danger and the heart is not at peace. One must do everything to protect one's heart, mind, and soul by constant prayer. Surrender those negative thoughts to the Lord. The apostle Paul told us, *"Set your minds on things that are above, not on things that are on earth"* (Colossians 3:2). When we focus on the things above, we can experience the joy and the peace given to us by the Lord. On the contrary, when unpleasant thoughts burden us, we are not living in the freedom of Christ.

If we stay connected to God, we are not shaken by the terror of the night nor the arrow that flies by day (see Psalm 91:5). Because we remember God's promises to those who know Him, He will rescue and honor us (see Psalm 91:14-15). We should pray to always be optimistic. Let us turn our eyes and hearts to Heaven and abandon ourselves to divine Providence.

Action/Thought for Today: When your mind cannot escape the anxiety of this world, pick up your Bible and fill your mind with the Word of God. Intentionally bring scripture to mind and affirm to yourself words such as: *"I am a child of God, I have been set free, and I belong to God."*

Prayer: Lord Jesus, give us the grace to fix our minds and thoughts on You alone. In Your name we pray. Amen!

BE AN ESTHER!

Then Esther said in reply to Mordecai, "Go, gather all the Jews to be found in Susa, and hold a fast on my behalf and neither eat nor drink for three days, night or day. I and my maids will also fast as you do. After that I will go to the king, though it is against the law; and if I perish, I perish." Esther 4:15-16

* For the full scripture, see the book of Esther.

Esther was a young Jewish orphan who was raised by her cousin, Mordecai, after the death of her parents. When King Ahasuerus was displeased with his wife, beautiful young virgins were sought, among them Esther. King Ahasuerus delighted in Esther, for she was beautiful, and he chose her to be his queen. She was instructed by Mordecai not to reveal her identity as a Jew (see Esther 2:10).

When Mordecai learned that King Ahasuerus planned to destroy all the Jewish people, he asked Esther to intercede for her people before the King. That was very risky because no one could approach the King *"without being called; there is one law —all alike are to be put to death"* (Esther 4:11). Esther asked all her fellow Jews to pray and fast with her for three days. Then she went to the King, interceded for her people, found favor with him, and thus saved her people.

God had placed Esther in the king's palace for just such a time. She obeyed the Lord and was willing to sacrifice her life for her people. We must learn from Esther to take the risk to help others with God's grace. Are you right now placed in a situation where you should make a sacrifice to help others? What are you willing to risk? Be an Esther, be the voice of the voiceless. Be the strength of the weak and marginalized. Pray, fast, and ask the Lord for courage, like Esther.

Action/Thought for Today: What risk is the Lord asking you to take for Him?

Prayer: Lord, give me courage like Esther so that I can obey You and do the right thing. In Jesus' name I pray. Amen!

BE A RUTH!

Ruth said, "Do not press me to leave you or to turn back from following you! Where you go, I will go; where you lodge, I will lodge; your people shall be my people, and your God, my God. Where you die, I will die—there will I be buried." Ruth 1:15-17

* For the full detail, see the book of Ruth.

Naomi and her family had settled in Moab to escape the famine in Judah. Ruth and Orpah, Moabite women, married Naomi's sons. However, when the husbands of the three women had died, Naomi decided to return home to Bethlehem and advised her daughters-in-law to return home to their family. Orpah returned home, but Ruth refused to go back to Moab. Instead, she accompanied Naomi to Bethlehem and took good care of her. She placed her trust in the true God, accepting the God of Israel as her God. Ruth later married Boaz, a relative of Naomi's late husband. God blessed them with a son, Obed, who became the father of Jesse, and Jesse became the father of King David—all ancestors of Jesus (see Matthew 1:1-17).

Ruth's faithfulness and loyalty brought about a blessing from generation to generation. She left us a perfect example of how we must be faithful, kind, loving, and devoted to our families. She taught us to try our best to help those God places in our lives. Our effort will never be in vain, for God will surely bless us.

Action/Thought for Today: Are you willing to help others without reservation? If not, pray and ask the Lord to help you.

Prayer: Lord Jesus, thank You for the family You have given me. Please give me the grace to remain faithful and loving to them. In Jesus' name I pray. Amen!

BE A DEBORAH!

Barak said to her [Deborah]: "If you will go with me, I will go; but if you will not go with me, I will not go."   Judges 4:8

Deborah was a prophetess, wife of Lappidoth, and a judge in Israel. She listened to God's voice, and He used her to communicate His plan to the people of Israel. One day, God gave her instructions to summon Barak and promised to help him and the Israelites defeat Sisera, the Canaanite commander who oppressed Israel for twenty years. God heard the cry of the Israelites and planned to deliver them from their oppression.

After Barak received Deborah's message, he asked her to go with him and told her that he would only go if she did. Deborah, without hesitation, went with Barak. God used Deborah to set up the mission, for she believed in His words. She listened to His voice and stepped out in faith. She spoke to Barak and courageously went with him to face the enemy. And, of course, Israel won the battle.

Do you listen to God's voice to accomplish His purpose? Deborah showed us the true meaning of courage and willingness to follow God's voice. God speaks to us often. Do we take time to listen to God? He speaks to us through the Scriptures, during prayer, and through family and friends. He also speaks in the quietness of our hearts. Therefore, we must strive to be calm and peaceful in all circumstances to hear the gentle voice of God, obey His will, and bring glory to His name.

Action/Thought for Today: Are you willing to be a Deborah?

Prayer: Lord Jesus, give us Deborah's courage to listen to Your voice and step out in faith to accomplish Your will. It is in Your name I pray. Amen!

BE A MARY (THE MOTHER OF JESUS)!

When the wine gave out, the mother of Jesus said to him, "They have no wine." And Jesus said to her, "Women, what concern is that to you and to me? My hour has not yet come." His mother said to the servants, "Do whatever he tells you." John 2:3-5

* For the full scripture, see John 2:1-11.

At the wedding of Cana, Mary told Jesus when she realized that the wine had run out. She did not directly ask Him to do anything, but telling Him indicated that she believed He could solve this problem. Knowing that Jesus could intervene, Mary did not wait to act. She told a servant, *"Do whatever He tells you"* (John 1:5). Then Jesus, with a single command, directed the servant to pour water into the jar, but when it was poured, the water had turned into wine.

The miracle of Cana was Jesus' first public miracle and sign of His great glory. In today's world, Jesus continues to do miracles and turn the water of our lives into wine. This miracle shows God's goodness and how He continues to give us *"grace upon grace "* (John 1:16). Mary gave us the perfect example of an intercessor when she asked Jesus to intervene and turn water into wine. Just like Mary, Jesus has called each one of us to intercede for each other in prayer, fasting, and deeds.

Action/Thought for Today: Have you interceded for someone lately? Who needs your prayer today? Please intercede for those in need.

Prayer: Lord Jesus, help us intercede for those in need. Today, we pray for the sick, dying, homeless, those in prison, and all those who need a miracle. In Your name we pray. Amen!

BE AN ABIGAIL!

David said to Abigail, "Blessed be the LORD, the God of Israel, who sent you to meet me today!"

1 Samuel 25:32-33

* For the full scripture, see 1 Samuel 25.

Abigail, a beautiful, clever, and wise woman, was married to Nabal, an ill-tempered and mean man. David and six hundred of his loyal men were encamped near them and had previously guarded Nabal's shepherds and possessions. When David requested food and provisions, Nabal refused, angering David, who decided to kill him and all who belonged to him. When Abigail learned of her husband's conduct, she acted in good faith, gathering food and wine for David and his hungry man.

Abigail went herself to meet David, bowed down before him and asked for mercy for her husband. She offered what she had brought as a peace offering. David accepted her offer and recognized that Abigail had helped him to not take revenge on Nabal's household (see 1 Samuel 23:32-33). Abigail returned home and found her husband drunk, so she didn't tell him about her meeting with David. The next morning, when she told Nabal everything that had happened, *"His heart died within him and became like a stone."* About ten days later, he died (see 1 Samuel 25:37-38). When David heard that Nabal was dead, he blessed the Lord for stopping him from using his own hands to kill Nabal, sent for Abigail, and married her.

Abigail taught us to act with kindness and wisdom, be peacemakers, and to help others in any way possible. She also taught us great humility by bowing down to David. Helping David changed her life in a most significant way.

Action/Thought for Today: Are you willing
to follow the footsteps of Abigail?

Prayer: Lord Jesus, teach us to act with kindness, wisdom,
and peace. Teach us to help others in any way possible. We
thank and praise You. In Jesus' name we pray. Amen!

BE A LYDIA!

A certain woman named Lydia, a worshiper of God, was listening to us; she was from the City of Thyatira, and a dealer of purple cloth. The Lord opened her heart to listen eagerly to what was said by Paul. Acts 16:14

* For the full scripture, see Acts 16:11-40.

Lydia was a businesswoman from the City of Thyatira who sold purple cloth. She loved the Lord and worshiped Him by the side gate of the river, a place for worship, where she met Paul. Along with her household, she was baptized by Paul and was among the first converts in the New Testament. As Paul was preaching the Word of God and was a visitor in her town, Lydia invited him to stay in her home. She stated: *"If you have judged me to be faithful to the Lord, come and stay at my home"* (Acts 16:15). Paul agreed to stay with her.

Although Lydia was a businesswoman, she found time for prayer. In this world of social media, entertainment, and business, it is challenging to find time for God. We must not let our day-to-day living or business take over. God must be the Alpha and Omega of our lives.

In her search for the Lord, Lydia was receptive to God's words. We, too, must be open to the truth of the Gospel and devote ourselves to the daily reading of the Scriptures.

Lydia was hospitable; she offered her home to Paul and Silas after they were released from prison (see Acts 16:40). Like Lydia, we must not neglect hospitality to strangers (see Hebrews 13:2).

Action/Thought for Today: Are you finding enough time for prayer in your day? If not, ask the Lord to help you.

Prayer: Lord Jesus, give us the spirit of Lydia, to be faithful in prayer, to be receptive to Your words, and to be hospitable to others. In Your name we pray. Amen!

BE A MARTHA OR A MARY
(SISTERS OF LAZARUS)

The Lord answered her, Martha, Martha, you are worried and distracted by many things; there is need of only one thing. Mary has chosen the better part, which will not be taken away from her.
Luke 10:41-42

* For the full scripture, see Luke 10:38-42.

As Martha was busy preparing to host the Lord, Mary sat at His feet, listening to Him. When Martha complained to the Lord about Mary not helping her, He told Martha not to be anxious about things, but to be more like Mary, focusing on Him only. Jesus accepted Martha's love for Him but reminded her of what is essential. Indeed, everything else can wait, as we sit at the feet of Jesus. Let us make it a significant part of our lives to spend time with the Lord and fix our eyes, hearts, minds, all our being on Him.

We can relate this story to our lives. Sometimes, when we have guests, we may be so worried about making our homes perfect that we forget to spend quality time with them. That is what happened to Martha. The Lord warned Martha, as well as us: *"There is need for only one thing"* (Luke 10:42), and that is be with Him. It is indeed more important to spend precious time with my guests instead of worrying about how my home appears.

We do need Marthas in our lives, the ones who keep everything moving in our church communities, as well in our families. However, our activities should not take us away from the Lord. If we create time to be still and sit at His feet, our services to others will bear more fruit.

Action/Thought for Today: Do you wish you could be a Mary more often, sitting at the Lord's feet?

Prayer: Lord Jesus, give me the grace to sit at Your feet, listen to You, and serve You all the days of my life. In Your name I pray. Amen!

BE A HANNAH!

For this child I prayed; and the LORD has granted me the petition that I made to him. 1 Samuel 1:27

In the biblical books of Samuel, Hannah appears as an excellent example of a woman who hoped in the Lord. She was unable to conceive. Her husband loved her profoundly, yet her infertility caused her a great deal of suffering. Hannah hoped that the Lord would bless her with a child; so, she cried to the Lord in prayer, and her petition was granted (see Samuel 1:1-28).

Like Hannah, we may be hoping for something good in life. If we have many great expectations, when things are not going as planned, we may get disappointed or feel hopeless. Friends, let us hope in God's plan for us, for hope in God does not disappoint (see Romans 5:5). If you are unhappy with the direction of your life, go to the Lord in prayer, cry out to Him with confidence. Like Hannah, do not despair, and He will rescue you in due time. I invite you to keep the words of St. Padre Pio in your heart, especially when you feel that you are losing hope. He said, "Pray, hope, don't worry."[16] Then, expect the Master of life, our God, to bless you with the desire of your heart.

Action/Thought for Today: What are you hoping for? Ask the Lord with confidence for your heart's desires.

Prayer: Lord Jesus, thank You for the many petitions You have granted us. Please give us the grace to hope in You with all our hearts. In Your name we pray. Amen!

PEOPLE OF JOY!

Mary Magdalene went and announced to the disciples, "I have seen the Lord."   John 20:18

Imagine Mary Magdalene seeing Jesus on Easter morning. She must have felt an indescribable astonishment mixed with joy! She must have been at a loss for words. Do you share the same joy that Mary Magdalene experienced, knowing that the Lord, our Savior, has risen?

During Easter, the Church often reminds us that we are "Easter People" and "People of Joy." We should not simply say that we are "Easter People"; we must live out Easter's joy and message in our actions, hearts, and minds.

There is no need to be gloomy; Jesus bore our sins and infirmities on the cross, and *"by his bruises, we are healed"* (Isaiah 53:5). There is no need to be hopeless; Jesus intercedes to the Father for us. He went to prepare a home for us in Heaven (see John 14:1-7).

We have every reason to align our actions with Christ's teaching. He lives in our hearts forever. That is more reason to adore and worship the Lord with an undivided heart, for His love and mercy endures forever (see Psalm 136). Let us kneel with our hands raised to Him and sing a song of joy to the Lord: We will always praise You, Lord, for You have rescued us.

Action/Thought for Today: Are you living out the call to be Easter People?

Prayer: Lord Jesus, give us the grace to always live out the Easter joy. It is in Your name I pray. Amen!

Strength and dignity!

She is clothed with strength and dignity, and laughs at the days to come. She opens her mouth in wisdom; kindly instruction is on her tongue.   Proverbs 31:25-26, NABRE

Every year, on Mother's Day, this scripture is seen on cards, electronic messages, and memorabilia, etc. To me, it is the definition of motherhood, an honorable and priceless calling. Motherhood can be exhausting, discouraging, and requires great sacrifice, but God blesses mothers with exceptional gifts of dignity, selfless love, generosity, and strength to care for their children. With their wisdom, they teach their children to know, love, and serve the Lord, and also to respect and love their neighbors—the greatest gifts a mom can offer to a child.

Mothers who have a fear of the Lord are to be praised (see Proverbs 31:30). They are not concerned with their external beauty (see Proverbs 31:30), but with their children's spiritual and moral lives. They counsel through God's words and teach with kindness. They pray without ceasing. Children may choose to walk away from God, but hopefully, the memory of their mothers' words and example will bring them back to Him.

Some women have no children of their own, but they love and serve with the heart and hands of a mother. They take great pride in those God entrusted to them. They care for them as if they were their biological children. Indeed, they are great MOMs. Others are our spiritual mothers who bring us closer to Christ through their prayers, encouragement, and helping us grow in our faith journey. All mothers deserve to be honored and loved!

Action/Thought for Today: Say a prayer
of blessing for all mothers.

Prayer: Lord Jesus, thank You for the gift of
motherhood. In Your name we pray. Amen!

JESUS AND THE WOMAN WITH A FLASK OF OINTMENT!

She stood behind him at his feet, weeping, and began to bathe his feet with her tears and to dry them with her hair. Then she continued kissing his feet and anointing them with ointment.

Luke 7:38

* For the full scripture, see Luke 7:36-49.

Did you notice that this scene is silent? The woman did not speak. She wept over Jesus' feet and wiped them with her hair, kissed his feet, and anointed them with ointment. This woman was known by everyone to be a sinner, yet Jesus let her touch His feet. She must have known from others that He could restore her broken life and that she would find forgiveness and salvation in Him. She offered Jesus what she had, her tears and ointment, without speaking a word. She washed His feet and then anointed them with perfume. In this way, she showed the Lord her love for Him and her desire to change and be renewed.

Jesus did not judge or condemn this woman but said to her: *"Your sins are forgiven"* (Luke 7:48). *"Your faith has saved you; go in peace"* (Luke 7:50). This woman's love and faith moved God. Her many sins were forgiven, and her life was changed forever. Jesus invites us to sit at His feet daily in prayer, and to ask for forgiveness with a firm resolution to change. He will transform us daily and bring us closer to His heart.[17]

Action/Thought for Today: Cry out to the Lord today for the forgiveness of your sins and the world's.

Prayer: Lord Jesus, please transform us to experience a new life in You. We thank and praise You. In Jesus' name we pray. Amen!

JESUS AND THE SAMARITAN WOMAN!

A Samaritan woman came to draw water, and Jesus said to her, "Give me a drink." The Samaritan woman said to him, "How is it that you, a Jew, ask a drink of me, a woman of Samaria?" John 4:7-9

* For the full scripture, see John 4:4-42.

Tired from the trip, Jesus decided to rest by Jacob's well in the Samaritan city, Sychar, while the disciples found food. A Samaritan woman came to draw some water, and Jesus asked her for some. The woman reminded Jesus that Jews and Samaritans did not get along. As the conversation continued, Jesus proceeded to ask her about her husband and told her about her past—that she had had five husbands and now was living with a man to whom she was not married.

Although Jesus knew the Samaritan woman's life, He spoke to her with compassion, offering her living water, eternal life (see John 4:10). Jesus did not ask her to change her life; He allowed her to decide to change her life. The woman went into her town and told everyone about Jesus, and many came to believe in the Lord. Jesus here gives us an example of love and forgiveness.

Often we tend to judge and condemn others, wanting them to conform to our standards. We choose our associates based on their way of life, without giving them a chance to change. Jesus sought out sinners, desiring to bring everyone to the Father. He accepted the woman as she was and let His unconditional love transform her.

We, too, should reach out to those in need of conversion with love, not telling them what to do, but letting Jesus do the rest. Jesus does not look at our past sins but accepts us as we are, hoping that we will accept Him as the Christ, the Savior of the world.[18]

Action/Thought for Today: Reflect on God's love for you.

Prayer: Lord Jesus, please teach us to treat others with love, compassion, and without judgment. Give us living water, eternal life. Help us believe that You are the Christ, the Savior of the world. In Your name we pray. Amen!

May 13

Jesus and the Woman Caught in Adultery

Jesus straightened up and said to her, "Women where are they? Has no one condemned you?" She said, "No one sir." And Jesus said, "Neither do I condemn you. Go your way and from now on do not sin again."

John 8:10-11

* For the full scripture, see John 8:2-11.

While Jesus was teaching in the Temple, the scribes and Pharisees brought to Him a woman who had been caught in the act of adultery. They made her stand in front of everyone and said that according to the Law of Moses she should be stoned. Jesus remained silent, writing on the ground. The Scriptures do not tell us what He wrote. When the scribes and Pharisees kept questioning Jesus, He said to them: *"Let anyone among you who is without sin be the first to throw a stone at her"* (John 8:7). At this, one by one, they all went away. Jesus is the only one without sin, yet He did not throw a stone. In His love and mercy, He could not condemn the woman because He came to redeem us.

Jesus did not approve of the act of adultery, but He is showing us to be careful about denouncing others' sins. In our society, we may not throw stones, but we do throw judgment and criticism. Let's look deeper into the mirror of our hearts. Then we will see that we must not condemn others, but, instead, ask the Lord to pardon our sins and shortcomings.

When Jesus said to the woman, *"Go and do not sin again,"* He gave her the confidence to start afresh, hope again, be free in the sight of God, and live a life of dignity and grace. We should allow others to start anew. This is easier said than done, but all is possible with prayer.[19]

Action/Thought for Today: How many stones have we thrown at others?

Prayer: Lord Jesus, give us the grace not to throw judgment and criticism at others. Instead, help us look into the mirror of our hearts and ask pardon for our own sins. In Jesus' name we pray. Amen!

WHO ARE THE TEACHERS?

Not many of you should become teachers, my brothers, for you realize that we will be judged more strictly, for we all fall short in many respects.   James 3:1-2, NABRE

* For the full reference, see James 3:1-10.

Teachers are not only in the classroom. Priests, pastors, evangelists, and ministry leaders teach the words of God. Parents and grandparents instruct their children or other family members in God's way and offer wisdom for life. Husbands and wives and good friends do the same for each other. We also teach in our professional lives. We may wear a different hat, but we all are teachers in some way. How are we doing as teachers? We must teach in word, deed, and example. Therefore, our actions and speech must be gracious, or others may rebuke us, and we will be judged more strictly. Remember, we must not only "talk the talk" but practice what we preach.

"No man can tame the tongue—a restless evil, full of deadly poison. With it, we bless the Lord and Father, and with it, we curse those who are made in the likeness of God" (James 3:8-9). We use our tongues to instruct, yet also to hurt others. Let us ask the Lord to guard our tongues and take over our conversations, as we all stumble in what we say. God is the only One who can give us the self-control to speak kindly, mindfully, truthfully, and wisely.

Action/Thought for Today: Let us pray for the Lord to guide our conversations.

Prayer: Lord Jesus, *"Set a guard over my mouth, O Lord; keep watch over the door of my lips"* (Psalm 141:3). Let my speech be gracious, O Lord. In Your name I pray. Amen!

DEEP WATERS

When you pass through the waters I will be with you; and through the rivers, they shall not overwhelm you; when you walk through fire you shall not be burned, and the flame shall not consume you. Isaiah 43:2, RSV

Have you ever felt that you are in deep water and dry land is impossible to reach? You may be crying, anxious, and only thinking of the possible adverse outcomes of your problems.

Early in our marriage, my husband and I invested in a rental property. Months later, a tenant chose not to pay the rent and damaged the property. Around that time, my dad was fighting a terminal cancer diagnosis. It was one problem after another, and I felt like I was drowning. Although spiritually I was not equipped to deal with these issues, Psalm 23 was on my lips. God was gracious. He provided for our every need. We sold the property, and God gave us peace with the loss. I now realize that God was with us all along, and He continues to bless us.

Friends, I assure you that God will never leave nor forsake us (see Deuteronomy 31:6). Always remember the truth of His promises as you meditate on these verses:

- *"Have no anxiety about anything, but in everything by prayer and supplication with thanksgiving let your requests be made known to God. And the peace of God, which passes all understanding, will keep your hearts and your minds in Christ Jesus"* (Philippians 4:6-7, RSV).
- *"He reached from on high, he took me, he drew me out of many waters"* (Psalm 18:16, RSV).

Action/Thought for Today: Meditate on these scriptures.

Prayer: Lord Jesus, when I am in the deep waters
of life, please help me navigate them with joy
and peace. In Your name I pray. Amen!

BLESSED ARE THOSE ...

Blessed rather are those who hear the word of God and keep it.
Luke 11:28, RSV

Sometimes, we read God's words and they speak to us immediately. At other times, we hear the words carelessly. God promises that we will receive His blessing if we obey His words. He guides us through His words, so we must enter His words daily and keep them in the depth of our hearts. God's words are a gift. He reveals Himself to us in the Scriptures, especially when we are troubled. The Bible speaks of the importance of God' words:

- *"And the Word became flesh and dwelt among us"* (John 1:14, RSV).
- *"In the beginning was the Word, and the Word was with God, and the Word was God"* (John 1:1, RSV).
- *"Heaven and earth will pass away, but my words will not pass away"* (Matthew 24:35, RSV).
- *"Man shall not live by bread alone, but by every word that proceeds from the mouth of God"* (Matthew 4:4, RSV).
- *"All scripture is inspired by God and profitable for teaching, for reproof, for correction, and for training in righteousness"* (2 Timothy 3:16, RSV).
- *"Your Word is a lamp to my feet and a light to my path"* (Psalm 119:105, RSV).

Action/Thought for Today: Do you read God's words daily? How does His Word bless you?

Prayers: Father, give me the desire to turn my eyes to Your words daily. Help me live according to Your will. It is in Jesus' name that I pray. Amen!

CONQUEROR OR LOSER?

For whatever is born of God overcomes the world. And this is the victory that overcomes the world, our faith.   1 John 5:4

- Suppose your spiritual life is in danger because of the nature of your job, and you decide to leave a high position at work, taking a lesser one with decreased pay to abide in the Lord and be present in your family life. Are you a conqueror or a loser?
- Suppose one has a terminal illness, death is imminent, but you he or she remains steadfast in the Lord and keeps the faith. Is this one a conqueror or a loser?
- Suppose you lack financial means and someone at work tells you to do something that compromises your moral and spiritual values for a promotion. You refuse and get fired. Are you a conqueror or a loser?

We are losers when we let the enemy take away our joy, peace, and love for God and others. We are losers when we live according to worldly standards and not God's ways. If we are in the faith and abide in the Lord, we are always victorious, no matter what happens in this life. We are victorious, for we have God, and nothing can separate us from His love. We may lose our physical life, but God will raise us on the last day. We may lack financial resources, but God will always provide for us. Friends, believe in this truth. We are victorious in the Lord! Alleluia and Amen are our songs!

Action/Thought for Today: Let us
reflect on the questions above.

Prayer: Lord Jesus, give me the grace to fix my eyes on You alone. Help me experience Your joy and peace, no matter where life takes me. It is in Your name that I pray. Amen!

MAY 18

DO YOU REMEMBER?

They forgot the God who had saved them, who had done great deeds in Egypt, amazing deeds in the land of Ham, fearsome deeds at the Red Sea. Psalm 106:21-22, NABRE

After God had delivered the people of Israel from slavery, after He had shown them His mighty power, they forgot about the works of His hands. *"They made a calf at Horeb and worshiped a cast image. They exchanged the glory of God for the image of an ox that eats grass"* (Psalm 106:19-20). History continues to repeat itself in our midst as we are no better than our Old Testament ancestors who had short-term memory issues. Some of us, too, forget God's mighty works in our lives.

- We are the people who do not recall God's power, no matter how much He has shown us.
- We are the people who tremble and resort to alcohol, hobbies, drugs, anything that can help us soothe pain, instead of waiting for God, even after He has done miracles in our past life.
- We are the people who forget about God when life is smooth, and all is well.
- We are the people who forget His commandments from time to time.

However, God remembers his covenant with us and shows us compassion due to the abundance of his steadfast love (see Psalm 106:45). Let us pray for the grace never to turn away from Him.

Action/Thought for Today: Meditate on and pray Psalm 106.

Prayer: Heavenly Father, even though we may not remember Your merciful and mighty works, do not forget us. Father, continue to show us favor and do not turn Your face away from us. In Jesus' name we pray. Amen!

WORDS HAVE POWER!

Death and life are in the power of the tongue, and those who love it will eat its fruits.　　　　　　　　　　Proverbs 18:21, RSV

Words have power. *"God said, 'let there be light'; and there was light"* (Genesis 1:3, RSV). Can you speak things into existence as God did? Many believe in speaking good things into existence. Some have a "motivation board (or notebook)," which is excellent for hope and inspiration. However, we must believe in God and have faith in order for our words to have power. We cannot just say "I am going to get this" or "I desire that" and expect to speak it into existence without faith. *"For truly, I say to you, if you have faith as a grain of mustard seed, you will say to this mountain, 'Move from here to there,' and it will move; and nothing will be impossible to you"* (Matthew 17:20-21, RSV).

As God told Moses to direct Aaron and his sons to bless the sons of Israel (see Numbers 6:22-27), I encourage you to speak blessing into your lives and those of your family members, friends, and acquaintances. Speak God's blessing into your problems, and chains will be broken. Speak God's words of courage and strength into the mountain of your lives, and they will move. As you speak the words of God, wait and watch God's miracles and power in your lives. But the words you speak will only have divine power if you abide in God and trust in Him.

Action/Thought for Today: Try to intentionally speak blessing into your life and the lives of your loved ones.

Prayer: Lord Jesus, thank You for giving us the ability to speak words of blessing upon ourselves and others. May our words always be encouraging and comforting to others. In Your name I pray. Amen!

LET THE LITTLE CHILDREN COME!

*Let the children come to me, do not hinder them; for to such belongs
the kingdom of God.*   Mark 10:14, RSV

Children were brought to Jesus for Him to lay His hands on them.
The disciples attempted to stop them from going to Jesus, but He
told the disciples, *"Let the children come to me"* (Mark 10:14 RSV).
Jesus loves little children. He blessed and laid hands upon them (see
Mark 10:16). We, too, must love children and do everything in our
power to protect them. How magnificent is the love of God for the
children and for us as well!

The Lord calls us to be childlike. He told the disciples and us,
*"Whoever does not receive the kingdom of God like a child shall not
enter it"* (Mark 10:15, RSV). What is so attractive about little children
that we must imitate them? They are carefree, trusting, and loving.
The innocence, purity, and simplicity of a child are to be desired. In
what areas in your life is the Lord calling you to be a child?

- Is He calling you to cast your cares, problems, and trials upon
  Him as little children depend on their parents for everything?
- Is He calling you to stop being anxious and worried but to live
  carefree as you bring your concerns to Him?
- Is He calling you to be more joyful and loving as you trust Him
  more?
- Is He calling you to live a life of simplicity and purity, like a
  child?

Let us strive to be a child in the classroom of Jesus as He transforms
our hearts and minds.

Action/Thought for Today: Pray and
reflect on the above questions.

Prayer: Lord Jesus, give us the heart of little Jesus.
Please help us to be innocent, pure, and simple
as a child. In Your name I pray. Amen!

There Shall Be No Divisions!

Now I appeal to you, brothers and sisters, by the name of our Lord Jesus Christ, that all of you be in agreement and that there be no divisions among you, but that you be united in the same mind and the same purpose. 1 Corinthians 1:10

In addition to weekly participation in mass, church, or worship services, it is essential to be part of Christian communities such as Bible study, prayer group, ministries, etc. One to two hours of weekly church service is not enough. Small groups help us learn more, stay connected with others, be accountable in our walk with Christ, and build each other's faith.

I have had many conversations with family and friends who refuse to participate in such communities. Most of them have lost faith in their brothers and sisters in Christ. The attitudes and behaviors of others have wounded their hearts. We are all children of God, and when we behave in ways contrary to God's teaching, we can push others away from the Lord. When we hurt others in our ministries, we can damage skeptical and weak faith. As Christians, we have a responsibility to:

- Bring others closer to Christ by enlightening them.
- Encourage others to use their God-giving gifts and talents.
- Treat others with kindness and love.

Therefore, *"Let us then pursue what makes for peace and for mutual upbuilding"* (Romans 14:19) for the glory of God.

Action/Thought for Today: What steps will you take to keep joy and peace in your ministry or small Christian group?

Prayer: Lord Jesus, I am sorry for the times I have hurt others in their walk with You. Please give me the grace to always keep peace and joy in my environment. In Your name I pray. Amen!

We All Need a Friend!

Finally, all of you, have unity of spirit, sympathy, love for one another, a tender heart, and a humble mind. Do not repay evil for evil or abuse for abuse; but on the contrary, repay with a blessing.   1 Peter 3:8-9

I don't know about you, but more than ever, I welcome encouragement and prayer from my friends. Life is chaotic and uncertain, with little uplifting in the news or social media. Hatred and unfairness are no longer undercover. Injustice, prejudice, and bigotry are out of the closet. However, I know *"love never ends"* (1 Corinthian 13:8) because Jesus is love, and He gives us friends to encourage and love us.

Love is the friend who lifts us in trying times. Love is the friend with whom we can honestly share our hearts, joy, and pain. It is the friend who helps us see Christ's light and truth. Love is the friend who can be the voice of reason while encouraging us to walk humbly with God. It is also the friend who does not point fingers or judge but meets us at our weakest point with prayer, love, and support.

Jesus knows that we cannot travel life alone. Hence, He places good friends in our lives to help us hope and love. *"Therefore, encourage one another and build up each other, as indeed you are doing"* (1 Thessalonians 5:11).

Action/Thought for Today: Reach out to a friend and let him or her know that you care.

Prayer: Lord Jesus, thank You for my friends. Please give me the grace to encourage them in times of need and love them like You do. In Jesus' name I pray. Amen!

REACH OUT AND ENCOURAGE DAILY!

But exhort one another every day, as long as it called "today," so
that none of you may be hardened by the deceitfulness of sins.

Hebrews 3:13

Encouragement is good medicine for the soul, one that can heal many wounds and heartaches. It costs nothing, and yet it is priceless. It requires a little effort, but it is worth more than gold. It is as simple as a smile, hug, kind word, or sharing a scripture or an inspiration with someone.

One day, when I called a friend, she answered the phone and started to cry. She had just had a painful experience, and she shared it with me through her tears. We talked and prayed over the phone, and at the end of the conversation, she regained her hope and peace. We all need to encourage each other daily in prayer and actions. Do not wait for only special occasions to reach out to others. You never know what difficulties or crises they may be secretly suffering, and you may be the only source of comfort and love for that person. If the Lord places someone on your heart today, reach out, and be Jesus to them. Through your encouragement, you may refresh another's soul and spirit.

Action/Thought for Today: Send a scripture
of encouragement to someone today. Ask the
Lord to lead you to the right person.

Prayer: Lord Jesus, You know that we will need the
medicine called encouragement. Therefore, You send
friends and family to bless us with love, gentleness,
and kindness. Thank You for always providing us with
what we need in life. In Your name we pray. Amen!

A LIFE LESSON!

Let no evil talk come out of your mouths, but only what is useful for building up, as there is need, so that your words may give grace to those who hear. Ephesians 4:29

My parents taught me that if I could not speak with kindness and gentleness, I should remain silent unless it was necessary to talk. I don't always observe these words of wisdom and prudence from my parents, but when I do put their advice into practice, it prevents me from significant disagreements with others. Through prayer, God blesses us with spiritual insight to act with peace in all situations: *"The wisdom from above is first pure, then peaceable, gentle, open to reason, full of mercy and good fruits, impartial and sincere"* (James 3:17, ESV).

Speaking with kindness is a life lesson that I carry daily in my heart. When I react with gentleness toward those who have offended me, I can see God's grace and mercy upon me. Staying silent may cause pain sometimes, but it is better to suffer than to use sharp words. Our words can soften or harden hearts; they can heal or hurt souls. They can bless or curse someone. We must always strive to build up others with our words instead of bringing them down, rejecting, or deceiving them.

Action/Thought for Today: When someone is not kind to you, what are some steps you can or will take to respond with love and gentleness?

Prayer: Lord Jesus, put a guard over my mouth. Please help me choose my words wisely. Bless me with wisdom and sacred silence when I don't have anything nice to say. I thank and praise You, Lord. In Your name I pray. Amen!

PRAY AND THINK BEFORE YOU CLICK "SEND"!

We who are strong ought to put up with the failings of the weak, and not to please ourselves. Each of us must please our neighbor for the good purpose of building up the neighbor.

Romans 15:1-2

Back in the day, people used to speak with each other more. Now we use text, email, and other electronic forms of communication. Social media can be used for good, but it can also poison the soul and discourage us when not used with care, wisdom, and love.

Recently, after receiving an unkind email message, I typed an answer three times, but because I felt that it sounded harsh, I didn't send it. Instead, I called on the Holy Spirit, and although I was upset, I was able to reply with simplicity and kindness. The email's originator responded with gratitude. All I could think of was, "What a change of heart!"

In this electronic age, while some have no consideration of what they send to others, I encourage you to think twice before responding to unpleasant messages. Please do not give in to ill-temper. Delay your response for a little while. You may have to sleep on the issue; your response will be softer the next day. *"A soft answer turns away wrath, but a harsh word stirs up anger"* (Proverbs 15:1). Regardless of how you feel, try to reply with love, gentleness, and kindness, and you will win the heart of your opponent.

Action/Thought for Today: When you receive an unkind message, let your anger settle before you respond. Pray for grace.

Prayer: Lord Jesus, I am not always kind in my response to others. I seek You for the grace to let my anger settle before I attempt to resolve a dispute. Please help me, dear Lord. In Your name I pray. Amen!

JUST LISTEN AND PRAY!

May our Lord Jesus Christ himself and God our Father, who has loved us and given us everlasting encouragement and good hope through his grace, encourage your hearts and strengthen them in every good deed and word. 2 Thessalonians 2:16-17, NABRE

I have a friend who was faced with many difficulties, but every time I encouraged her, she got upset. By God's grace, I realized what was going on, and as difficult as it was, whenever she complained, I just listened. Sometimes, in my effort to encourage others, I tend to say too much. For someone going through a difficult time in life—the diagnosis of a life-threatening illness, the loss of a loved one, the loss of a job or a divorce—even kindly-intended words may be painful to hear. For instance, Romans 8:28: *"We know all things work together for good for those who love God, who are called according to his purpose,"* is a very true scripture, but it may be unbearable to a hurting heart. Sometimes, a simple "I care" or "What can I do?" can be more encouraging than you could ever have imagined. If you do not know what to say to someone who is suffering, then give a hug, a holy kiss, and be present as you pray quietly for that person.

Action/Thought for Today: Encourage someone through your prayers today.

Prayer: Lord Jesus, I don't always know what to say to others in difficult times. Please give me the grace to bring encouragement and joy to others and not hurt a suffering heart. Teach me to speak only when I should. In Your name I pray. Amen!

THE GIFT OF FRIENDSHIP!

Every good and perfect gift is from above, coming down from the Father of lights.   James 1:17, NIV

Jesus had friends on Earth—the disciples, Lazarus, Martha, and Mary (see John 11:1-45). He also calls us friends (see John 15:15) and gives us earthly friends. Friendship is a precious gift from Him, a source of encouragement, joy, love, and support. It requires commitment from both parties. Let us reflect on a few principles of friendship:

- **Be honest:** *"Let your Yes mean Yes and your No mean No"* (Matthew 5:37, NABRE).
- **Be a good example:** *"Do not be deceived: 'Bad company ruins good morals'"* (1 Corinthians 15:33).
- **Choose carefully:** *"Make no friends with those given to anger, and do not associate with hotheads, or you may learn their way and entangle yourself in a snare"* (Proverbs 22:24-25).
- **Forgive them:** *"One who forgives an affront fosters friendship, but one who dwells on disputes will alienate a friend"* (Proverbs 17:9).
- **Reason for friendship:** *"A friend loves at all times, and a brother is born for a time of adversity"* (Proverbs 17:17, NIV).
- **Treat them well:** *"As God's chosen ones, holy and beloved, clothe yourselves with compassion, kindness, humility, meekness, and patience"* (Colossians 3:12).

Action/Thought for Today: Let us pray
for and cherish our friends.

Prayer: Lord Jesus, thank You for being my
Friend. Please teach me to love and cherish my
earthly friends. In Your name I pray. Amen!

LOVE THEM ALWAYS!

But I say to you that listen, love your enemies, do good to those who hate you, bless those who curse you, pray for those who abuse you. Luke 6:27

* For the full scripture, see Luke 6:27-31.

Many are disappointed and hurt by the mistreatment of others. Some shut the doors of their hearts to prevent future painful experiences. No matter the pain others have caused us, we must never cease loving them well and consistently.

- When others take our hospitality for granted, we must never stop being hospitable and genuine (see Romans 12:13, Hebrews 13:1-2, and 1 Peter 4:8-10).
- When others mock or are cruel to us, we must never stop forgiving them. Forgive as our heavenly Father has forgiven us (see Matthew 6:14).
- When we face unkind people, we must be kind anyway (see 1 Corinthians 13:4).
- When others take our generosity for granted, we must continue to give (see Luke 6:38).

Even if you are always the one to compromise, to maintain tranquility and avoid a quarrel, never stop being a peacemaker, for you will be called a child of God (see Matthew 5:9). Remember that the Lord was abused, ridiculed, and hung on the cross without cause. He never stopped loving us. Indeed, He asked the Father for forgiveness for us (see Luke 23:34).

Action/Thought for Today: It is not easy to let go of others' offenses, but our Heavenly Father wants to help us. Let us ask Him for the grace to forgive.

Prayer: Lord Jesus, thank You for showing us how to love and live. Please give us the grace to always forgive and love. In Your name we pray. Amen!

WHO ARE OUR NEIGHBORS?

Jesus asked, "Which of these three, do you think, was a neighbor to the man who fell into the hands of the robbers?" He [an expert in the Law] said, "The one who showed him mercy." Jesus said to him, "Go and do likewise."

Luke 10:36-37

*For the full scripture reference, see Luke 10:25-37.

In the story of the Good Samaritan, a Jew was beaten, robbed, and left to die on the side of the road. A priest and a Levite passed him but did not stop to help. A Samaritan traveling along the way saw the man, stopped, cared for his wounds, and brought him to an inn. He gave money to the innkeeper to care for him. Historically, Jews and Samaritans did not get along, yet this Samaritan stopped to save the life of a Jew.

Are you able to help your enemy? We often want to take revenge on our enemy, but the Samaritan taught us to love our enemies. We must follow in his footsteps. We sometimes fail to help others because we don't know them. Our neighbors are not solely those in our community but everyone. Therefore, we must strive to act kindly toward all. We often don't offer help because of the differences between us, but we all have one Father, God. We are created equal and are one in the Lord. Therefore, we must help those in need—regardless of race, language, and socioeconomic class. We sometimes neglect our neighbors because we're too busy and expect someone else to care for them. Don't always expect someone else to respond to God's call. It is our responsibility to be charitable to all.

Action/Thought for Today: Who are you in the story: the priest, the Levite, or the Samaritan? Ask the Lord to help you be more like the Good Samaritan.

Prayer: Lord Jesus, teach us to be more loving and merciful. It is in Your name I pray. Amen!

RETALIATION, NO MORE!

You have heard that it was said, "An eye for an eye and a tooth for a tooth." But I say to you, Do not resist an evildoer. But if anyone strikes you on the right cheek, turn the other also.

Matthew 5:38-39

"*An eye for an eye and a tooth for a tooth*" was a law of the past, but some still believe in it. They teach their preschoolers to hit back at any kids who kick them. Many are ready to fight back at any sign of conflict or offense. But the Lord teaches us not to repay evil for evil but to show mercy. "*Love your enemies and pray for those who persecute you, so that you may be children of your Father in heaven*" (Matthew 5:44-45).

When Nelson Mandela became part of the government of South Africa, he did not repay those who had put him in jail. He renounced vengeance. Through his peaceful approach, he was able to achieve the end of Apartheid, and the reconciliation and peaceful coexistence of the races in South Africa.[20] Can you imagine what Mandela could have done with his power to those who had afflicted him?

Jesus demands mercy. With His death, He took upon Himself humanity's offenses without repayment. Therefore, we must practice mercy as Christ did. Mercy calls us to action in word and deed. It calls us to forgive a neighbor who has hurt us, extend a helping hand to one who has wrongly treated us and continue to help someone who has shown past ingratitude. Mercy requires that we give to the poor, feed the hungry, and help the oppressed. It is kind, compassionate, and loving.

Action/Thought for Today: Practice one of the acts of mercy above.

Prayer: Lord Jesus, give me Your heart so I, too, can have a merciful spirit. In Your name I pray. Amen!

JUDGE NO MORE!

Therefore, do not pronounce judgment before the time, before the Lord comes, who will bring to light the things now hidden in darkness and will disclose the purposes of the heart. Then each one will receive commendation from God. 1 Corinthians 4:5

When you witness someone going through a hardship, do you conclude that "they must be reaping what they sowed," or "God is punishing them." Sometimes, God lets us go to trial for unknown reasons, not because of wrongdoings. When Job suffered great misfortunes from the devil, his friends accused him of being unrighteous and believed that was the cause of his suffering. Job was righteous, and he attempted to defend himself, but his friends still condemned him (see the Book of Job). God rebuked Job's friends for not speaking of Him rightfully. God told them to ask Job to pray for them, so He would not punish them (see Job 42:7-9).

Friends, be careful not to judge someone who suffers a misfortune. You do not know the cause of their sorrows. Only God knows the depth of the heart. If God keeps us from trials, it is not because we are perfect but because He is merciful. He loves us so much that He may spare us from tribulations, even after we make many wrong choices. Therefore, be grateful for God's grace and pray for those facing adversity.

Action/Thought for Today: With God's grace, let us resolve to participate in the suffering of others without judging them.

Prayer: Heavenly Father, please forgive me for the times I have judged my neighbors. Lord, I strongly ask for a spirit of compassion and love for others. In Jesus' name I pray. Amen!

I HAVE SINNED AGAINST YOU!

*For I know my transgressions, and my sin is ever before me.
Against you, you alone, have I sinned, and done that which is
evil in your sight.*   Psalm 51:3-4, RSV

I sometimes feel like this psalmist, crying out, "I have sinned against You." In my walk with God, I have often sinned against Him. Every time we cause pain to our brothers or sisters and fail to act according to God's ways, we sin against the Lord.

When I face my sins, I sometimes question, "Lord, why did You let me fall?" God, in His mercy, never ceases to love me—regardless of my faults. He never revokes His covenant with me nor takes His blessings from me. He only wants me to acknowledge and confess my sins and strive to do better.

Sometimes, through His grace and mercy, God prevents me from sinning. At other times, He lets me fall to teach me to change my ways, repent, or be humble. Either way, God acts out of love for me. He enters daily into my messy life to repair my brokenness and weaknesses. I can genuinely say that although I am broken, I am neither forsaken nor forgotten, but redeemed and saved by Jesus Christ. We should all take solace in the fact that we are loved, redeemed, and saved.

Action/Thought for Today: Let us ask for
forgiveness for our sins. Pray Psalm 51.

Prayer: Lord Jesus, thank You for not forsaking me every time I sin. I ask for forgiveness of all my sins. Please help me repent and bring me to everlasting life. In Your name I pray. Amen!

IT IS WELL!

Deep calls to deep at the thunder of your cataracts; all your waves and your billows have gone over me. By day the LORD commands his steadfast love, and at night his song is with me, a prayer to the God of my life. Psalm 42:7-8

Sometimes we are full of devotion to the Lord because everything is going well in life. Then, when trials and tribulation arise, we become desolate and lose faith. Some may even get upset at the Lord for their misfortunes. Job did not turn away from God when he lost his children, servants, property, health, and wealth. He accepted the will of God (see Job 1 and 2). Imitating Job's gracious attitude may be challenging for us, but the Lord can give us the grace to abide in Him and say, "It is well" despite any hardship.

The Lord is present and compassionate in both our joys and our sorrows. Sometimes He permits us to experience trials for unknown reasons or to teach us a lesson, but He does not rejoice in our sufferings. He grieves with us, just as He wept with His friends, Mary and Martha, when Lazarus had died (see John 11:35). Hence, we must allow the Lord to share our suffering by blindly trusting Him.

In our darkest moments, Jesus makes all things well in seen or unseen ways. He may remain silent, but He is near us to comfort, strengthen, and give us peace. Let us surrender our joys and pain to Him and pray for the grace always to exclaim, "It is well with my soul."

Action/Thought for Today: Can you honestly say "it is well" in a difficult time? Pray for that grace.

Prayer: Lord Jesus, fill me with Your grace to accept Your holy will. In Your name I pray. Amen!

GOD, OUR HELP IN ALL!

God is our refuge and strength, a very present help in trouble.
Therefore we will not fear, though the earth should change, though
the mountains shake in the heart of the sea.　　　Psalm 46:1-2

It is very comforting to know that the Lord will help us in times of trouble. Why do we remain fearful when the Lord has clearly said that He is our refuge and strength? Why do we not abide in the Lord and trust in His words?

The apostle Paul told us: *"We do not wage war according to human standards, for the weapons of our warfare are not merely human, but they have divine power to destroy strongholds. We destroy arguments, and every proud obstacle raised up against the knowledge of God, and we take every thought captive to obey Christ"* (2 Corinthians 10:3-5). Ceaseless prayer and fasting are effective weapons in spiritual warfare during trials, tribulations, and uncertainties. Through these weapons, God's heart is open to deliver us from our miseries. And when we walk through the valley of death, we should fear no evil (see Psalm 23:4), but walk confidently in God's care. The enemies' weapons formed against us will not prosper (see Isaiah 54:17). Words spoken against us have no power in our lives, and we are not shaken by the darkness of this world. God has defeated our enemies, and we are victorious. Let us pray with an honest heart, without hesitation, and bring all our concerns to the Lord, the Creator of all.

Action/Thought for Today: Pray an extra five minutes today.

Prayer: O Lord, You are my Deliverer, Shield,
Protector, Refuge, and Strength. Give me the
grace to believe in Your promise that You are with
me always. In Your name I pray. Amen!

THROUGH GOD'S EYES!

For the LORD does not see as mortals see; they look on the outward appearance, but the LORD looks on the heart.

1 Samuel 16:7

I know of an extraordinary person who is always grateful for any act of kindness extended toward him. If a person who had been good to him turns against him, he continues to remember the goodness of that person. I strive to emulate this man. How many of us remember the goodness of those who have hurt us? Or do we forget it once they offend us? It seems as if one's offenses erase one's virtue.

We often remember the pain caused by others, but charity and mercy call us to forgive. Therefore, let us strive to focus on the goodness of others instead of dwelling on their shortcomings. We must pray for the grace to see our defects in the mirror of our hearts. Only then can we overlook others' shortcomings. If we see the goodness of others, then our own virtues become more evident to us. We are all created in God's image and He loves us—regardless of our shortcomings and sins. Therefore, let us pray not to look at anyone from a worldly point of view but through the lens of God's eyes.

Action/Thought for Today: How can I see God in others?

Prayer: Lord Jesus, help me see others through the lens of Your eyes. In Your name I pray. Amen!

Jesus, Our Refuge!

For you have been a refuge to the poor, a refuge to the needy in their distress; shelter from the rain, shade from heat. When the blast of the ruthless was like a winter rain, the roar of strangers like heat in the desert, you subdued the heat with shade of a cloud, the rain of the tyrants was vanquished.   Isaiah 25:4-5, NABRE

In times of crisis and in this troubled world, let us seek refuge in the shelter of the Lord. *"For He will deliver you from the snare of the fowler and from the deadly pestilence; he will cover you with his pinions, and under his wings you will find refuge, his faithfulness is a shield and buckler"* (Psalm 91:3-4). When the storms of life are blazing, we need to remember that we are not alone. The Lord is always with us. He will never leave or forsake us. God will fight all of our battles if we leave them up to Him. Victory is from our God. Therefore, let us fix our eyes and hearts on Him and surrender all to Him.

Abandoning all to God is not easy, but we can do it with His grace and prayer. Therefore, *"Do not be anxious about anything, but in every situation, by prayer and petition, with thanksgiving, present your requests to God. And the peace of God, which transcends all understanding, will guard your hearts and your minds in Christ Jesus"* (Philippians 4:6-7, NIV).

Action/Thought for Today: Pray for those who are anxious, troubled, and fearful.

Prayer: Lord Jesus, we surrender our all to You. Please deliver and heal this world from diseases, war, and anxiety. You are the divine Healer, and nothing is impossible with You. Therefore, we humbly implore You for Your mercy and protection. In Your name I pray. Amen!

IN THE MIDST OF TRIALS AND UNCERTAINTIES!

Praise be to the God and Father of our Lord Jesus Christ, the Father of compassion and the God of all comfort, who comforts us in all our troubles, so that we can comfort those in any trouble with the comfort we ourselves receive from God.   2 Corinthians 1:3-4, NIV

Crosses and trials? Anxiety and fears? Too much to bear? Prayer and fasting are always the answer! Bend your knees in supplication, raise your hands in praise and thanksgiving to God, the Master of your life, and abandon yourself to Him. Ceaseless prayer is essential to counteract the world's dangers, anxieties, and uncertainties. Prayer is our weapon to fight the attacks of the enemy. We cannot resist the enemy's tricks and the trials of this world if we do not pray. Therefore, let us ask the Lord for the courage and grace to pray without ceasing.

Friends, I encourage you to pray from the depths of your heart with confidence and trust that the Lord will answer your prayers. Remember to cheer, comfort, and support those who are troubled and fearful. *"May the God who gives endurance and encouragement give you the same attitude of mind toward each other that Christ Jesus had"* (Romans 15:5, NIV).

Action/Thought for Today: Pray or fast for someone experiencing fear and anxiety over life's issues.

Prayer: Lord Jesus, shield us with Your protection in difficult times. Give us peace, courage, and grace to pray without ceasing, especially in times of trial and tribulation. We surrender all our trials to You; please take care of everything. Lord, all is possible with You. Increase our faith and trust in You. In Your name we pray. Amen!

JOY AMID TRIALS AND UNCERTAINTIES!

A cheerful heart is good medicine, but a crushed spirit dries up the bones. Proverb 17:22, NIV

As Christians, we should not be discouraged or saddened by life's uncertainties, trials, and troubles, but rather rejoice in the Lord for His overflowing mercy and grace. The apostle Paul tells us: *"Rejoice in the Lord always, again I will say, rejoice"* (Philippians 4:4). We must always try to have a cheerful heart, not because everything is great in life, but because *"the joy of the LORD is your strength"* (Nehemiah 8:10, NIV).

A crushed spirit is used by the enemy's to distract us from God's presence, peace, hope, joy, and love. If you are cheerful, share your spirit of joy with those in your life and let them know the glory of God. If you are sad or troubled, decide to take back your joy from the enemy in Jesus' name. Pray for the grace to remain cheerful despite life's crises or problems. Let us rejoice in hope, knowing that the Lord is with us always and will deliver us from all evils. We can do all things through Christ who gives us strength (see Philippians 4:13).

Action/Thought for Today: Make every effort to cheer someone today.

Prayer: Lord Jesus, please grant me a cheerful heart in all circumstances. Please give me Your supernatural peace so that I can remain cheerful always. Thank You, Lord, for Your grace, joy, and kindness. I praise and adore You, O Lord. In Your name I pray. Amen!

Jesus and Matthew!

As Jesus was walking along, he saw a man called Matthew sitting at the tax booth; and he said to him, "Follow me." And he got up and followed him.

Matthew 9:9

The Story of Matthew (see Matthew 9:9-13) is a story of a life-changing encounter with Christ. Matthew was a tax collector. In those days, a tax collector's position was loathed; no one spoke to or ate with them. Even the disciples hated tax collectors. Jesus did not judge. He gazed at Matthew with mercy and love, and this moved Matthew to follow Him and change his life forever.

Consider how the action of Jesus in calling Matthew demonstrated God's mercy and love. That was an important lesson for Matthew, the Pharisees, and the disciples. Matthew noted, in his Gospel: *"When the Pharisees saw this, they said to his disciples, " 'Why does your teacher eat with tax collectors and sinners?' On hearing this, Jesus said, 'It is not the healthy who need a doctor, but the sick.' But go and learn what this means: 'I desire mercy, not sacrifice. For I have not come to call the righteous, but sinners'"* (Matthew 9:11-13, NIV).

Like Matthew, Jesus came to clothe us with righteousness. He calls each one of us to be cleansed from our sins and be justified. Let us allow Him to give us a new life, to make us a new person and a disciple of Christ, bringing others to Christ instead of judging them.[21]

Action/Thought for Today: Are you willing to leave your tax booth and follow Jesus today? He is calling you.

Prayer: Lord Jesus, please help me change my life and follow You with my all. I praise and thank You. In Your name I pray. Amen!

JESUS AND ZACCHAEUS!

"Zacchaeus, hurry and come down; for I must stay at your house today."   Luke 19:5

* For the full scripture, see Luke 19:1-10.

As a tax collector, Zacchaeus was probably not loved in his town. He was considered unfair, dishonest, and lacking moral principles. Yet Jesus gazed at him with love and called him to come down from the tree so that He might go to his home and dine with him. Jesus did not accept Zacchaeus' fraudulent practices; He came to change Zacchaeus and all of us.

Jesus did not ask Zacchaeus to cleanse or purify himself; He did not ask him to change his profession as a tax collector or do penance. Zacchaeus felt the merciful and unconditional love of Jesus and received his love with joy. This love was so profound that his life was transformed. Without instructions from Jesus, Zacchaeus showed mercy by giving half of his belongings to the poor and restoring fourfold to anyone he had cheated.

Zacchaeus' conversion was the consequence of the love of Jesus. His merciful love is so powerful that, having been loved by Jesus first, Zacchaeus understood the need to turn toward others, pay back those he had defrauded, and respect and love them. We must let Jesus come and dine with us despite our sins and shortcomings. Like Zacchaeus, we must be willing to accept Jesus' deep love for us and let Him help us treat others with kindness and fairness.[22]

Action/Thought for Today: Are you willing
to let Jesus profoundly gaze at you?

Prayer: Lord Jesus, thank You for giving us an
example of true conversion in Zacchaeus. Give us
a contrite heart. In Your name we pray. Amen!

JESUS AND PAUL!

"Saul, Saul, why do you persecute me?" He asked "Who are you, Lord?" The reply came, "I am Jesus, whom you are persecuting."

Acts 9:4-5

* For the full scripture, see Acts 9:1-19.

Saul, later known as Paul, a persecutor of the early Christians, received permission from the High Priest to bring any followers of Jesus from Damascus back to Jerusalem in chains. On his journey to Damascus, a powerful light overwhelmed him, knocking him to the ground, and he heard a voice say, *"Saul, Saul, why are you persecuting me?"* He asked, *"Who a`re you, Sir?"*, then heard the reply, *"I am Jesus, whom you are persecuting."* Told to go into the city, he got up, realized that he was blind, and was led to the city, where he neither ate nor drank for three days.

The Lord told Ananias, a disciple, in a vision, to lay his hands upon Saul to restore his sight. He was reluctant, having heard of Saul's reputation, but the Lord told him that Saul was His chosen instrument to carry His name before Gentiles, kings, and Israelites (see Acts 9:10-15). Ananias did as he was bid, and Saul regained his sight and was baptized. He preached the Gospel of God far and wide and accepted suffering for the sake of Jesus' name.

The story of Saul should give us hope. If the Lord can take His persecutor and make him a disciple of Christ, He can save anyone. There is no one the Lord cannot transform and forgive unless they refuse His forgiveness, mercy, and grace. Let us make every effort to know the Lord, to let Him transform us, and to be more like Him. As the apostle Paul said, *"I want to know Christ and the power of his resurrection and the sharing of his suffering by becoming like him in his death, if somehow I may attain the resurrection from the dead"* (Philippians 3:10-11).

Action/Thought for Today: What is your conversion story? Share it with someone who needs to experience the Lord more deeply.

Prayer: Lord Jesus, we accept Your forgiveness, mercy, and grace. Create in us a pure heart, O God, and put a new and right spirit within us (see Psalm 51:10). In Your name we pray. Amen!

BE A BARNABAS!

There was a Levite, a native of Cyprus, Joseph, to whom the apostles gave the name Barnabas (which means "son of encouragement"). He sold a field that belonged to him, then brought the money, and laid it at the apostles' feet. Act 4:36-37

Barnabas encouraged the disciples with his financial resources, and most likely with prayer and words as well. Although we can use our words to cheer up others, sometimes we may have to go the extra mile, using our resources to help those in need. You may give a meal to the sick. You may spend time visiting the sick, lowly, and those who are mourning. You may provide some of your resources to the poor. You may be the voice for the marginalized or those who suffer from injustice. All these examples are ways we can bless others.

We must encourage one another in the Lord. He wants us to encourage each other, not only when someone is down, but also when someone is doing well. When others inspire us, we become more resolved to walk with the Lord. Many people walk away from the Lord because of a lack of encouragement. Therefore, let us strive to welcome others in our lives, ministries, and churches. Let us go into the world and be a Barnabas!

Action/Thought for Today: If you know of someone who needs assistance, help her or him bear the burden and encourage her or him with your resources, time, and prayers.

Prayer: Lord Jesus, help us encourage someone today, a person in need of a shoulder to lean on. Let that person see You through us. I thank You, Lord, for the word of grace and blessing that You continue to bestow on us daily. In Your name I pray. Amen!

JESUS AND US!

After this he went out and saw a tax collector named Levi sitting at the tax booth, and he said to him, "Follow me." And he got up, left everything, and followed him.　　　　Luke 5:27-28

Levi, the tax collector, left everything behind to follow Jesus. In our spiritual lives, we are tax collectors in many ways, depriving the Lord of the holy lives that He has given us. Jesus may not be calling us to leave material things behind, but rather the spiritual defilements that are stopping us from being one with Him. Like Levi, He calls all of us to a new life in Him, requiring us to let go of our wickedness and ungodly behaviors.

Put to death, then, the parts of you that are earthly: immorality, impurity, passion, evil desire, and the greed that is idolatry.
　　　　Colossians 3:5, NABRE

But now you must put them all away: anger, fury, malice, slander, and obscene language out of your mouths. Stop lying to one another.　　　　Colossians 3:8-9, NABRE

Fornicators, idolaters, adulterers, male prostitutes, sodomites, thieves, the greedy, drunkards, revilers, robbers—none of these will inherit the kingdom of God.　　　　1 Corinthians 6:9-10

Jesus, in His mercy, will cleanse us if we come to Him with a contrite heart, for *"You were washed, you were sanctified, you were justified in the name of the Lord Jesus Christ and in the Spirit of our God"* (1 Corinthians 6:11). Let us journey together, leaving everything behind to follow the Lord.

Action/Thought for Today: What is it that Jesus is calling you to leave behind to follow Him?

Prayer: Lord Jesus, please help me put to death my old self and live according to Your ways. Thank You for cleansing, purifying, and sanctifying me in the name of the Lord Jesus Christ. Amen!

HONOR THY FATHER!

Honor your father and your mother, that you may have a long life in the land the LORD your God is giving you.

Exodus 20:12, NABRE

Fatherhood is a noble profession and a gift from God. Fathers are role models to their children and can influence their lives positively or negatively. It is not enough for a dad to provide financial support for his children or have fun with them. It is of the utmost importance that every dad prays with and for his kids, teaches them to read the Scriptures, and lives a godly life.

Many know the joy of having faithful fathers who are devoted to God and their families. Some are blessed with adoptive or spiritual fathers who have raised and cherished them. Others may have dads who did not care for them and left them with emotional scars, which is truly unfortunate.

"Honor your father and your mother" is, however, the first commandment with a promise (see Ephesians 6:2). Therefore, whether our fathers are caring or uncaring, compassionate or heartless, considerate or selfish, famous or unknown, joyful or sad, rich or poor, strict or lenient, talented or inept, virtuous or morally lax, young or old, teachers of integrity, honor, and respect, or not, we must love, honor, and forgive them. God will bless us abundantly.

Action/Thought for Today: Pray for a blessing for all the fathers in this world.

Prayer: Father God, thank You for the gift of fatherhood. Help all fathers imitate You and teach their children what is right and just. May all children honor and love their fathers. In Jesus' name we pray. Amen!

FATHER GOD!

See what love the Father has bestowed on us that we may be called the children of God. Yet so we are. 1 John 3:1, NABRE

John 3:16 is a very commonly quoted scripture: *"For God so loved the world that He gave His only Son, so that everyone who believes in Him may not perish but might have eternal life"* (NABRE). I am sure we all have intellectual knowledge of God's love from the Scriptures and other spiritual books. But have you sat down with God and meditated on His love for you? Do you really understand that He gave His only son to save you? Have you moved your intellectual knowledge of God's love to the depth of your heart? Have you accepted His love?

God loves us so much that He created us in His image (see Genesis 1:27). Even before He formed us in the womb, He knew us. He set us apart before we were born (see Jeremiah 1:5) and planned all the details of our lives. Even the hairs on our heads are all counted by Him (see Luke 12:7). He also reminds us in Isaiah 43:4 that we are precious in His sight, honored, and He loves us so much that He will give people in return for us and nations in exchange for our lives. Even if our birth father and mother forsake us, the Lord will care for us (see Psalm 27:10).

We may not comprehend the grandeur and profoundness of God's love, but if we pray for grace, He will help us open our hearts to see and understand the depth of His love for us. We must pray to accept His love and deepen our relationship with Him.

Action/Thought for Today: Reflect on these questions.

Prayer: Father God, thank You for Your merciful and steadfast love. It is in Jesus' name that I pray. Amen!

FATHER JOB!

For I know that my Redeemer lives, and that at last he will stand upon the earth, and after my skin has been thus destroyed, then in my flesh I shall see God. Job 19:25-26

* For the full reference, see the book of Job.

Job was a righteous man who feared the Lord (see Job 1:1). Satan told God that Job was only faithful because he was doing well. But God knew that Job was His trusted servant. God permitted Satan to do whatever he wanted with Job, except take his life (see Job 1:12). In one day, Job lost everything—his ten children, his servants, livestock, and property—due to natural disasters. In Job's suffering and grief, he did not curse the name of the Lord nor charge Him with wrongdoing (see Job 1:22). Job surrendered all to the Lord, blessed Him, and said, *"The LORD gave, and the LORD has taken away; blessed be the name of the LORD"* (Job 1: 21).

Satan then attacked Job's health and caused sores on his entire body. Job's wife advised him to curse God and die. But he replied, *"Shall we receive the good at the hand of God, and not receive the bad?"* (Job 2:1-9). Friends also criticized Job, yet he kept his faith in God, the Redeemer, who would speak on his behalf. Because of Job's humility, faith, and fear of the Lord, God restored his health and fortunes twofold (see Job 42:10). It is easy to doubt and curse God when life is difficult, but Job taught us to praise Him in the storm. Let us pray to imitate Job.

Action/Thought for Today: Pray for the grace to praise God in all circumstances.

Prayer: Lord Jesus, amid trials and tribulations, give me the grace to accept Your will and praise You. It is in Your name that I pray. Amen!

FATHER JOSEPH

Joseph, son of David, do not be afraid to take Mary as your wife, for the child conceived in her is from the Holy Spirit.   Matthew 1:20

Joseph is a quiet figure in the Bible, but we cannot underestimate his role in God's work of salvation. God entrusted Joseph with the gift of being the adoptive father of Jesus, our Savior. Let us reflect on some lessons from Joseph:

When Joseph found that Mary was pregnant before they lived together, he planned to dismiss her quietly to prevent embarrassing her (see Matthew 1:19). Instead of judging Mary, Joseph showed a great deal of compassion. How many of us would have spared Mary this embarrassment?

When the angel announced to Joseph that Mary's child was conceived through the Holy Spirit, Joseph agreed to stay with her without questioning the Lord (see Matthew 1:20-25). How many of us would have doubted the angel's message?

When Herod wanted to kill Jesus, Joseph fled to Egypt with Him and Mary as the Lord commanded him and remained there until the death of Herod (see Matthew 2:13-15). Amid adversity, he showed strength and courage. How many of us would have complained about our situation?

Throughout Jesus' life, Joseph cared for Jesus and loved Him. He sacrificed his life for his family. We must follow the example of Joseph, his compassion, obedience, and faithfulness to God, and his selfless love for Jesus and Mary.

Action/Thought for Today: What can you learn from Joseph?

Prayer: Lord Jesus, help me be more obedient and faithful in all You ask of me. I pray in Your name. Amen!

FATHER ABRAHAM!

Now the Lord said to Abram, "Go from your country and your kindred and your father's house to the land that I will show you. I will make of you a great nation, and I will bless you, and make your name great, so that you will be a blessing." Genesis 12:1-2

When Abraham was seventy-five years old, God called him to leave his country and go to a land He would show him (see Genesis 12:1 and 4). Without questioning the Lord, Abraham got up and went. The Lord blessed him and made him the father of nations.

It is never too late to serve the Lord. God can call us at any age, and all we must do is say yes. If God calls you today to go to an unknown land, would you accept His invitation? To work for God, we must be willing to leave our comfort zone and go where He leads us.

Abraham and Sarah were barren. In their old age, the Lord blessed them with a son, Isaac. The Lord then put Abraham to the test and asked him to sacrifice Isaac, his beloved son. Again, Abraham obeyed the Lord. As he was about to sacrifice his son, the angel of the Lord stopped him and sent a ram to replace Isaac (see Genesis 18, 21 and 22). Suppose the Lord asked you to give all your possessions for His service. Would you question the Lord and worry about your future, or submit to His will? Do you believe that the Lord would provide for your needs (see Genesis 22:8)? To follow Christ, we must be willing to follow His commands.

Abraham's life was exemplary for his faith, obedience, and trust in the Lord. We must pray for the grace to imitate his footsteps.

Action/Thought for Today: Do you have faith like Father Abraham? Pray for grace.

Prayer: Lord Jesus, help me respond to You with faith when You call me. I pray in Your name. Amen!

June 18

Father Noah!

Noah found favor in the sight of the LORD. Genesis 6:8

Noah was a righteous man who walked with God (see Genesis 6:9). God saw man's wickedness on Earth and wanted to wipe out every human being, but Noah pleased God. He chose Noah to build an ark to save humanity. He commanded Noah, *"You shall come into the ark, you, your sons, your wife, and your sons' wives with you. And of every living thing, of all flesh, you shall bring two of every kind into the ark, to keep them alive with you; they shall be male and female"* (Genesis 6:18-19).

After Noah built the ark and all were in it, it rained for forty days and nights (see Genesis 7:12). The water on the Earth swelled for one hundred and fifty days (see Genesis 7:24). Everyone died, and everything else perished except for Noah and his family and the animals he had brought into the ark.

God trusted Noah enough to ask him to build an ark. Noah did not doubt and did what God asked of him. Can the Lord trust you with a great mission? What would be your response if He asked you to do something radical, something difficult to comprehend? Would you answer yes to God's request? The Lord could have saved the world without Noah's assistance, but he wanted Noah to be part of his work of salvation. Let us follow Noah's legacy.

Action/Thought for Today: Let us reflect together on these questions.

Prayer: Lord Jesus, I want to be part of Your work of salvation, but sometimes I doubt Your request. Please help me do what You ask of me. I pray in Your name. Amen!

FATHER DAVID

Have mercy on me, O God, according to your steadfast love; according to your abundant mercy blot out my transgressions. Psalm 51:1

David was a great king and a man after God's heart because he carried out His wishes (see Act 13:22). However, David sinned against God when He committed adultery with Bathsheba, the wife of Uriah, who became pregnant with David's child. David then had Uriah killed by placing him in the forefront of the most brutal battle, after which David married Bathsheba (see 2 Samuel 11 and 12).

God was not pleased with David's actions, so He sent the prophet Nathan to condemn David for them. Nathan told David that the Lord would raise trouble against him from within his own house, his neighbor would lie with his wives in his sight, and Bathsheba's child would die (see 2 Samuel 12).

David recognized his sins and said to Nathan, *"I have sinned against the LORD"* (2 Samuel 12:13). He then fasted and prayed, but the child died after seven days. After the child had died, David rose from the ground, anointed himself, and worshiped the Lord. He did not curse the Lord. He recognized his transgressions and plead for God's grace and mercy.

Many with great power or leadership roles refuse to acknowledge their sins against others. Regardless of our status in life, we must recognize our sins and ask God to cleanse and purify us. David could have offered God many sacrifices, but He knew that what the Lord requires is a *"broken spirit; a broken and contrite heart"* (Psalm 51:17). Let us imitate David, humble ourselves, and ask for God's forgiveness and mercy.

Action/Thought for Today: Meditate on and pray Psalm 51.

Prayer: Lord Jesus, help me recognize my sins. *"Create in me a clean heart, O God, and put a new and right spirit within me"* (Psalm 51:10). In Your name I pray. Amen!

BE A SOLOMON!

Give your servant therefore an understanding mind to govern your people, able to discern between good and evil; for who can govern this your great people?   *1 King 3:9*

* Solomon's prayer for wisdom. For the full reference, see 1 Kings 3.

Solomon asked God for wisdom and a discerning mind to lead his people. He did not ask for anything for himself. Therefore, God blessed Him with both riches and honor and made him the greatest king. No other king rose to his level. When we pray, we should ask for the Holy Spirit's gifts and fruits to serve well and walk humbly with God and others. When you seek God's righteousness, He will bless you with all the necessities of this life and bestow on you the Kingdom that He has promised to those who love Him.

As we can see in 1 King 3:13-14, Solomon only asked for wisdom, and yet God favored him. He said, *"I give you also what you have not asked, both riches and honor all your life, no other king shall compare with you. If you walk in my ways, keeping my statutes and my commandments, as your father David walked, then I will lengthen your life."* Therefore, let us follow Solomon's footsteps and seek only to serve the Lord and others.

Action/Thought for Today: Is your prayer motivated only by your needs or those of others?

Prayer: Lord Jesus, give us the grace to seek the things above. Let our prayers be motivated, not by self-interests, but by seeking to serve You and others. We pray in the holy and blessed name of Jesus. Amen!

JUNE 21

JESUS, HELP ME BE A SIMON!

As they led him away, they seized a man, Simon of Cyrene, who was coming from the country, and they laid the cross on him, and make him carry it behind Jesus.   Luke 23:26

Simon helped Jesus carry His cross. Although Simon did not choose this duty, he accepted it. He, therefore, is the perfect example of discipleship. He did what Jesus asks us to do daily: *"Pick up your cross and follow me"* (Matthew 16:24). We, too, must help others with their crosses through our prayers, encouragement, and deeds.

Simon and Jesus did not meet under the best of circumstances, but by God's divine Providence. Simon's life must have changed forever, for when we meet Jesus, we change. Likewise, others can bring us a life-changing experience as we help them. Therefore, let us strive to assist those in our path of life. Through reflection and prayer, the Lord taught me how to be a Simon:

- Do not be afraid to help a stranger in the street.
- Do not regret the good you do for others.
- Do good continuously, no matter the price.
- Do not boast about the good you do. Instead, boast in the Lord.

If we are open to serving others, God will give us the grace and resources to do His work. So, let us ask the Lord to be a Simon.

Action/Thought for Today: Are you willing to be a Simon?

Prayer: Lord Jesus, help me be a Simon. Open my heart to help others. I pray in Your name. Amen!

FATHERHOOD!

As a father has compassion for his children, so the Lord has compassion for those who fear him.   Psalm 103:13

Every child needs a father as we need God, our Father in Heaven. A father is the anchor of the family. He complements a mother's courage and love to make a three-fold cord to keep the family stable and protected. Dads are caring and loving, and they keep their family functional in distress or chaos. Dads are firm, yet they prepare their children for life. Dads discipline when necessary, yet they are the cheerleaders of their sons and daughters in every sense of the word. Dads embrace the joy and pain of fatherhood.

Unfortunately, some children do not have a dad, but God promises that even if one's mother or father forsakes them, He will take care of them (see Psalm 27:10). I hope that we hold on to God's promises, especially for those lacking a father figure in their lives. I encourage:

- Fathers, be an exceptional example of love, faith, and virtue to your sons so they can mimic your footsteps.
- Mothers, pray blessings for your husband and sons to become outstanding husbands and fathers.
- Sons and daughters, honor your fathers and pass on God's teaching from generation to generation.

Action/Thought for Today: Say a prayer of
blessing for all men in the world.

Prayer: Lord Jesus, thank You for being a good Father
to us. I ask that You bless all fathers with Your wisdom,
guidance, and grace to lead their families closer to
You and raise their sons and daughters with dignity
and love. It is in Your name we pray. Amen!

JUNE 23

THE CALL OF THE FIRST DISCIPLES!

As he [Jesus] passed by the Sea of Galilee, he saw Simon and his brother Andrew casting their nets into the sea; they were fishermen. Jesus said to them, "Come after me, and I will make you fishers of men." Then they abandoned their nets and followed him. Mark 1:16-18, NABRE

Jesus called the disciples to leave their profession as fishermen to follow Him. Being a fisherman was very profitable in those days, yet the disciples were willing to abandon their nets for the Lord. Some people are called to leave their profession and become church leaders—priests, preachers, evangelists, missionaries, and volunteers in full-time ministry. While the Lord may not ask all of us to do the same, He invites us to follow Him and be fishers of men in one way or another. The Lord calls ordinary people like you and me:

- To become fishers of men in our daily lives.
- To evangelize and bring the Good News of Jesus Christ to all whom we encounter.
- To intercede and pray for others and the world.
- To comfort the sick and those who mourn.
- To serve the poor and those in need.

Following the Lord requires sacrifice and a decision to leave our former life for a new life in Christ, a life of prayer and humble service. Let us pray to recognize the Lord's call and abandon our nets without looking back.

Action/Thought for Today: Are you willing to abandon your nets, go after the Lord, and be a fisher of men?

Prayer: Lord Jesus, You call us all by name to follow You and be fishers of men. Please give us the grace and wisdom to hear Your call, follow after You, and serve You with all our souls, minds, and hearts. We pray in Your name. Amen!

SPEAK TO ME, MY LORD AND MY GOD!

The LORD came and stood there, calling out as before: "Samuel, Samuel!" Samuel answered, "Speak, for your servant is listening."
1 Samuel 3: 10, NABRE

Are you paying attention to God's call and direction? If we take time in prayer to say, like Samuel, *"Speak, Lord, for your servant is listening,"* I am sure we will hear the Lord speaking to us. He desires to express His love to us, as well as to reveal Himself to us. The Lord is willing to point us in the right direction ... if only we take the time to listen. He wants to show us mighty things which we do not know (see Jeremiah 33:3).

In 2016, in the middle of the night, I heard the Lord within my soul, and He asked me to start a retreat/conference team within my Haitian community. Through prayers and the movement of the Holy Spirit, I confirmed the message. When I stepped out in faith, the Lord sent faith-filled brothers and sisters to start this project with me. To this day, all of us continue to work in this ministry. Whether or not we serve in any ministry, the Lord daily calls us to be more loving, compassionate, generous, faithful, prayerful, and serve Him and our neighbors. Therefore, our ministry is LOVE. Are you listening to the Lord and answering His call?

Action/Thought for Today: In your daily prayer, stay still for five minutes or longer, and say to the Lord: "Speak Lord, your servant is listening." Then, please pay attention to His call? He might surprise you.

Prayer: Lord Jesus, give us the grace to be still in prayer, hear Your voice, and answer Your call. Teach us, Lord, to follow Your commands. In Jesus' name we pray. Amen!

HERE I AM, LORD!

When the LORD saw that he [Moses] had turned aside to look, God called out to him from the bush: "Moses! Moses!" He answered, "Here I am."   Exodus 3:4, NABRE

When the Lord called Moses to send him to Pharaoh so that the Israelites could be delivered from their Egyptian oppressors, Moses hesitated and said to the Lord, *"Who am I that I should go to Pharaoh and bring the Israelites out of Egypt?"* (Exodus 3:11). But the Lord assured Moses that He would be with him and gave him signs confirming that He had sent him (see Exodus 3:12).

If the Lord calls you today, will you answer, "Here I am, Lord," and leave the world behind you? Or will you feel like Moses, not ready for the task? I want to reassure you that God does not call only qualified people, but He qualifies those whom He calls. He equips us with every spiritual gift and blessing to do the work that He entrusts to us. *"God chose what is foolish in the world to shame the wise; God chose what is weak in the world to shame the strong"* (1 Corinthian 1:27), *"so that no one might boast in the presence of God"* (1 Corinthian 1:29). Let this answer, "Here I am, Lord," be one of our prayers. The Lord has important works for us. Therefore, let us say Yes to His call without reservation.

Action/Thought for Today: What are the things that stop you from serving the Lord?

Prayer: Lord Jesus, help me answer Your call without reservation. I need Your grace to leave the world behind and follow You. Help me, dear Lord, for I desire to say Yes to You. In Your name I pray. Amen!

GOD IS CALLING YOU TODAY!

Then I heard the voice of the LORD saying, "Whom shall I send? And who will go for us?" And I said, "Here am I. Send me!"

Isaiah 6:8

The Lord had an important message to deliver to the people of Judah. He asked who would go for Him, and Isaiah answered the call. Before the Lord's call, Isaiah had a vision of God in the Temple and saw the Lord in His glory. Then Isaiah acknowledged his sins and brokenness, *"Woe is me! I am lost, for I am a man of unclean lips, and I live among a people of unclean lips; yet my eyes have seen the Kings, the LORD of hosts!"* (Isaiah 6:5). The Lord sent a seraph to cleanse his mouth of wickedness, enabling him to answer God's call (see Isaiah 6).

Are you willing to say, "Here I am, Lord, send me," if He calls you today? And if you do not answer the Lord, why not? Are you worried that you are not worthy of delivering the Lord's message? Just like Isaiah, we must acknowledge our faults and ask the Lord to purify us to serve Him freely. In today's world, the Lord needs you—yes, you! The Lord needs you to proclaim His Good News to the poor and freedom to the captives (see Isaiah 61:1). He has sent you to bind up the brokenhearted (see Isaiah 61:1) to help the blind see and set the oppressed free (see Luke 4:18). He needs you to make His truth known and to shine His light into the world.

Action/Thought for Today: How easy or difficult is it for you to answer God's call?

Prayer: Lord Jesus, when You asked for a volunteer, I heard the call and backed away. Lord, give me the willingness to say Yes when You call me. Lead and guide me in Your ways. In Your name we pray. Amen!

Lord, I Am Yours, Please Lead Me!

Then I said, "Here I am, I have come—it is written about me in the scroll. I desire to do your will, my God; your law is within my heart." Psalm 40:7-8, NIV

How do you know when God calls you to do His will? In your daily prayer, offer yourself to the Lord: "Here I am to do your will, I am Yours. Please lead me, Lord." If you make yourself available to the Lord, He will direct you on how to serve others. The Lord will lead you to do your part in His work of salvation to bring others closer to Him through your prayers and your ministry. He said, *"I will give you as a light to the nations, that my salvation may reach to the end of the earth"* (Isaiah 49:6). This message applies to us if we open ourselves to the Lord's service.

Furthermore, the good Lord will give you the desire and motivation to use your inspirations, talents, resources, time, money, and strength in His service for the good of all. He will increase the knowledge and understanding of your call through prayer, the Scriptures, and affirmation from others. Let us continue to pray for the Lord to reveal His call and bless us with the grace to do whatever He wants.

Action/Thought for Today: What inspiration has the Lord given you lately in prayer?

Prayer: Lord Jesus, here I am. I come to do Your will. Please help me see and hear Your call in my life and *"let it be with me according to your word"* (Luke 1:38). Lord, give me the grace not to say "Here I am" lightly, but to mean it. Father, I praise and thank You. In Your name I pray. Amen!

WHAT IS YOUR MISSION IN LIFE?

But you are "a chosen race, a royal priesthood, a holy nation, a people of his own, so that you may announce the praises" of him who called you out of darkness into his wonderful light.

1 Peter 2:9, NABRE

Each of us is called and chosen by God for a specific mission. He has chosen and brought us out of darkness to announce His praise and glory and to do His works in this world. For those who know their vocation or calling, pray that the Spirit of God helps you work diligently. For those waiting for God to reveal His plan, don't worry. Know that your task is assigned to you only, and God has not given it to anyone else. Therefore, focus not so much on the mission but on God, who calls you.

As we wait to hear from God, let us walk humbly with Him in our daily lives and do the small and simple things He calls us to do well.

Let us always do what is good without ulterior motives.

Let us be peacemakers as much as possible.

Let us try to live by the truth, regardless of the cost.

Let us declutter our lives, so we can be free to hear God's calling and fulfill our life's mission.

Most of all, let us strive to accept and respect His commandments and teachings.

Action/Thought for Today: How do you respond to God's call in your life?

Prayer: Lord Jesus, thank You for calling us Your people. Please give us the grace to wait for Your call patiently as we walk with You. In Your name I pray. Amen!

FILL ME WITH PATIENCE!

I am confident of this, that the one who began a good work among you will bring it to completion by the day of Jesus Christ.
Philippians 1:6

Are you eager to start a ministry, but you have not received approval from God? Or have you created a ministry, but nothing seems to be working? Please don't lose hope or be discouraged, for we all have a mission in life. As you wait to hear from the Lord, He may be blessing you with the gift of patience and courage. If your ministry is not flourishing, He may be transforming you to serve Him better. In the waiting process, work hard for Him wherever you are. The Lord prepares, purifies, guides, and slowly changes us to accomplish His mission here on Earth. He will complete the work that He has begun in us (see Philippians 1:6). Remember that God uses every circumstance to teach and instruct us. No good deed will go to waste.

Although the Lord may seem silent, He will work everything for good for those who love Him (see Roman 8:28). Therefore, surrender yourself to Him with joy as you prayerfully say, "Here I am, Lord." Friends, know that God can provide you with every blessing in abundance so that you may always have enough of everything for every good work (see 2 Corinthian 9:8).

Action/Thought for Today: Pray for the gift of patience.

Prayer: Lord Jesus, I am eager and anxious to do Your work. Fill me with patience and courage to wait for You. May Your will be done in me. In Your name I pray. Amen!

LOVE ON THE CROSS!

Surely, he [Jesus] has borne our griefs and carried our sorrows; yet we esteemed him stricken, smitten by God, and afflicted.

Isaiah 53:3, RSV

The meaning of the cross is personal for everyone. We are unique individuals, yet all created by God. Although the cross is personal, it is collective because of what Jesus has done for each of us. The cross is more than a piece of wood; it signifies the price of our salvation. It was stained with the Messiah's precious blood to bring new life, hope, and joy to humanity.

What do you see on the cross?

On the cross, I see the crushed body of Christ and the blood and water gushing from His pierced side, washing away my sins and defilement. God's infinite and passionate love and mercy for you and me were on that cross.

On the cross, I recognize the holy God Almighty who would do anything for you and me. The humble Lord heals, restores, and redeems us on the cross.

On the cross, He calls me to enter the depth of His love and experience the light of His salvation. My amazing God has used the cross as a vessel to resurrect me from the pit of life and make me whole again.

While on the cross, with every man's rejection and mockery, in sorrow and grief, Jesus He cried out, "I love you, My child." The profound mystery of the crucified Lord has removed me from the shadow of death, and restores everyone to our identities as beloved children of God. Let us live out the death and resurrection of Jesus Christ so we can deeply experience Him and be more like Him.

Action/Thought for Today: Reflect on the meaning of the cross.

Prayer: Lord Jesus, help me experience the depth of Your love for me on the cross. It is in Your name I pray. Amen!

God Wants You to Be Free of Clutter!

For God is not a God of disorder but of peace.

1 Corinthian 14:33, NIV

What is clutter? According to the Oxford online dictionary, clutter is "a collection of things lying about in an untidy mass."[23] We have clutter in our lives, hearts, minds, and homes that prevents us from praying and living in God's freedom. Lately, the Lord has been telling me to declutter my life. I am not good at organizing, but He has been gentle and patient with me and allows me to take the process slowly. I do not feel overwhelmed, for with the Lord by my side, I am ready to declutter my life according to His plan.

To declutter any area of our lives, whether our hearts or homes, God has to be the One in charge of the process. Why? Because He does everything well. The clutter around us prevents us from seeing His work in our day-to-day living. It stops us from praying and living in peace. Give God the keys to your life and allow Him to cleanse you of all the things that prevent you from being one with Him. Let Him pour fresh water over your life and make you new again.

Action/Thought for Today: Before you begin organizing your life, say a prayer, asking the Lord to show you the areas that need decluttering.

Prayer: Lord Jesus, please help me declutter my life, to make more room for You. I need help. I cannot do it alone. Lord, I praise and thank You. In Your name I pray. Amen!

Declutter Your Mind!

Finally, beloved, whatever is true, whatever is honorable, whatever is just, whatever is pure, whatever is pleasing, whatever is commendable, if there is any excellence and if there is anything worthy of praise, think about these things. Philippians 4:8

What occupies your mind—your calendar, family issues, work deadlines, stress, social media, or all the other extra things on your plate? With the busyness of our lives, we think and talk simultaneously. We move at a hundred miles an hour and lose focus on what matters most in life—loving God and our neighbors, serving Him, and praying and meditating on His words.

Last week, I spoke with many people, and everyone seemed to have something in common—the daily stress of life. Their minds were so full, leaving little or no room to think of God. I had hoped it was otherwise for me, but I realized I was no different than any of the people I encountered. I was bombarded with stress over something beyond my control and was so overwhelmed that I couldn't even pray. I read the Psalms because that was all I could do. It was hard to get any direction from the Lord because this concern overpowered my mind. Once I surrendered the matter to God, He gave me consolation and guidance.

We cannot escape certain life events and demands, but with prayer and fasting, we can make the best of them, while having an uncluttered mind to continue our journey with God.

Action/Thought for Today: Take five minutes
and ask God to help you clear your mind
from worries and life's daily demands.

Prayer: Lord Jesus, I implore You for the grace to think
only of You. Declutter my mind, O Lord, from worries
and things of this world. In Your name I pray. Amen!

DECLUTTER YOUR HEART!

Since we have these promises, beloved, let us cleanse ourselves from every defilement of body and of spirit, making holiness perfect in the fear of God.　　　　2 Corinthians 7:1

What is in your heart—anger, bitterness, envy, hatred, hurt, regret, shame, or unforgiveness? This type of clutter (I call them bad company) breaks our spirits and stops us from experiencing the joy of the Lord. We must get rid of these companions as soon as they enter the door of our hearts. If we do not, we run the risk of having them move in and become rooted in our lives, creating more pain and heartache. When I am hurting or feeling angry and bitter, I quickly go to the Lord and ask Him to take over my heart. He always comes to my rescue.

God wants a heart that is free of this clutter so that we can serve, praise, adore, and love Him unconditionally. Our hearts are not open and healed when full of bad companions, and we cannot fully serve and love others. *"For you were called for freedom, brothers. But do not use this freedom as an opportunity for the flesh, rather, serve one another through love"* (Galatians 5:13, NABRE). An uncluttered heart serves freely, without limit, and with grace and mercy. In prayer, ask God to show you the clutter in your heart and give you the grace to accept His teaching as you walk in His freedom.

Action/Though for Today: Pick one or more bad companies from the list above and ask God to help you get rid of them today. Then pick another one each day until your heart is free of clutter.

Prayer: Lord Jesus, many times I hang on to past hurts and pains. Please give me the strength to declutter my heart and to walk in Your freedom. In Your name I pray. Amen!

CHRIST SETS US FREE!

For freedom Christ has set us free; stand fast therefore, and do not submit again to a yoke of slavery.   Galatians 5:1, RSV

On Independence Day, we are grateful for our freedoms and that we are no longer under the chain of slavery. I am thankful to God and to our forefathers who paved the way to liberty, justice, and peace. Some say they have freedom but do not understand the actual meaning of it. Some experience freedom in certain aspects of life but not in its entirety. According to the dictionary, freedom is "liberation from slavery or restraint or from the power of another."[24]

One of my friends was in an unfortunate marriage. Her husband forbade her to pursue a degree, to get a job, or to go out without his permission. She could neither shop alone nor choose her clothing, such that she forgot her size at one point. When he bought her oversized dresses, she had to wear them without complaint and could only wear her hair how he wanted it. She couldn't even go to the doctor. After many prayers, God intervened, and she escaped.

After the divorce, my friend told everyone, "I am free," whether they knew her story or not. She is truly free. She refused to let her experience make her bitter or resentful. She did not speak ill of her ex-husband. She is peaceful, carries the joy of the Lord with her, and never misses an opportunity to proclaim the name of the Lord. She posts inspirational messages on her social media page to encourage others. She went back to school and completed her degree while holding a job. I call this true freedom.

So many are not truly free. For some, our experiences keep us enslaved as we continuously dwell on the past. Does our freedom of speech give us the right to speak untruthfully or hurt others? No! My friend chooses not to speak ill of her ex-husband. Are we free of bitterness or resentment although we are part of the history of slavery or have experienced discrimination or mistreatment? Do you feel that "liberty, justice, and peace" belong to a particular group of people and not you? If our freedom causes us to sin, and the compensation is death, then this freedom means nothing. Let us pray for the grace to experience God's supernatural freedom from sins and spiritual slavery.

Action/Thought for Today: What does freedom mean to you?

Prayer: Lord Jesus, help me to experience true freedom in You. In Your name I pray. Amen!

DECLUTTER YOUR PANTRY!

Do not be among winebibbers or among gluttonous eaters of meat; for the drunkard and the gluttons will come to poverty, and drowsiness will clothe them with rags.   Proverbs 23:20-21

Do the tasty and empty-calorie foods in your pantry hold you captive? I know I should go to God when I am hurting, yet I go to sweets. However, if I don't have sweets in my pantry, I am able to resist the temptation, looking to the Lord for help. Therefore, removing unhealthy food from our homes and setting boundaries for eating healthier are essential. Those sweet, high-calorie, and fatty foods cannot make us happy, and they create adverse health effects such as diabetes, obesity, heart disease, cancer, pain, emotional issues, etc.

Attachment to food can keep us away from God. Therefore, we must resolve to declutter our pantries of unhealthy food. We are not immune to the temptation of food and drink. We must ask the Lord to empower us with self-control and renew our spirits. He will help us, for He, too, was tempted (see Hebrews 4:14-15), and He defeated the evil one. The avoidance of bad food should not be only for our physical, but also for our spiritual well-being. Once we declutter our pantries of non-nutritious foods, we must make a lifelong decision to keep it clean and continue to ask the Lord for help. *"But put on the Lord Jesus Christ and make no provision for the desire of the flesh"* (Romans 13:14, NABRE).

Action/Thought for Today: As much as possible, commit to eliminating unhealthy foods from your pantry.

Prayer: Lord Jesus, give me the grace to set limits on the food and drink I consume. Please help me to observe my boundaries. In Your name I pray. Amen!

DECLUTTER YOURSELF FROM ACTIVITIES!

I am the vine, you are the branches. Whoever remains in me and I in him will bear much fruit, because without me you can do nothing.   John 15:5, NABRE

All God-centered activities are good for us. Sometimes we are so busy with social activities and ministries that we forget about God. However, we cannot bear good fruits without being deeply grounded in Him. During the Covid-19 Pandemic, while we were in quarantine, I reevaluated myself and my involvement in church and social activities. I realized that I needed to get closer to God and spend more time with my family. I knew it would be hard to step away from some activities and ministries, but, through prayer, God directed me.

Sometimes, when we are too busy, we miss out on what God wants to do in our lives. The distractions can stop us from hearing His calling and, as a result, missing our next assignment. Our busyness may keep us from being present in our family's life. Therefore, I invite you to slow down and listen to God's whisper. I encourage you to be still, rest on God's shoulders, and let Him love you. Do not let social activities or ministries take over your life. Make every effort to allow God to fill the most significant part of your life and let Him guide you. We must seek to have a sincere and deep relationship with Him.

Action/Thought for Today: If you are involved
in many activities, strive to slow down from
time to time and be still in God's arms.

Prayer: Lord, I want more of You. Fill me with Your love,
joy, peace, grace, and mercy. In Your name I pray. Amen!

THE LORD FILLS US WITH GOOD THINGS!

May the God of hope fill you with all joy and peace as you trust in him, so that you may overflow with hope by the power of the Holy Spirit.   Romans 15:13, NIV

After we have decluttered and organized every aspect of our lives, we may feel a void. We must pray to the Lord to deliver us from the temptation to refill those empty spaces with TV, social media, the Internet, sports, etc. Instead, let us invite the Lord to meet us in daily prayer and fill us supernaturally, to help us remain free of all clutter. We must ask Him to coach us to walk away from ungodly things and get closer to Him.

As the Lord enters the empty and most profound spaces of our hearts and souls, we must look forward to experiencing His goodness, unfailing love, faithfulness, peace, hope, mercy, grace, and joy. If we ask the Lord, He will fill us with good things, help us in all our needs, cleanse us from all defilements, complete the spiritual and physical decluttering process, and bless us with a consistent prayer life. The good and merciful Lord satisfied the thirsty and fills the hungry with good things (see Psalm 107:9).

Action/Thought for Today: In prayer today,
ask the Lord for a consistent prayer life.

Prayer: Lord Jesus, please help me stay close to You and fill me with every good gift and blessing for my faith journey. Teach me to let go of worldly things and deepen my love for You. I thank and praise You. In Your name I pray. Amen!

Let Nothing Disturb You!

Do all things without grumbling or questioning.
Philippians 2:14, NABRE

How challenging is your life? Do you find yourself complaining about it—your marriage, children, work, church, etc.? Is there something in your life right now that irritates you?

One day, I came across a spiritual reading instructing me that murmuring is a sin, and I needed to hear that, for I complain from time to time. These are the times I forget that Jesus is my Savior, and I want to take charge of my life instead of surrendering my concerns to Him. If you find yourself complaining about life, it's time to have a one-on-one conversation with the Lord and examine your relationship with Him. Where is God in your life? Is He at the center or the bottom of your heart?

When we put God at the center of our lives, everything falls into place. We may still have difficult moments, but He is there to give us peace, direct us, and help us navigate through the ups and downs of life. I echo St. Teresa of Avila, "Let nothing disturb you. Let nothing frighten you. All things pass. God does not change. Patience achieves everything. Whoever has God lacks nothing; God alone suffices."[25]

Action/Thought for Today: Are you in the
habit of complaining about life? If you are, ask
God for help and cast your cares on Him.

Prayer: Lord Jesus, help me not to complain about
anything or react to the grumblings of others, but to fully
surrender my all to You. In Your name I pray. Amen!

LIVING YOUR CHRISTIANITY AT WORK!

I will make you a light to the nations, that my salvation may reach to the ends of the earth. Isaiah 49:6, NABRE

You may be working at a place where prayer, spirituality, or religion are not welcome. Or you may be working with some individuals who want nothing to do with God. If you are in this situation, praise God, for you can evangelize the loudest without saying a word. God will use you to bring light into the darkness. Let us ask Him to help us exercise our Christianity wherever we are. Here are some suggestions:

- Avoid talking negatively or complaining. *"Do not grumble against one another, brothers, so that you may not be judged; behold, the Judge is standing at the door"* (James 5:9, ESV).
- Be courteous, joyful, kind, patient, and punctual.
- Be honest in everything.
- Pray to be peaceful and calm, despite any work chaos.
- Do your work with all your heart as for God and not for men (see Colossians 3:23).
- As much as possible, give a smile, a hug, and kind words.
- Help your co-workers as much as you can.
- Pray for your co-workers.

Through your attitude, your co-workers will know that you are a Christian, and many will follow your footsteps and come to believe in the Lord.

Action/Thought for Today: Are you an excellent example to your co-workers? Ask God to help you.

Prayer: Lord Jesus, give me the grace to reflect Your characteristics in my life every day. Thank You for my co-workers and my work. In Your name I pray. Amen!

"GOD KNOWS, I TRIED!"

Two are better than one: They get a good wage for their toil. If the one falls, the other will help the fallen one. But woe to the solitary person! If that one should fall, there is no other to help.

Ecclesiastes 4:9-10, NABRE

Two is better than one, but how can we be at our best when our marriage is falling apart? We must start with prayer for the Lord to sustain us, for prayer changes everything. Then invest in the relationship as much as possible:

- Compliment him/her for the simple things, accomplishments, etc.
- Celebrate the good times and reject painful memories.
- Pray for the grace to serve your spouse as if you were serving the Lord.
- Spend quality time with your mate and date again.
- Seek the help of a marriage counselor, spiritual advisor, or religious leader.
- Try not to look at how much you invest into the relationship.
- Don't dwell on his or her mistakes or shortcomings. No one is perfect. Concentrate on your own failings.

Relationships require the efforts of both individuals. However, we have to be willing to meet each other halfway. When we exhaust all our options and nothing works, we can honestly say, "God knows, I tried my best." Know that Jesus is with you always. Confide your broken heart to the Lord. Let Him meet you at your greatest need, and He will fill you with the everlasting joy of His salvation.

Action/Thought for Today: Invite your spouse on a date. If this is not possible, pray about what you can do to improve the relationship.

Prayer: Lord Jesus, I present all marriages to you. Please help us be the best spouse we can be. Open our hearts to love more like You. In Your name I pray. Amen!

SURRENDER THEM TO HIM!

Children are a heritage from the LORD, offspring a reward from Him.   Psalm 127:3, NIV

Parenting is a beautiful gift, but it requires guidance from the Lord. As parents, we feel responsible for our children's emotional, physical, and spiritual well-being. When they are well, we are happy and at peace. When they are not at their best, we bear their pains and sufferings.

When my children were young, I worried less, for I had more control over their lives. As they get older, I struggle with the fear of "what if something happens to them"? I have less control over them, and my stress increased. I have to often remind myself that I am my children's guardian and that God had entrusted them to me. Once I accepted that God was in charge of their lives, I prayed more for them, surrendered them to the Lord freely, and God blessed me with peace.

Beloved parents, when concerns arise in our children's lives, we must draw our strength and courage from the Lord. Knock on the door of God's hearts without ceasing. Keep coming to Him and plead your cause like the persistent widow (see Luke 18:1-8). Implore the Lord through prayer and fasting. God can do the impossible in their lives. He has a plan for them. Therefore, let us approach the throne of God with confidence as we present our children to Him, and He will surely grant us the desire of our hearts.

Action/Thought for Today: Offer a prayer
of thanksgiving for your children.

Prayer: Lord Jesus, we thank You for our children,
and we present them to You. Bless them in every
area of their lives. In Your name we pray. Amen!

CHANGE NOT!

Jesus Christ is the same yesterday, today, and forever.

Hebrews 13:8

Do you remain faithful in prayer or give up during trials, tribulations, or challenging moments in life? Do you stop praying or going to prayer meetings and church because you are discouraged? Know that Jesus is always present in our joy and suffering, good health and illness, hope and despair, success and failure. He does not change. Jesus will never leave us or forsake us (see Psalm 94:14). We can count on the Good Shepherd, for He laid down his life for us (see John 10:11-18).

When things are difficult in life, we should NEVER change our prayer life. We must continue all our spiritual practices, such as our daily prayers, attending praying meetings, mass, or church services. We should pray more and ask others to intercede for us and with us. For those who belong to a sacramental church, receiving the Sacrament more often is of utmost importance. Fidelity, faithfulness, and consistency in prayer strengthens, purifies, consoles, and helps us accept the will of God. In everything, *"trust in the LORD with all your heart"* (Proverb 3:5).

Action/Thought for Today: Do you remain faithful in prayer during challenging times and unforeseen circumstances? Ask the Lord to help you pray always.

Prayer: Lord Jesus, I tend to give up on my prayer life when I am weary and suffering. Please help me worship and adore You even amid trials and tribulations. It is in Your name I pray. Amen!

PRAYER AND MENTAL HEALTH!

Come to me, all you who labor and are burdened, and I will give you rest. Matthew 11:28, NABRE

Are you suffering from a mental illness? Anxiety, depression, and other psychological diseases affect many people's lives. Some are willing to seek mental health care. Many suffer in silence. Others are reluctant to speak to a mental health provider because they are concerned about the stigma attached to a mental health diagnosis. If you have mental illness, you are not alone, you are not a failure, and you should not be ashamed. Those who are not ill should assist, support, show love, and reach out often to those who have mental health conditions.

The Lord does not want us to suffer. He blesses us with mental health professionals, family support, healing and deliverance ministries to help us navigate the illness. God also wants us to lean on Him as we go through the hardships of this life. He invites us to come to Him for healing. Prayer and mental health care should go hand in hand for treating psychological diseases, for God is the Divine Healer. If you pray and trust in God, He will help you seek professional help, accept the diagnosis and treatment, share with others your daily struggles, and give you everlasting peace. Therefore, let us abide in the Lord and pray for healing.

Action/Thought for Today: Pray for and support all who have mental illness.

Prayer: Lord Jesus, we pray for blessing, healing, and peace for all those affected by psychological illnesses. In Your name we pray. Amen!

GOD, THE SOURCE OF OUR JOY!

You have turned my mourning into dancing; you have taken off my sackcloth and clothed me with joy, so that my soul may praise you and not be silent. O LORD my God, I will give thanks to you forever.　　　　　　　　　　　　　　　Psalm 30:11-12

God is the Source of all our joy. The joy He gives is not temporary, and no one can take it away from us. The joy of the Lord gives us strength (see Nehemiah 8:10) and courage in the midst of trials and tribulations. God wants to provide us with His joy and sustain us in every pain and grief: *"When anxiety was great within me, your consolation brought me joy"* (Psalm 94:19, NIV). He wants to turn our darkness into light and enlighten us with His truth, love, joy, and peace.

Although life is difficult and our problems are sometimes long-lasting, as Christians, let us pray for the grace not to complain and lament, but to trust in the Father's care for us. He is ready to relieve our mourning and make our joy complete by filling us with the peace and courage to move on in life. Let us open our hearts to the Lord and accept His joy without reservation. Let us be thankful for the gift of joy and sing praises to the Lord.

Action/Thought for Today: Will you let the Lord bring His joy into your mourning and make you complete?

Prayer: Lord Jesus, through Your love, mercy, and compassion, bring healing, joy, and peace to us, our nation, and the whole world. Please help us to trust You and believe in Your promise that dancing comes after mourning. We thank and praise you, Lord Jesus Christ. We pray in Your holy name. Amen!

WE ARE GOD'S CREATION!

Yet, LORD, you are our father; we are the clay and you our potter: we are all the work of your hand. Do not be so very angry, LORD, do not remember our crimes forever; look upon us, who are all your people!   Isaiah 64:7-8, NABRE

We are God's creation, and we must acknowledge that we are the work of His hands. The Lord created us in His image and wants to shape us daily to be more like Him, imitating His ways. He wants to lead us in every area of our lives. Although we are God's creation, He has given us free will. Therefore, we should ask God to lead us. We should open ourselves to accept His guidance and let Him bring us deeper into His merciful heart. Pray for the grace to let the Lord mold you. May you follow Him with your heart and whole being. He will always take care of you, for He cares for you. Let us thank God for creating and loving us. Let us appreciate the gift of life. *"Oh come, let us worship and bow down; let us kneel before the LORD, our Maker!"* (Psalm 95:6).

Action/Thought for Today: Are you accepting the Lord's guidance, or are you being guided by the world?

Prayer: O Lord, sometimes we forget that You have created us and fail to live up to Your expectations. Have mercy on us and do not remember our iniquity forever. Lord, forgive our sins, bring us back to You, and give us the grace to acknowledge that we are Your creation and must adore You and glorify You. In Your name we pray. Amen!

SECOND CHANCES!

The Lord is not slow about his promises, as some think of slowness, but is patient with you, not wanting any to perish, but all to come to repentance.   2 Peter 3:9

Are you in favor of second chances? Is there someone in your life who deserves a second chance? Paul was known for persecuting Christians. After he converted to Christianity, he *"attempted to join the disciples,"* but *"they were all afraid of him, for they did not believe that he was a disciple"* (Act 9:26). Barnabas, known as the *"son of encouragement"* (Acts 4:36), took Paul to the disciples and spoke highly of him, informing them that Paul had seen the Lord and had spoken boldly in His name (see Acts 9:27). Barnabas gave Paul a second chance.

Like Paul, someone in our lives may have changed for the better, yet we still avoid that person. Therefore, we must ask the Holy Spirit to help us discern others' actions and intentions. Let us determine to give others another chance, for all of us have fallen short of the glory of God (see Romans 3:23). We all have been beneficiaries of second, third, and many more chances by God and others. Every time we sin, if we go to God and repent, He takes us back without preconditions. He is very patient with us (see 2 Peter 3:9). Healing occurs when we give others a second chance. Life is more meaningful when we forgive, love, and show compassion.

Action/Thought for Today: Reflect on a time in your life when you received an undeserved second chance. Thank the Lord for this grace.

Prayer: Lord Jesus, open my heart to give a second chance to those around me. In Your name I pray. Amen!

SINCERE COMPASSION!

The LORD is gracious and merciful, slow to anger and abounding in steadfast love. The LORD is good to all, and his compassion is over all that He has made. Psalm 145:8-9

Life has more meaning when we help those who are in need or suffering. If you want to live a purposeful life, start imitating Jesus Christ by living a life of sacrifice, caring for others, and showing compassion and love. Sometimes we are blind to the suffering of others. Sometimes we do not know what to do, or we are unwilling to make sacrifices for others. At other times, we are so preoccupied with our lives that we forget or neglect the needs of others. Therefore, we must pray for the Spirit of God to guide and lead us to those who need a helping hand, a caring and listening heart.

Sincere compassion is entering into the suffering of another, which leads us to take action to alleviate their pain and empower them to change for the better. Hence, like Christ, we must die to ourselves and suffer a little for the good of others, most importantly for the salvation of souls. Therefore, let us imitate Jesus' selfless love by not ignoring the suffering of others but responding with compassion and generosity to all.

Action/Thought for Today: Who needs a little compassion from you today? Pray for the grace to help alleviate that person's suffering or pain.

Prayer: Lord Jesus, give me the grace to enter the suffering of my brothers and sisters. Teach me to be compassionate and merciful like You. It is in Your name I pray. Amen!

July 18

Let Go of Regrets!

For godly grief produces a repentance that leads to salvation and brings no regret, but worldly grief produces death.

2 Corinthians 7:10

Are you living with regrets? Do you wish you could take back your past actions and mistakes? Many people carry past burdens and hurts, failing to understand that they cannot change the past. It will permanently be part of our history. However, we must reject the things that keep us from being joyful and peaceful. Many aspects of our lives can be affected when we live with regrets. No matter the heartache of the past or present age, there is no condemnation for those who are in Christ. He has freed us from sin and death (see Romans 8:1-2).

The antidote for regret is forgiveness. Therefore, ask God for forgiveness. Forgive yourself and others. Ask Him to heal your heart, and to help you let go of the hurts and live in the present moment. Renounce the spirit of regrets in Jesus' name. Let God replace your regrets with His joy and peace. When we let go of regrets, life is more meaningful, for we can better appreciate God's blessing, goodness, and kindness. When we reject guilt, we can accept our mistakes, learn from them, and resolve to do better.

Action/Thought for Today: What are your regrets? Pray to let go of your shame.

Prayer: Lord Jesus, fill me with Your grace and peace so that I can live without regrets. It is in Your name I pray. Amen!

FINDING MEANING IN SUFFERING!

For just as we share abundantly in the sufferings of Christ, so also our comfort abounds through Christ.

2 Corinthians 1:5, NIV

Suffering is challenging, difficult to accept, and hard to understand. Jesus suffered on the cross for us. We, too, cannot escape suffering in this life. Let us not waste our suffering by being discontent or bitter; instead, let us turn it into love and sacrifice by sharing our cross with the Lord. When we unite our suffering with Christ, He helps us with the struggles of life. He leads and guides us to safe pastures. He gives us the strength, courage, and patience to accept the suffering.

A few years ago, I visited a friend who was dying of cancer. In her suffering, she told me, "Either way, life or death, I will be fine because God is with me." My friend knew well that God lived within her, and He suffered with her. Her self-surrender to the Lord made her suffering and dying a peaceful process.

Jesus offered his suffering to the Father for the salvation of all souls as He called out, *"Father, into your hands I commit my spirit"* (Luke 23:46, NRSVUE). We must imitate Him by offering our suffering as intercessory prayer for our families and friends and the redemption of the world. Let us ask God to give us the grace to accept our suffering and find meaning in it.

Action/Thought for Today: The next time you face difficulties, offer your suffering for someone in your life or for the salvation of the world.

Prayer: Lord Jesus, thank You for laying down Your life for me. I offer You my suffering for the salvation of the world. It is in Your name I pray. Amen!

JULY 20

STRIVE FOR CONTENTMENT!

Not that I am referring to being in need; for I have learned to be content with whatever I have. Philippians 4:11

Some are very successful in their personal and professional lives, yet still not happy. Others settle for less, but they complain about their situation. Many feel that if they were rich, had a big home, a better car, or did not have to work, they would be much happier. However, even if all these wishes came true, satisfaction is not guaranteed because true contentment is in the Lord.

Contentment is also a choice. It should not come with what we *have* or where we *are* in life. We should be content regardless of our situation because we have Christ, and He is our All-in-All. I know people who are content in life, and their secrets are that they:

- Abide and live with the Lord in the present moment.
- Are grateful for everyone in their lives and everything they have.
- Do not compromise their spiritual life for worldly things.
- Do not let negativity bring them down.
- Recognize that God is in charge.
- Strive to be at peace with everyone.
- Use their God-given talents to serve God and others.

So, let us abide in the Lord, be filled with His grace and joy, as we imitate the apostle Paul, by being content with whatever we have (see Philippians 4:11-13).

Action/Thought for Today: Are you content with your life? Take a few minutes to pray and reflect.

Prayer: Lord Jesus, when I am dissatisfied, remind me of all the blessings You have bestowed upon me and give me the grace to be grateful. It is in Your name I pray. Amen!

MAKING THE BEST OF TIME!

So teach us to count our days that we may gain a wise heart.

Psalm 90:12

Sometimes, I look back at my day and wonder where the time went. Time goes by quickly and does not wait for us. It is a valuable gift from God. It is precious and unpredictable, and we cannot regain lost time. Therefore, let us not waste our time on unnecessary things. Instead, let us use it in the service of God and others, and cherish those around us. Whether at home, at work, or in the community, our time should always be centered and grounded in Christ.

How we spend our time gives meaning to life. When we use time wisely, we don't have to wish for more time at the end of our life's journey or look back with regret. Instead, we can peacefully rest in the Lord. So, how do you use your time?

- Are you making the most of your time or wasting it on meaningless activities or overworking?
- Do you use your time in useless talk or being idle while you could be praying?
- Do you use your time for yourself only, not caring for those in need?
- Do you use your time complaining instead of being grateful?

Action/Thought for Today: Reflect on these questions and ask the Lord for His help.

Prayer: Father God, thank You for the gift of time. Help us use our time wisely in Your service and for the good of others, and may we leave a legacy of time well spent. It is in Jesus' name I pray. Amen!

TRUST IN GOD'S DIVINE PROVIDENCE!

The LORD has established his throne in the heavens, and his kingdom rules over all.   Psalm 103:19

Sometimes we experience the heartache and disappointment of this life, forgetting that only trusting in God's divine providence can help us be at peace and make sense of it all. Trusting in God's divine providence can be seen:

- When life is challenging, but we trust God's plan in life (see Jeremiah 29:11) and submit to His will.
- When we are tired or weary, but instead of losing heart, we meditate on God's words: *"Come to me, all you who labor and are burdened, and I will give you rest"* (Matthew 11:28, NABRE).
- When we face spiritual battle, but we remain strong by using God's armor of protection (see Ephesians 6:10-18).
- When we lack life's necessities, yet we remain at peace, knowing that God will always provide (see Philippians 4:19, Matthew 6:31-32 and Luke 12:24).
- When we start a new chapter in life, not knowing what tomorrows hold, but we continue to hope in the Lord and not rely on our understanding (see Proverbs 3:5).
- When we trust in the Lord's protection in all situations (see Psalm 91).
- When we wake up in the morning, and instead of worrying about what awaits us, we thank the Lord for a new day.

Action/Thought for Today: Are you trusting
in God's divine providence?

Prayer: Lord Jesus, give me the grace to trust in Your divine providence. It is in Your name that I pray. Amen!

DO YOU KEEP THE SABBATH HOLY?

Remember the sabbath day, and keep it holy. Exodus 20:8

God said in Exodus 20:9-10, "*Six days you shall labor and do all your work. But the seventh day is a sabbath to the LORD your God; you shall not do any work.*" God showed us an example by resting on the seventh day after completing the work of creation (see Genesis 2:2-3). Therefore, we must try to keep the day of the Lord holy. Go to church, worship the Lord, pray, reflect, and reboot for the new week ahead. We should try to rest, relax, and avoid any unnecessary work. I encourage you to call or visit family and friends, especially the elderly.

Jesus healed people on the Sabbath (see John 5:1-18, Mark 3:1-6, and Luke 13:10-17), and He teaches us to help those in need on His day. God will be pleased that we don't rest on the Lord's Day if we save someone's life or help someone in an emergency. Many, such as hospital workers, police officers, firefighters, etc., have to work on Sunday. If we must work, let us strive to remember God during the day. For instance, use our lunchtime to pray and offer our work as a sacrifice of love. The Lord will see our efforts as an acceptable sacrifice.

Action/Thought for Today: Call or visit someone next Sunday.

Prayer: Lord Jesus, thank You for giving me the Sabbath as a day of rest. Teach me to keep Your day holy. In Your name I pray. Amen!

July 24

A Sleepless Night!

He who keeps Israel will neither slumber nor sleep. The LORD is your keeper.   Psalm 121:4-5

Have you ever had a sleepless night? If so, have you become frustrated or lost patience as you lie awake? You may have been thinking about whatever happened that day. Instead of dwelling on the past day, say a prayer of gratitude for the past day, ask for forgiveness for any failure and resolve to make tomorrow better with God's grace.

Your mind may also shift to your plan for tomorrow and life in general. Surrender those details to God. Pick up your Bible and meditate on God's words. Allow Him to fill you gently, and in peace you will sleep and rest, for the Lord will make you lie down in safety (see Psalm 4:8).

Remember, the Lord who watches over you does not sleep. Invite Him to your sleepless night. Speak to Him. Listen to the whisper of His voice and let Him love you. Maybe God wants to speak to you in the stillness of the night when you are quiet. For me, when I cannot sleep, I pray intercessory prayers for whomever God brings to my mind, and often I fall back asleep. At other times, I stay awake, but I pray for strength and courage for the next day. The Lord, in His mercy, refreshes my soul.

Action/Thought for Today: The next time you have a sleepless night, pray and rest in the Lord.

Prayer: Lord Jesus, thank You for giving me the nights to rest and for watching over me. In Your name I pray. Amen!

TEACH ME TO PRAY AND REST, O LORD!

Make me to know your ways, O LORD; teach me your paths. Lead me in your truth, and teach me, for you are the God of my salvation; for you I wait all day long. Psalm 25:4-5

Are you unable to rest because of life's demands? Are you a multi-tasker who takes no time for God and yourself? Life can be hectic. We get bombarded with our family's needs, work deadlines, and so many other things thrown at us during the day that we may place God and self-care on the back burner. But God can come to the rescue.

We must ask God to help us to faithfully fulfill our duties and find the time for Him and self-care. If we ask, He will teach us how to organize, prioritize, and maintain peace in our days to serve Him and others better. To help us relax, let us evaluate our lives, see what tasks are urgent versus unnecessary, and learn to delegate to others. This may be asking family members to help with the dishes or other chores. We can take a prayerful walk or ask family to give us a few minutes alone to recharge. We can invite a friend for coffee or dinner.

I don't know about you, but it is challenging for me to pray when I am tired because I fall asleep in prayer. Therefore, let us ask the Lord to direct us. If we offer our days to Him, we will be surprised at how much we can accomplish in a day.

Action/Thought for Today: Take a prayerful walk today.

Prayer: Lord Jesus, help me prioritize my life to spend more time with You and my family. In Your name I pray. Amen!

A SPIRITUAL GET-AWAY!

My soul thirsts for God, for the living God. When can I go and
meet with God?   Psalm 42:2, NIV

I often hear from others, "I need a vacation," especially when things are not going well at home or work. The body needs rest from time to time. That is why our employer gives us annual time off, or we take a family vacation. How about a spiritual retreat or conference to refresh your soul? Have you attended one lately?

Years ago, I attended a women's weekend retreat at my church. At first, I was reluctant about spending the weekend away, but my soul was thirsty for the Lord, and I needed to rest in Him. As I fellowshipped with other women, we all agreed that we needed that time to refresh and recharge in the Lord. After the retreat, everyone at home and work wanted to know why I was so joyful. Indeed, I experienced God's grace and mercy in a more profound way than words could impossibly describe.

A spiritual retreat does not only benefit us, but also those around us. It changes us to serve them better. Some discern God's call in their lives; others receive God's grace to move on in the chaotic world, as well as receiving healing. Let us make an effort to attend a spiritual retreat from time to time, even for half a day. Trust me, friends, you will not regret it.

Action/Thought for Today: Pray about
attending a spiritual retreat soon.

Prayer: Lord Jesus, I thirst for You. Please give me the grace to spend quality time with You. In Your name I pray. Amen!

SACRED SILENCE!

For God alone my soul waits in silence; from him comes my salvation. Psalm 62:1

Our world is filled with so much noise and so many interruptions that we sometimes forget how vital silence is to the spiritual life. Some are afraid of, or uncomfortable, in silence. From the time we wake up, we are surrounded by noise—the phone, TV, social media, traffic noise, and, for those who work, the busyness of the workplace. Then, we go home to the activity of the evening, turn on the news or the computer and catch up with family and friends. Bedtime comes quickly, and the cycle starts over the next day. It is an unending process if we fail to find silence.

Silence is sacred. Silence is a gift from God, and this is where we find Him profoundly. He whispers to us in the stillness. His voice is more evident when we are silent. God knows that the world will not offer the luxury of silence. Therefore, He instructed us: *"Be still and know that I am God"* (Psalm 46:10). Hence, one must be active in making space for solitude and silence and getting away from noise, to turn the heart and soul to the Lord and rest in Him. Let us devote a few minutes in stillness daily to hear God's voice. He is waiting for you in the silence of the heart.

Action/Thought for Today: Spend five minutes in silence today.

Prayer: Lord Jesus, teach me to be still in Your presence. In Your name I pray. Amen!

IS GOD ON VACATION?

Be careful then how you live, not as unwise people but as wise, making the most of the time, because the days are evil.

Ephesian 5:15-16

Vacation is a time to relax, alone or with family and friends. We visit new places, pack the day with fun-filled activities—sightsee, visit a local restaurant, enjoy new dishes, etc. And at the end of the day, we return to the hotel exhausted but filled with excitement, looking forward to the next day, we may neglect our evening prayers. Even Christians can fall into the trap of not praying and worshiping the Lord while vacationing.

Where is God while you are vacationing? Do you make time to pray a little longer since you are on vacation and have no time constraints? Do you attend church while vacationing? Or do you put God on vacation, too, until you return home to your routine?

For some, vacation is not only a break from work, but also from God and Church. Some forget about their obligations—spending time in prayer with God and worshiping on the Lord's Day. We cannot fully enjoy peace and rest if God is not part of it, for He sustains us in everything. Let us always be mindful that vacation is a gift from God, for He gives us both the time and money to rest and relax. Therefore, let us make the best use of our time and not neglect prayer.

Action/Thought for Today: Next time you are on vacation, find a church where you can worship on the Lord's Day.

Prayer: Lord Jesus, thank You for the gift of vacation. Please give me the grace to use my time wisely. In Your name I pray. Amen!

JULY 29

EVERLASTING PEACE!

You will keep in perfect peace those whose minds are steadfast, because they trust in you. Trust in the LORD forever, for the LORD, the LORD himself, is the Rock eternal.   Isaiah 26:3-4, NIV

Worldwide, people are seeking the peace which only God can provide. And we cannot rest until we have His everlasting peace. Do you let things beyond your control bother you? Is there someone in your life robbing you of your peace? Once, I had someone who challenged me. With God's grace, I tried to stay calm. The Scriptures tell us to try to always make and keep the peace (see Hebrews 12:14) and avoid any quarrels (see Proverbs 20:3). As much as I wanted peace, my heart remained heavy. So, I resorted to more prayer, and the Lord said to me, "Let Me be your peace." His message was to focus on Him for strength and courage in this matter.

Indeed, everlasting peace is from God. Therefore, *"Do not be anxious about anything, but in every situation, by prayer and petition, with thanksgiving, present your requests to God. And the peace of God, which transcends all understanding, will guard your hearts and your minds in Christ Jesus"* (Philippians 4:6-7, NIV). We cannot change people or certain life circumstances. We can pray for them. We must change or adjust how we react to others and life events, and let God gives us the peace and joy promised to us (see John 14:27). Be grateful for His peace!

Action /Thought for Today: What is stopping you from experiencing the peace of the Lord?

Prayer: Lord Jesus, help me experience Your peace beyond understanding. In Your name I pray. Amen!

PEACE IN THE MIDST OF TRIALS AND TRIBULATIONS!

Peace I leave with you; my peace I give to you. I do not give to you as the world gives. Do not let your hearts be troubled and do not let them be afraid.   John 14:27

Are you looking for peace in the world? The world offers empty promises—power, fame, and riches—but cannot provide lasting happiness or peace. Money, wealth, and good health cannot buy peace and joy. The only lasting peace and joy are from the Lord, and we receive them through prayer, trust, and abiding in Him. Your heart will be forever peaceful and joyful with God, despite the many hardships and uncertainties of life. The Lord's promises are true and everlasting, and He will keep in perfect peace those whose minds are steadfast because they trust in Him (see Isaiah 26:3). Let us lean on God's words, run to our Creator and Father, God, to find and maintain a spirit of peace at all times.

Action/Thought for Today: Pray for those who are fearful and anxious about their life's circumstances.

Prayer: Lord Jesus, with a grateful heart, I come to You today in search of Your peace that surpasses all understanding. Please fill me with Your peace and allow me to remain joyful and peaceful when the world around me seems to be falling apart. Thank You, Lord, for Your love and mercy. It is in Your name I pray. Amen!

THE POWER OF GOD'S GRACE!

May grace and peace be multiplied to you in the knowledge of God and of Jesus our Lord. 2 Peter 1:2, RSV

Grace upon grace is a blessing and unmerited favor from the Lord!

Grace makes us beloved children of God.

Grace is God's love.

Grace is His mercy.

Grace sets us free.

God's grace shall be food for my soul.

His grace shall be my guiding light.

His grace I need every day.

His grace shall be all I need.

Lord, give me the wisdom to embrace Your grace.

I shall breathe by God's grace.

I shall live by His grace.

I shall walk by His grace.

I shall fear no evil under His grace.

Lord, help me to be grateful for Your grace.

Only by God's grace can I be holy.

Only by His grace can I be righteous.

Only by His grace can I follow His laws and precepts.

Only by His grace can I be whole.

Lord, let Your amazing grace reside in me.

Action/Thought for Today: Reflect on God's grace in your life.

Prayer: Lord Jesus, thank You for Your unfailing love and mercy. In Your name I pray. Amen!

ALL THINGS WORK TOGETHER!

Have I not commanded you? Be strong and of good courage; be not frightened, neither be dismayed; for the LORD your God is with you wherever you go. Joshua 1:9, RSV

Have you ever heard a message from the Lord that caused you to worry? One morning in my prayer, the Lord spoke to my heart, *"Be strong and courageous; the LORD your God is with you wherever you go."* Instead of thanking God for His presence, the message left me a little concerned.

Half an hour later, I received a worrisome email. My heart became heavy, and I was unsettled for a few minutes. However, when I remembered the message from the Lord, I felt a peace that surpassed all understanding. This peace from the Lord strengthened my spirit and gave me clarity. I then regained my composure and moved on with my day. God was preparing me to focus on Him and trust in Him. The problem was still there, but the Holy Spirit was with me.

God's messages can be scary or intimidating at times. He does not want to frighten us. He wants to remind us of His presence in our lives and that He will be with us through it all. At the same time, He gives us the grace to endure whatever life brings. Remember, all things work together for good for those who love God (see Romans 8:28).

Action/Thought for Today: Pray for the grace to thank God when He speaks to you instead of worrying.

Prayer: Lord Jesus, thank You for sending Your Spirit to speak within us. Help us listen to Your voice and accept Your message. In Your name I pray. Amen!

SACRIFICE JOYFULLY!

Even if I am to be poured out as a drink offering upon the sacrificial offering of your faith, I am glad and rejoice with you all.
Philippians 2:17, ESV

Have you heard the proverb, "You can't have your cake and eat it too," meaning you can't have it both ways. This proverb also holds in the spiritual life, which requires daily dying to self to follow the Lord. We cannot:

- Be victorious without walking humbly with Jesus, letting Him fight our battles.
- Be Jesus' disciples without picking up our cross and following Him (see Matthew 16:24).
- Desire Jesus' promises without trusting in Him. His promises give us hope for a new day (see Jeremiah 29:11).
- Enter Heaven without striving to walk the narrow path (see Luke 13:23-25 and Matthew 7:13-14).
- Have a deep relationship with Christ without loving, submitting to, and surrendering ourselves to Him (see Luke 10:27).
- Have an Easter without a Good Friday, the reflection of God's love for us (see John 3:16).
- Move the mountain of life without faith (see Mark 11:23).
- Want to be like Jesus but be unwilling to spend time with Him in prayer, follow His commands, and change our old ways.

Our willingness to sacrifice for the Lord will bring us everlasting joy, life, and peace. The small sacrifices we perform here on Earth are nothing compared to what the Lord has done for us. Therefore, let us rejoice in being a living sacrifice to the Lord.

Action/Thought for Today: What choices are
you willing to make to be a friend of Jesus?

Prayer: Lord Jesus, help me choose You above
all things. In Your name I pray. Amen!

AN APPEAL TO BE DETACHED!

What profit is there for one to gain the whole world yet lose or forfeit himself? Luke 9:25, NABRE

Are you struggling with life's choices? Are you compromising your state of life for worldly things? Luke 9:25 is an appeal to be detached from the things of this world. As I was praying and reflecting on this scripture, the Spirit of God revealed to me that I must ask for the grace to:

- Desire what God desires
- Live out His will
- Love what He loves
- Seek Him constantly
- Want what He wants

God created us to know, love, and serve Him. Therefore, as we glorify Him, we must accept His will in all things. We must strive to be indifferent to our circumstances of life and be content with where we are, regardless of the hardship. This requires denying ourselves and picking up our crosses, as we follow Christ (see Luke 9:23). Jesus reminded us, *"Whoever loses his life for my sake will save it"* (Luke 9:24, NABRE). We can be confident that our reward will be in Heaven. However, steadfast prayer is required to receive the grace to always choose to obey God. Only then can we be free from worldly desires.

Action/Thought for Today: In what area of your life is God asking you to accept His will? Can you be indifferent to your own desires and trust God's plan instead? Pray for the freedom to choose God in all things.

Prayer: Lord Jesus, help me choose You above all things and be one with You. In Your name I pray. Amen!

ASK, SEEK, AND KNOCK!

Ask, and it will be given you; search, and you will find; knock, and the door will be opened for you. For everyone who asks receives, and everyone who searches finds, and for everyone who knocks, the door will be opened. Matthew 7:7-8

The Scriptures tell us: *"Ask, and you shall receive."* Do you get angry at God when He does not answer your prayer? We can trust God. He is faithful and He will give us what is good for us. He does not provide things that will hurt our souls or are not advantageous. We ought to pray for our hearts' desires to align with God's will. For instance:

- Do you want a big house because your family has grown or to compete with others?
- Do you want a promotion at work to serve the Lord and others or to control others?
- Do you want a degree or profession for God's glory or to gain respect and honor from others?
- Do you want to get married just because all your friends are married, when you are unsure if married life is your vocation?

When your prayers are not answered, continue to seek God. Ask Him for wisdom to discern and accept His will and surrender all to Him. Friends, know that God may not give us what we request, but He always gives us the best.

Action/Thought for Today: If you are a parent, do you give your children everything they ask for, even if these things are not suitable for their life?

Prayer: Lord Jesus, I praise and thank You for always caring and providing for me. In Your name I pray. Amen!

Let's Choose Humility!

Do nothing out of selfishness or out of vainglory; rather, humbly regard others as more important than yourselves, each looking out not for his own interests, but [also] everyone for those of others.
Philippians 2:3-4, NABRE

Pride is an illness of the soul, and if not cured, it may kill you spiritually. Pride tells you that life is all about "me, myself and I," because you are more important than others. Pride leads you to inflate your self-image, even if it means lying to others. Pride gets irritated when things don't work your way, for the prideful like to control every situation. Pride does not admit its faults, and cannot say, "I'm sorry." Why? Because pride is never wrong. Pride doesn't do the lowly jobs. Pride loves to be praised by others, forgetting that all praise and glory are only due to God, our Creator and Father. If left unchecked, pride will cause you to fall.

In contrast, humility calls us to trust in God and not rely on our own efforts. Humility challenges us neither to gossip nor make negative comments, nor to see ourselves as better than others. Humility helps us to admit our faults, find ways to ask for forgiveness, and correct our failures with God's grace. Humility helps us not to seek praise from others, but rather, to direct all praise to God. Humility leads us to say, *"I can do all things through Him [Christ] who strengthens me"* (Philippians 4:13) because we find our aspirations, accomplishments, and success only in the Lord.

Action/Thought for Today: Let us practice humility today.

Prayer: Precious Lord, teach me humility. Let my thoughts, words and actions be humble before You and others. In Your name I pray. Amen!

GOD MUST INCREASE; I MUST DECREASE!

Humble yourself therefore under the mighty hand of God, so that he may exalt you in due time. Cast all your anxieties on him, because He cares for you. 1 Peter 5:6-7

When I surrender a concern to the Lord and submit to His will, it always works out well. Sometimes, I may not get the expected outcome, but still, it works for the best. In effect, my trust and faith are strengthened in God. The Scriptures tell us that *"all things work together for good for those who love God"* (Romans 8:28). Surrendering our lives to God requires humility. It allows us to give over the wheel, be a backseat passenger, and let God be the Captain of our lives. Humility reminds us that we are not in control of our lives, and we must submit to the Master of Life— God. It reminds us that we depend on Him for every breath and heartbeat. We must trust in God and never lose sight of Him. Humility helps us acknowledge that God is our Creator, and all things exist because He created them. It helps us to desire and accept the will of God in all things. We must pray ardently for the gift of humility, which will lead us closer to the Father's heart.

Action/Thought for Today: Pray for the gift of humility.

Prayer: Lord Jesus, You are Alpha and Omega, the Beginning, and the End. You must increase in honor, power, and glory, and we must decrease before You. O God, You are our Creator, and without You, we are nothing. Give us the grace to surrender to You, ourselves, our will, hearts, and minds, desires, and emotions—all that we have. Jesus, Humble of Heart, let our hearts be one with Yours. We exalt You, O Lord! In Your name we pray. Amen!

HOW DOES GOD FEEL ABOUT THE PRIDEFUL?

A person's pride will bring humiliation, but one who is lowly in spirit will obtain honor. Proverbs 29:23

God resists the proud but favors the humble (see James 4:6). This scripture is a warning to the prideful but is full of hope and blessing for the humble and meek. God will lift the lowly. God's words are truthful, and He keeps His promises. Therefore, we must pay close attention to His teachings.

Pride is the main instrument of the devil to disrupt the Holy Spirit's work in our lives. Pride prevents us from receiving God's grace and growing in virtue. It alienates us from God and others. When pride is at work, it can affect our relationships in the family and community, since we may behave in ways that diminish others. It causes us to be selfish, and to seek glory from others. Therefore, we must pray and ask the Lord to bless us with the gift of humility. We must ask Him to remove every bit of pride from us, for pride is the root of all evil (see Genesis 3:5). The Lord guides the humble in what is right and teaches them his way (see Psalm 25:9).

Action/Thought for Today: With God's grace, what can we do to become humble? Reflect on your actions and words toward others and choose to be humble.

Prayer: In Jesus' holy name, I renounce the spirit of pride, and I seek a spirit of humility, love, compassion, and wisdom. Lord, I exalt, glorify, and praise You. It is in Your name I pray. Amen!

Let Us Imitate the Lord's Humility!

He [Jesus] emptied himself, taking the form of a slave, coming in human likeness; and found human in appearance, he humbled himself, becoming obedient to death, even death on a cross.

Philippians 2:7-8, NABRE

The Lord Jesus is humble of heart. He emptied Himself and accepted death on the cross to save us. He did not complain about the cross; He remained silent and asked the Father to forgive us. Many cannot bear the smallest humiliation or injustice without fighting back or being resentful. Yet, although He committed no crime and no fault was found in Him, our Lord was scourged and a crown of thorns was placed on His head (see John 19:1-4).

Jesus is the King of kings, yet He washed the disciples' feet (see John 13:1-17) to show us how to serve and love. Many put themselves first, before others, but Jesus gave us many examples of self-giving. Even when He was tired, He ministered to the Samaritan woman (see John 4:4-26). He did not focus on His own health or need for rest or hunger. The path to humility is to strive to imitate Jesus' way of life—His sacrifice to save us, His genuine love for others, and His characteristics. We ought to conform to His image (see Romans 8:29) and collaborate with Him, as He transforms us to react with love and kindness toward others.

Thought/Action for Today: Let us pray for the grace to submit to God's holy will with humility, courage, and perseverance.

Prayer: Lord Jesus, You showed us a great example of humility by accepting death on the cross to save us. Please give us the grace, courage, and strength to be humble, just like You. Thank You, Lord, for Your ultimate sacrifice to save us. Praise You, O Lord. In Your name we pray. Amen!

GOD WANTS A HUMBLE HEART!

For all those who exalt themselves will be humbled, and those who humble themselves will be exalted.   Luke 18:14, NIV

*For the full scripture, see Luke 18:9-14.

God wants a humble heart. Our prayer should not be to glorify ourselves. God knows what we do for Him and for others. In Luke 18:11-12, a Pharisee glorified himself: *"God, I thank you that I am not like other people—robbers, evildoers, adulterers—or even like this tax collector. I fast twice a week and give a tenth of all I get"* (NIV). God knew the Pharisee's heart. His prayer was prideful, and he was not justified before the Lord. Our prayer should be more like the tax collector, *"God, have mercy on me, a sinner"* (Luke 18:13, NIV) and the Lord will accept it. The tax collector was forgiven and exalted by the Lord, for He favors a humble heart (see James 4:6).

Therefore, we ought to come to God as we are, accepting our fallen nature. Although it is difficult, we must admit our sins and shortcomings to the Lord and ask for His mercy and forgiveness. He is willing to forgive us. In prayer, we must recognize that God is God. Therefore, let us bow down in praise and worship in front of the Master of the Universe and ask for the grace to be humble. If humble, our prayer will unite us to the Lord more profoundly.

Action/Thought for Today: Acknowledge your sins and ask the Lord for mercy and forgiveness.

Prayer: Lord Jesus, have mercy on me, a sinner. Help me to be humble and to admit my sins to You in prayer. Lord, I praise and thank You. In Your name I pray. Amen!

THE KEY TO HOLINESS AND GRACE!

As God's chosen ones, holy and beloved, clothe yourselves with compassion, kindness, humility, meekness, and patience.

Colossians 3:12

Humility is the key to holiness and grace; therefore, we should strive to seek this virtue. God commanded us to be holy. He said: *"Be holy, for I am holy"* (Leviticus 11:44). Without holiness, we cannot see the Lord (see Hebrews 12:14). One who strives to be holy must pray without ceasing to be humble, resist the temptation of pride, submit to God's will, and be open to receive God's grace. The closer we are to God, the more we will have a pure and humble heart.

Humility helps us to be aware of God's grace in our lives and the gifts that God has given us. We must be grateful for these gifts. We must use them with a humble heart and for the benefit of others. Without humility, we cannot use our God-given gifts to full potential because we are relying on ourselves and not on God. God's grace is sufficient for us (see 2 Corinthians 12:9). We must rely only on His grace for all our needs and service to others at home and work, and in the community and ministry.

Action/Thought for Today: Reflect on your daily life to see where you can improve with the virtue of humility. Ask the Lord to help you.

Prayer: Lord Jesus, I know I can do all things with Your grace. Help me choose humility with all my heart, and teach me to be humble in my daily life. Teach me to be holy and to have a pure heart. Lord, thank You for the many graces You have given me. In Your name I pray. Amen!

ARE YOU DETERMINED TO PURSUE THE VIRTUE OF HUMILITY?

He has told you, O mortal, what is good; and what does the Lord require of you but to do justice, and to love kindness, and to walk humbly with your God. Micah 6:8

Being humble is very difficult and requires perseverance to succeed. Prayer and humility are imperative in one's spiritual life. Therefore, we should pray without ceasing and ask the Lord to help us understand the true meaning of humility, as well as how to practice it. We should also decide to follow the example of the Lord's humility. It will require that we accept being despised and rejected, as Jesus did (see Isaiah 53:3). We must bear injuries and criticism without retaliation and, despite all, serve like Jesus.

As we become more humble, God will help us perform our daily duties with fidelity, as we lean on Him for assistance in all things. With God's grace, we will better know ourselves, gifts, and defects, and resolve to start anew every time we fall. We will be able to stay silent when we must and speak out when necessary. We will be able to glorify and accept the Lord's will in all circumstances. We will serve with our hearts, not for others to see, but because it is the right thing. We are very weak, but the impossible can become possible with God's help. Let us focus on God's grace to acquire the gift of humility.

Action/Thought for Today: Are you determined to pursue the virtue of humility? Ask the Lord for His help.

Prayer: Lord Jesus, we resolve to pursue the gift of humility. Help us to accept small injuries and criticism without retaliation. Help us perform our daily duties with humility and peace. Thank You, Lord, for granting us the gift of humility. In Jesus' name I pray. Amen!

BE WATCHFUL!

Be on your guard, stand firm in the faith, be courageous, be strong. 1 Corinthian 16:13, NABRE

What is vigilance? According to Oxford's online dictionary, "vigilance is the action or state of keeping careful watch for possible danger or difficulties."[26] We should not only be vigilant for potential day-to-day risks or dangers. We must also be watchful in our Christian life for the state of our spiritual wellbeing. Hence, we must examine ourselves to see whether we are in the faith (see 2 Corinthians 13:5) and living according to God's ways. We must prayerfully strive to be mindful of and reflect on our behaviors and attitudes from time to time to see where we have fallen short of God's glory. Then sincerely ask the Lord for forgiveness and take immediate action to follow God's teachings and commandments. He wants us to be perfect like Him (see Matthew 5:48). Our lives must be Christ-centered. Therefore, watch and pray for Christ's characteristics in you, and make every effort to live and love like Christ consistently.

Action/Thought for Today: Are you reflecting God's characteristics? Ask the Lord to help you.

Prayer: Lord Jesus, help us make every effort to reflect God's characteristics every single day of our lives. Teach us to be more like You. In Your name we pray. Amen!

LIFE IS SHORT!

For you yourselves know very well that the day of the Lord will come like a thief in the night. 1 Thessalonians 5:2

Some people live freely, eating and drinking, not thinking of God. Some don't know Him, and others have no interest in knowing Him. I hope and pray that God keeps us vigilant to remain near Him, for we must be ready when He comes. Remember, He will come as a thief, unexpected. Let us not sleep as the rest do, but let us stay alert, sober, and prayerful (see 1 Thessalonians 5:6).

This life is short, today is what counts, and tomorrow is not promised. Be vigilant in how you live, serve, and treat others. Be vigilant in the big and little things you do every day, and be steadfast in your prayers and relationship with God. Bring joy and peace wherever you go, and make every effort to bless others. Live a life of obedience to God and be humble before Him. By doing so, when the Lord comes, you can honestly say, "Father, I did my best." Therefore, let us ask the Father for the grace to remain vigilant and receive salvation through Jesus' mercy and love.

Action/Thought for Today: What would you do if the Lord were to come today? Are you ready to meet Him?

Prayer: Lord, keep us alert for that day when You will come in Your glory. Lord, You told us, "*As you go, make this proclamation: 'The kingdom of heaven is at hand'*" (Matthew 10:7, NABRE). Give us the courage to guide others to You. Teach us to pray for those who do not know You. Lord Jesus, we thank You and adore You. In Your name we pray. Amen!

BE VIGILANT AND PRAY!

Discipline yourselves, keep alert. Like a roaring lion your adversary the devil prowls around, looking for someone to devour. Resist him, steadfast in your faith, for you know that your brothers and sisters in all the world are undergoing the same kinds of suffering. 1 Peter 5:8-9, NABRE

The devil is always trying to destroy us. He even attacks us in our churches, creating confusion within the Christian family, to discourage us from serving the Lord or others. Resist the evil one, and serve God ardently. The adversary wants to destroy families, friendships, and marriages, and he turns children away from their parents. He is happy when we decide to stop being active in the family and when we stop loving and forgiving others. He creates division to isolate us from those we love. Resist the evil one, forgive others and love more.

The enemy knows that the flesh is weak, and he offers worldly desires. When I am on a spiritual fast, the cookies smell sweeter, and I struggle more with various life issues. I encourage you, despite the struggles in your walk with Christ, to resist the enemy. Cry out to the Lord for His help.

Be vigilant, with your spiritual eyes open, to understand and see the schemes of the adversary. Submit yourselves to and abide in God. Our God will always give you the strength and courage to fight the enemy, if you remain in Him.

Action/Thought for Today: Make a concrete plan to resist the devil when he attacks you in family life or community.

Prayer: Lord Jesus, give us a sober spirit, help us resist the devil, and keep us abiding in You. We thank and praise You, Lord. In Your name we pray. Amen!

Be Vigilant and Keep Awake!

But about that day or hour no one knows, neither the angels in heaven, nor the Son, but only the Father. Beware, keep alert, for you do not know when the time will come. Mark 13:32-33

When a hurricane, storm, or snow is approaching, we prepare our homes, communicate a safety plan with family, seek safe shelter, and stay on guard. We must do the same with our spiritual well-being because we do not know when the Lord is coming. Luke 12:40 teaches us: *"You also must be ready, for the Son of Man is coming at an unexpected hour."*

Therefore, in preparation for the Lord's coming, we must stay awake and live like today is the last day. We ought to try to live in the light and truth of Christ at all times. We must continue to proclaim the message of hope, love, and faith to everyone we encounter. We should strive to use the gifts the Lord has given us to the fullest to serve and encourage others, bringing them to Christ. Are you preparing your minds and your hearts for Christ? Friends, please, stay awake for the Lord and be vigilant!

Action/Thought for Today: Are you alert?
Are you strong in the faith of Christ? Are you
vigilant in prayer and the Lord's ways?

Prayer: Lord Jesus, I want to remain awake and vigilant,
but I can only do this by Your grace and mercy. Lord,
keep my focus on You day and night, and prepare me
for Your coming. In Your name I pray. Amen!

CHOOSE THE NARROW GATE!

Enter through the narrow gate; for the gate is wide and the road is easy that leads to destruction, and there are many who take it. For the gate is narrow and the road is hard that leads to life, and there are few who find it. Matthew 7:13-14

Vigilance keeps us on the alert. It also leads us to the way of God, the way to salvation. There are just two ways, no middle way. One way leads us to Christ, and the other leads to destruction. Therefore, let us be among the few who choose the narrow gate to Heaven.

The way of salvation is not easy; it requires dying to self to follow Christ's path. It requires us to be a martyr for Christ daily as we continue our journey with Him. It also requires us not to conform to this world's pattern, but to test and approve what is God's will for us (see Romans 12:2). Therefore, let us pray for the grace to follow the road that leads to salvation, no matter what comes our way and how difficult it may be. I am confident that we will find the way ... if we are abiding in the Lord.

Action/Thought for Today: Meditate for five to ten minutes on the message of Matthew 7:13-14.

Prayer: Lord Jesus, gives us strength and courage to go in the narrow gate and receive the gift of eternal life. Help us find the way that leads to You. We praise and thank You, Lord. In Your name I pray. Amen!

BE ALERT AND AWARE!

Devote yourselves to prayer, keeping alert in it with thanksgiving.
Colossians 4:2

The evil one has a way of throwing rotten tomatoes at us, sometimes from many different directions. Events in life can be unexpected, painful, and fearful. As we keep watch, we must remember to lean on God in good and bad times. Be vigilant and remember that we must respond with prayers of praise and thanksgiving when the enemy throws rocks at us. When I am having a bad day or rough times, I sometimes get discouraged. If I start listening to upbeat spiritual or Gospel music or read the Psalms, I usually regain my peace and joy.

We must be alert to know what to do in adversity, such as remaining strong in Christ through prayer and abiding in His ways. During times of difficulty, let us try not to change our prayer life. Instead, fast, pray, and meditate on God's words more fervently to remain connected with Him, and you will be able to resist anything that comes your way. Talking to a trusted spiritual friend or mentor can also bring clarity in times of darkness. These active acts will strengthen us to sustain life's storms, without losing hope and courage, and remind us of God's goodness and mercy.

Action/Thought for Today: Make a mental note to pray more in times of adversity.

Prayer: Lord Jesus, You know how easy it is for me to lose hope. Please give me the grace to offer You my heart with songs and prayers of praise and thanksgiving in times of adversity. In Your name I pray. Amen!

Vigilance in the Christian's Life!

Come to a sober and right mind, and sin no more; for some people have no knowledge of God.   1 Corinthian 15:34

Vigilance is essential in the life of a Christian. It helps keep our minds on Christ. It guards our hearts and minds against the world's pleasures and beliefs. The devil always wants to distort the truth. However, vigilance in Christ helps us differentiate the good from the evil and the truth from the lies. It reminds us to always pray, so God will direct us. If we trust in the Lord with all our hearts and do not rely on our own understanding, He will make straight our paths (see Proverbs 3:5).

When you partner vigilance, fasting, and prayer, you can fight the daily battle of life by not accepting the world's way but seeking God's way in everything. Ask God for the grace to remain vigilant, keep watchful, submit to Him, and gain salvation through Jesus Christ. He said: *"Ask, and you shall receive"* (Matthew 7:7-8).

Action/Thought for Today: Take a few minutes
to pray to remain vigilant in the Lord, and also
pray for those who do not know God.

Prayer: Lord Jesus, teach me not to rely on my understanding,
but to be vigilant and consult You in all my affairs. Open
my eyes and heart to seek Your truth and way and to
keep me close to You. In Your name I pray. Amen!

WHAT IS COURAGE?

Wait for the LORD, be strong and let your heart take courage;
wait for the LORD.   Psalm 27:14

According to the online Merriam-Webster dictionary, "courage is mental and moral strength to venture, persevere, and withstand danger, fear, or difficulty."[27] Courage and strength are needed:

- To acknowledge Christ, be His disciples, and serve Him with all our being, despite the setbacks or misfortunes of life.
- To do the right thing, even if we are mocked, ridiculed, or everyone is against us.
- To face adversity in this world of chaos, illness, and uncertainty.
- To stand for our brothers and sisters who are abused, rejected, and oppressed.
- To wait on and hope in the Lord to fight our battles, to stay silent when necessary, and create an environment of peace during quarrels and misunderstandings.

Do you lack strength and courage? Are you discouraged? We are reminded in Ephesians 6:10 to draw our strength from the Lord and His mighty power. He is the only Supplier of the courage necessary to survive in this world. Therefore, let us pray for the gift of courage. The Lord will grant it to us if we earnestly seek Him for it.

Action/Thought for Today: In what area of your life
do you lack courage? Ask the Lord to help you.

Prayer: Lord Jesus, please grant us the gift of courage to
survive in this chaotic world. Thank You, Lord, for giving
us Your strength and power to face adversity. Praise
You, Lord. It is in Your name that we pray. Amen!

COURAGE TO FACE DEATH!

Strengthen the weak hands and make firm the feeble knees. Say to those who are of a fearful heart, "Be strong, do not fear! Here is your God. He will come with vengeance, with terrible recompense. He will come and save you." Isaiah 35:3-4

On my way back home from a funeral, the thought of my own unavoidable death came to mind. I did not want to think about it, but I knew that I must face the reality of dying one day. I never pondered my death when I was younger, but now, I understand that death is inevitable. Hence, it made me realize the importance of preparing for the end of my life today and not tomorrow. What would those left behind have learned from me? Would my footsteps leave a mark, or would others want to erase them quickly? Would I receive eternal life in Christ? Reflecting on these thoughts led me to pray for a courageous life and death in Christ, the grace to accept the prospect of dying and receive the gift of salvation.

Sooner or later, we must all face death. How are you preparing for your future death? What legacy will you leave behind? Of course, our eulogies may be embellished by those who love us, but what will God say about our lives? Let us strengthen the weak hands and feeble knees in prayer so that our lives can reflect a living sacrifice and labor of love acceptable to the Lord.

Action/Thought for Today: Reflect on one or more of these questions. Ask God to help you.

Prayer: Lord Jesus, help us live and die for You and with You. Please bless us with the gift of salvation. It is in Your name that I pray. Amen!

"TAKE COURAGE, IT IS I!"

At once [Jesus] spoke to them, "Take courage, it is I; do not be afraid." Matthew 14:27, NABRE

* For the full scripture reference, see Matthew 14:22-33.

When the disciples saw Jesus walking on the sea, they were afraid because they thought they were seeing a ghost. But Jesus said to them, *"Take courage, it is I; do not be afraid."* The disciples were terrified because they were not focusing on Jesus. Life is full of ghosts—our fears, pain, troubles, and worries. In the face of these adversities, we must pray for the courage to focus on Jesus and not our problems.

Are you facing difficulties that require courage to move on? The Lord is saying to you today: "Do not focus on the storm of life, but take courage, I am with you always! It is I, walking with you, keep your gaze on me!" We must hold on to God's words and promises when we feel that we have no more strength and courage to go on in life. Pray and be courageous, for you are no longer a slave to fear, discouragement, nor problems. You are a child of God. Let us hold on to Jesus' hand as we walk courageously by faith in the storms of life. He will strengthen us, and our boats will arrive safely to shore.

Action/Thought for Today: What are your worries or fears? Ask the Lord to help you let go of your problems and focus on Him.

Prayer: In Jesus' name, we renounce the spirit of fear, and we pray for a spirit of courage, strength, power, and love. We thank and praise You, Lord. In Your name we pray. Amen!

COURAGE UNDER PRESSURE!

Be strong and steadfast; have no fear or dread of them, for it is the Lord, Your God, who marches with you; he will never fail you or forsake you. Deuteronomy 31:6, NABRE

Have you ever been pressured to behave a certain way because it was popular? Have you ever been told to reject your religious belief or affiliation? Because we naturally want to please others, we sometimes put aside or modify our beliefs to comply with the world. As hard as it is, we cannot give in to the world or the people who want us to conform to ungodly behaviors or ways. We must pray for the ability to stand firm and to kindly reject any invitation that does not advance our spiritual life.

I was invited to a place once, and I kindly rejected the invitation because the environment did not adhere to my Christian principles. Some mocked me, but with God's grace, I stood firm in my decision. As Christians, we should not make any excuses for choosing to do the right thing. As we strive to follow God's commands, He will bless us with the courage to carry on. Know that we will never be able to please everyone, and that's okay. What is essential is pleasing and honoring God in all things. Let us pray for that grace.

Action/Thought for Today: What are your barriers to following the Lord? Let us reflect and pray for the grace to do the right thing.

Prayer: Lord Jesus, please give us the grace and courage to do the right thing in all circumstances. It is in Your name that we pray. Amen!

When Life Is Hard, Keep Moving!

For God alone my soul waits in silence; from him comes my salvation. He alone is my rock and my salvation, my fortress; I shall never be shaken. Psalm 62:1-2, NABRE

When life is uncertain, do you want to run away and hide? Do you think you will be better if you let go of your heartaches without facing them? Sometimes life is so difficult that we want to give up. It may be a complicated relationship, a long-lasting illness, or a rocky job that makes us discouraged.

Friends, when life is hard, PRAY, keep pushing, and don't give up. God is faithful. He will neither leave nor forsake you. We must pray to face life's challenges with courage and strength. God did not give us a spirit of cowardice but a spirit of power to conquer and be victorious. If we continue to push forward despite life's difficulties, we will prevail. Therefore, let us make every effort to press on when things are hard, be patient during our sufferings, and rejoice in the Lord. Let us persevere to attain our heart's desires by working diligently toward our goals. Whether at home or at work, we were created to do great things. Hence, discouragement has no place in the Christian life, for we are victorious in Christ.

Action/Thought for Today: With God's grace, resolve to press on when life is difficult.

Prayer: Heavenly Father, often I get discouraged when things are not going my way. Lord, help me to move forward despite life's setbacks and never to give up. In Jesus' name I pray. Amen!

A Plea for Courage!

Hear my voice, LORD, when I call; have mercy on me and answer me. Psalm 27:7, NABRE

Lord Jesus, life is messy and unpredictable. Courage is needed to survive in this world. Grant us the courage to face day-to-day setbacks and to start afresh.

In difficult and confusing situations, give us the courage to do the right thing—regardless of the cost.

Life's difficulties may stop us from dreaming. Give us the courage to live a meaningful life.

When we are at our weakest point, put Your strength in us.

When we are spiritually lost or desolate, grant us the courage to find our way back to You.

When we face loss through life's misfortunes, give us the courage to find hope and trust in Your plan for us.

When we have nowhere else to turn, grant us the courage to turn to You always.

When all else fails, show us the way, dear Lord.

Action/Thought for Today: Write down your plea for courage and pray for the gift of courage.

Prayer: Lord Jesus, grant me courage so that I can continue my faith journey. In Your name I pray. Amen!

Faith Tested!

Therefore, I make a decree: Any people, nation, or language that utters blasphemy against the God of Shadrach, Meshach, and Abednego shall be torn limb from limb, and their houses laid in ruins; for there is no other god who is able to deliver in this way.
Daniel 3:29

In Daniel's time, King Nebuchadnezzar had a golden statue made and demanded that all his officials fall and worship it. Shadrach, Meshach, and Abednego, devout Jews who had been appointed administrators of Babylon, refused to serve the king's god or worship the statue. The king cast them into a white hot furnace, so hot that the men who threw them into it were devoured by the flames. The Lord sent an angel to accompany them as they sang God's praised while walking through the fire.

When Nebuchadnezzar saw that these men were not affected by the fire, he ordered them out of the furnace. The king recognized the greatness of the Most High God and called all his people to worship the God of Shadrach, Meshach, and Abednego (see Daniel 3:24-30). The courage of these three men made the king aware of the power of God and brought forth the king's conversion and that of many of his people.

Let us follow the footsteps of these brave men and pray for the courage to proclaim God's name in all circumstances, so that we change hearts of stone into flesh. These men did not give in to the pressure of the king and his minions, nor did they follow the world. Their faith was tested, but they conquered.

Action/Thought for Today: Like these men, our faith will be tested. Will we give in to the world or make a stand for Christ?

Prayer: Father, give me the grace to make a stand for Your name whenever necessary. In Jesus' name I pray. Amen!

DESTINED FOR SUCH A TIME!

So that no one would be unsettled by these trials. For you know quite well that we are destined for them.

1 Thessalonians 3:3, NIV

We are living in a turbulent time. Recently we have faced the Covid Pandemic, violence, war, and natural disasters. God has destined us for such a time in history. We may not be aware of the reason for our existence at this specific time, but God has a plan for us. Should we be discouraged? No! It is a time to seek God's mercy and rely on Him to help us carry our daily cross. Where there are problems and sorrows, God has also dispensed many graces to help us navigate through life.

Should we be afraid in such a time of uncertainty and tribulation? No! We were created to be the blessing the world needs and to support the weary and hopeless. Therefore, let us not be shaken by these trials. Trust God during the uncertainties of life and bring Him everything weighing on our hearts. God is in the midst of our daily troubles, and He is still in control. I am confident that He will use the evils of this world to transform hearts of stone into flesh and help us overcome sin.

Action/Thought for Today: What is heavy on your heart? Bring all your concerns to the Lord.

Prayer: Father, we are living in a time of trials and tribulations. Please fill us with Your grace to seek Your mercy and rely on You for everything. Help us always acknowledge that Your grace is sufficient for us (see 2 Corinthians 12:9). In Jesus' name we pray. Amen!

TAKE COURAGE!

But you, take courage! Do not let your hands be weak, for your work shall be rewarded. 2 Chronicles 15:7-9, RSV

Do you avoid essential projects or inspirations because they seem too difficult? Do you look at the amount of work you have to do and feel it is not achievable? Do your responsibilities make you anxious? In this chaotic world, we can easily be discouraged. The Lord wants us to be strong and of good courage. He promised us that He will always be with us. Therefore, let us consider His promises and be courageous in all things.

God did not create a spirit of cowardice within us, but rather a spirit of strength to accomplish anything that He has entrusted to us. Therefore, The Lord will fulfill our life's purpose because of His steadfast love for us (see Psalm 138:8). When things seem unachievable or when the hill seems too hard to climb, let us press forward to the finish line, as we meditate on God's promises in the Psalm 138:3: *"On the day I called, you answered me, you increased my strength of soul."*

Action/Thought for Today: What important projects and inspirations do you let go of because of anxiety and fear? Pray for the grace to never give up.

Prayer: Lord Jesus, give me the grace to remain steadfast in Your presence and not give up when the hill seems too hard to climb. In Your name I pray. Amen!

A WANDERING SOUL!

I have swept away your offenses like a cloud, your sins like the morning mist. Return to me, for I have redeemed you.

Isaiah 44:22, NIV

Do you know someone who has walked away from God—a family member, a close friend, or a church member who used to faithfully serve the Lord? All Christians want their loved ones to receive eternal life. When a loved one has wandered away from the Lord, we can get discouraged, upset, sad, and worried. However, we must persevere in prayer for our loved ones and hope in the Lord. God can bring that person back to His flock.

As we pray for those who have lost their faith, let us be patient and at peace with them. Let us be the light of Christ in their darkness. We can encourage them to return to church or prayer meetings. If they are not receptive to any invitation, evangelize them with deeds, not words. Stop nagging them. Instead, be supportive and loving. Know that even though someone stops praying or serving the Lord, He remains near and pursues them. We must take comfort knowing that God is ready to take us back whenever we repent and return to Him.

Action/Thought for Today: Fast and pray for those who have walked away from God to encourage them to return.

Prayer: Lord Jesus, please open the eyes of those who have wandered away from You and bring them back. Give them a strong desire to know, love, and serve You. In Your name we pray. Amen!

Perseverance!

And not only that, but we also boast in our sufferings, knowing that suffering produces endurance, and endurance produces character, and character produces hope.   Romans 5:3-4

How do you not give up when a family or friend is gravely ill or suddenly dies, a job is lost, or a relationship is broken? It is perseverance that helps us move on despite life's difficulties. Perseverance is a special grace from God. It is in our human nature to shake or crumble when life is difficult, but with God's help, we can continue to hope for the future.

Perseverance and determination are necessary for physical and spiritual life. It keeps us grounded in the Lord. Perseverance is vital when we are successful. One who has a flourishing ministry or vocation will find the grace to continue with zeal and give one's best. Perseverance helps us achieve success despite roadblocks and unforeseen fears. No matter the education, if we do not persevere, we cannot attain life's professional goals.

Perseverance helps us hope for the future, even if the present moment is not promising. Perseverance strengthens us to continue whatever we undertake, even if the enthusiasm has passed. Our Lord persevered during His passion and crucifixion. He did not give up, but He kept carrying the cross to save us. We must emulate His footsteps and never give up despite trials, discouragement, heartache, disappointments, and losses. Let us pray to persevere in good and bad times.

Action/Thought for Today: Pray for
the virtue of perseverance.

Prayer: Lord Jesus, bless us with perseverance and courage
in every walk of life. In Your name I pray. Amen!

PERSEVERE IN PRACTICING GOODNESS!

Do not be overcome by evil but overcome evil with good.

Romans 12:21

We are created in God's image, and God is good all the time. Therefore, we are created for goodness and are capable of doing good through God's grace. Although life is not always good to us, we must continually seek what is good and pure. Here are a few ways to practice goodness:

- Assist those who are suffering. The more we help others, the easier it becomes.
- Keep our promises toward those who often fail to help us.
- When experiencing discrimination, injustice, unfairness, or violence, strive to respond with the love of God.
- When others plot against us, do not retaliate. In return, God will take over the situation, for He said that no weapon formed against us shall prosper (see Isaiah 54:17)
- When others injure us, strive to see their goodness and not their defects.
- When we are victims of wrongdoing, we must surrender our pain to God and strive to live at peace. Then God will fight our battles. He said, *"Vengeance is Mine, I will repay"* (Romans 12:19).

We must persevere in practicing goodness, which is a fruit of the Spirit, until it becomes part of who we are, and others will experience the goodness of God through us.

Action/Thought for Today: Intentionally find something good in someone who has hurt you recently or in the past.

Prayer: Lord Jesus, help me see the goodness in You. Help me strive always to do good to others and see their goodness. In Your name I pray. Amen!

CALL UPON HIM!

Call on Me in the day of trouble; I will deliver you, and you shall glorify Me. Psalm 50:15

In the Parable of the Persistent Widow in Luke 18:1-8, the widow consistently approached a judge to seek a fair judgment. The judge had no compassion or respect for anyone. Initially, the judge rejected her request, but the widow persisted, and the judge granted her heart's desire. *"And will not God grant justice to his chosen ones who cry to him day and night? Will he delay long in helping them? I tell you that he will quickly grant justice to them"* (Luke 18:7-8). This parable is a clear example of the need to always pray and not give up (see Luke 18:1-8).

Do you have a concern that needs God's attention? Then, keep crying to the Lord without ceasing, *"Jesus, son of David, have mercy on me"* (Luke 18:38). If this is the only prayer you can say, keep crying out. We must persevere in supplication to our Heavenly Father because He is our Deliverer and Savior. One must seek to attain one heart's desire by praying and working diligently toward one's goal like this widow. Even if we do not receive what we pray for, let us not lose heart, for discouragement has no place in the Christian's life. We are all survivors in Christ.

Action/Thought for Today: Pray for
the virtue of perseverance.

Prayer: Lord Jesus, help us persevere in prayer despite
this life's many trials and tribulations. Thank You for
answering our prayers. It is in Your name we pray. Amen!

Finding Balance!

May our Lord Jesus Christ himself and God our Father, who has loved us and given us everlasting encouragement and good hope through his grace, encourage your hearts and strengthen them in every good deed and word.   2 Thessalonians 2:16-17, NABRE

How do you find a balance in this fast-paced and goal-oriented life? What is your priority? Is God first, family and friends next, then work, or vice versa? Do you feel you are running out of fuel sometimes? Life requires a balance for things to stay in order. A well-balanced life is healthy, peaceful, purposeful, and spiritually grounded in the Lord. Life is unstable and disordered when everything takes precedence over God, and we are more spiritually and physically exhausted.

If your job takes over your life and leaves you no room for God and family, you may have to make the difficult decision to find another job more suitable for your life.

If family life takes priority, one should evaluate the relationship with God and ask Him for the grace to place Him first. Family relationships are more stable when we are one in the Lord.

If it is a hobby or other activity that preoccupies you most of the time, examine yourself in prayer to see how you can change your schedule to place God first. Pray for the courage to change.

I encourage everyone to pray for an orderly and well-balanced life and, most importantly, to place God first.

Action/Thought for Today: Pray for
the grace to place God first.

Prayer: Lord Jesus, help me to have a balanced life
centered on You. It is in Your name I pray. Amen!

WHO ARE WE TO JUDGE?

Judge not, that you be not judged. For with the judgment you pronounce you will be judged, and the measure you give will be the measure you get.   Matthew 7:1-2, RSV

Do you struggle with being judgmental or critical? I am sure many of us have sinned by judging others. The Lord instructed us not to judge. Let us reflect on the following thoughts regarding being judgmental:

- What if the person we are judging has asked God for forgiveness and resolved to a new life in Christ without our knowledge? While God forgives this person, we continue to sin.
- We all have our flaws. What skeleton is hiding in the closet of your heart? Are you better than others? Are you able to throw the first stone (see John 8:7)?
- Judging others can make us prideful. God loves the humble (see James 4:6).

Only God is perfect and no one else. We must strive toward perfection with God's grace. Judging others will not get us closer to God. When tempted to criticize others, pray for them instead. Ask God to give them a new life. The more we pray for them, the more God will increase our capacity to love them and we will be less judgmental. *"Bless those who persecute you; bless and do not curse them"* (Romans 12:14).

Action/Thought for Today: Reflect on
your attitude toward others.

Prayer: Lord Jesus, eradicate any pride in me, and give
me the grace not to judge others but to pray more and
more for them. It is in Your name I pray. Amen!

WHAT IS TOLERANCE?

It [love] bears all things, believes all things, hopes all things, endures all things.   1 Corinthian 13:7

Tolerance does not mean accepting the wrongdoings of others or their beliefs, sins, standards, or way of life. It is to love and respect others as Christ loves us—despite our flaws. The world is in trouble these days because tolerance is in very short supply. There is no tolerance for others' mishaps or diversity. We look at the failure of others, forgetting to look at their inner beauty. We also forget that we are all children of God. We lose patience with others when they don't behave according to our norms.

- Some want to fight others because of their trivial actions or comments.
- Others' behaviors or actions get under our skin because we don't agree with them, or they're not part of our cultural or religious beliefs. We don't have to tolerate others' sinful behaviors, but we must love them.
- Sometimes we cannot tolerate the sound of someone's laughter. We call them "annoying" because they are lively and joyful.
- Sometimes we are unwilling to tolerate others' constant suffering. We complain that they are always depressed. "I can't deal with that," so we avoid them.

The world would be a better place if we try to accept and love each other unconditionally.

Action/Thought for Today: Pray for the grace to be respectful of others, despite their flaws or sins.

Prayer: Lord Jesus, help us love each other as You commanded. It is in Your name we pray. Amen!

SEPTEMBER 4

FEED YOUR SOUL TOO!

Take heed to yourselves and to all the flock, in which the Holy Spirit has made you overseers, to care for the church of God which he obtained with the blood of his own Son. Acts 20:28, RSV

Many busy themselves with ministry and evangelization but forget about the care of their souls. Imagine a mother feeding and caring for her family but who doesn't do the same for herself. How long can this mother be effective? God wants your soul, just as He wants the souls of those to whom you minister. What good would it be for you to forfeit your soul while striving to save others? Jesus said to all of us, as He did to Simon Peter, *"Feed my lambs, ... tend my sheep"* (John 21:15-16, ESV). However, we must also feed our own souls:

- Attend mass or church services as much as possible, at least on the Lord's Day.
- Attend a prayer retreat or spiritual conference from time to time, so you can be better equipped to teach, evangelize, and preach the Good News to others.
- Create sacred silence around you regularly to hear God's voice.
- Spend time daily in prayer with the Lord. Let Him love you so you can spread His love.

When we are filled with the Spirit of God, we are better stewards of the Lord. We can give ourselves to others without reservation. We can serve as an example to others as we imitate the characteristics of Christ.

Action/Thought for Today: What are your plans to feed your own soul?

Prayer: Lord Jesus, help me to always abide in You so I can be a good ambassador for Your Kingdom. In Your name I pray. Amen!

A PILGRIM'S LIFE!

Come, let us go up to the mountain of the LORD, to the house of the God of Jacob; that he may teach us his ways and that we may walk in his paths. Isaiah 2:3, RSV

A pilgrimage is "a journey to a sacred place."[28] This is often a foreign destination, where one takes time away from ordinary life to pray and seek God more profoundly. Paraphrase a pilgrimage prayer in one sentence: "Lord, if things do not go my way, help me remember that I am a pilgrim, not a tourist."[29] A pilgrimage doesn't always go according to our plan, especially when traveling in groups. In this life, little goes as planned, for our lives revolve around other people. Therefore, we are encouraged to:

- Bear inconvenience for the benefit of all.
- Remind ourselves from time to time that we are pilgrims on this Earth. Make a conscious effort to complain less and seek God more.
- Accept those suffering as the disciples did, focusing on what is essential, a quest for Christ.

It takes courage and grace to undertake a pilgrimage. When we are frustrated, tired, and weary in our life pilgrimage, let us imagine Christ on Calvary and imitate His footsteps, carrying our cross with courage. At the end of our life pilgrimage, may we joyfully meet the Lord and leave the gifts of hope, faith, love, and prayer as examples for those we left behind.

Action/Thought for Today: Are you willing to at least try living a pilgrim's life? Ask the Lord for His grace.

Prayer: Lord Jesus, give us the grace to search for You in the depth of our hearts. It is in Your name we pray. Amen!

LORD, GRANT ME SELF-CONTROL!

*A man without self-control is like a city broken into and left
without walls.* Proverbs 25:28, RSV

Although God gave us the Spirit of self-control (see 2 Timothy
1:7), we continue to need His grace to control our thoughts, words,
and actions. Self-control, a fruit of the Holy Spirit (see Galatians
5:23), is the grace to persevere in God's ordinances and resist the
desires of the flesh. It helps us live a well-balanced life. When we fail
to resist these desires, we can engender a guilty conscience, leading
to shame and self-doubt, hurting ourselves and those around us.

Years ago, I encountered a demeaning person who abused his authority and demanded that others adhere to his beliefs. I wanted
to fight back, but through much prayer, the Holy Spirit helped me
restrain my reactions. Let us fervently pray for this fruit of the Holy
Spirit.

There are many unbalanced areas of our lives in need of divine
intervention. Let us question ourselves and pray when facing
self-control issues:

- Is it God's will when I indulge in unhealthy eating or drink-
  ing behaviors?
- When my spouse or family members aggravate me, and I
  lack patience and fight back, do I ask myself, "What would
  Jesus do?"
- When someone is unkind to me, do I say a prayer and walk
  away before I react?
- Do I let God direct my actions, behaviors, and thoughts?

Action/Thought for Today: Reflect on these questions.

Prayer: Lord Jesus, I am weak; take over my actions,
thoughts, and words. Help me in every area of my life
that requires self-control. In Your name I pray. Amen!

THE FEAR OF THE LORD!

The fear of the LORD is the beginning of wisdom, and the knowledge of the Holy One is insight. Proverbs 9:10

When I visited the Rhine Falls in Switzerland, I was in awe of God's creation, the greatness of His handiwork, and who He truly is. This prompted me to reflect that if I did not have a fear of the Lord, my Master and the Creator of all things, what kind of life would I be living?

To me, the fear of the Lord is a "holy fear." It is not to be "afraid" of God but to love Him enough to never offend Him with our thoughts, words, and actions. It is also to be aware that God is watching us and wants the best from us.

I grew up in a small town where everyone knew each other, so I always tried to be on my best behavior to avoid offending my late earthly father. This is how we should strive to follow God's precepts and ordinances.

When we fear the Lord, we resort to asking Him for the grace to choose what is right every time we face temptation. A healthy fear of the Lord helps us live out His teachings despite the world's beliefs. It helps us to run to His mercy every time we fall short of His glory, allowing us to live our life according to His will. The fear of the Lord aids us in faithfully serving Him and others through our daily duties.

Christian wisdom and knowledge of God are grown from a healthy fear of the Lord, for the wise love what is right and just. Let us ask the Lord to bless us with a "holy fear" of Him.

Action/Thought for Today: Pray for the grace to have a holy fear.

Prayer: Lord Jesus, give us the grace to have a healthy fear of the Lord and grow in us the virtue of wisdom. It is Your name I pray. Amen!

You Have Said So!

"The Son of Man indeed goes, as it is written of him, but woe to that man by whom the Son of Man is betrayed. It would be better for that man if he had never been born." Then Judas, his betrayer, said in reply, "Surely it is not I, Rabbi?" He answered, "You have said so." Matthew 26:24-25, RSV

As Jesus discussed His betrayal with the disciples, Judas said, *"It is not I, Rabbi?"* Jesus replied, *"You have said so."* Judas knew his intention to hand over the Lord to the Jews. He must have known that his decision was wrong but gave in to temptation. Did Judas attempt to ask the Lord the meaning of his reply to him? Did he ask the Lord for help and reflect on Jesus's statement to him?

Sometimes we know we are about to do something wrong, but we still proceed like Judas. Do we ask Jesus to lead us to do the right thing? He is the light in our darkness. He can shine His light on us and lead us in the right direction. Let us always ask Him for help in all circumstances. Take a moment and raise your heart in prayer, "Lord, I am confused and tempted; please help me do the right thing. I don't want to offend You." I'm sure the Lord will help us.

When I ask the Lord to help me with my confusion or temptation, He helps me make the right decision and prevents me from sinning. *"He restores my soul"* (Psalm 23:3). He will do it for you, too. Let us call upon the Lord in all circumstances. Without doubt, He will rescue us.

Action/Thought for Today: Ask the Lord for the wisdom to call upon Him in your moments of weakness.

Prayer: Lord Jesus, help me always do the right thing. It is in Your name I pray. Amen!

DECLUTTER YOUR HOME!

Then he [Jesus] said to them, "Watch out! Be on your guard against all kinds of greed; life does not consist in an abundance of possessions. Luke 12:15, NIV

Do you have clothing, shoes, or things in your home that you have not used for a long time? One of my family members always says that if you haven't used something in six months or more, you have no use for it. Give it up. I agree. I recently decluttered three closets, and I felt a weight lift off of my shoulders. Something as simple as decluttering closets gave me a sense of freedom from worldly possessions and a special connection with the Lord. Can you imagine if I had decluttered my entire home?

The Lord does not want our lives to be filled only with earthly possessions. Instead, He wants us to be attached to Him, so that we can be a blessing to others. The clothing and shoes you don't wear could serve someone in need. The toys with which your children no longer play can be a joy to another child. A home free of clutter gives us the ability to spend more time with God, friends, and family. It also gives you time for yourself. Therefore, let us make an effort to declutter and, in the process, be generous with those in need.

Action/Thought for Today: When you are decluttering your home, try to listen to uplifting Christian music and invite the Lord to be with you. You will be amazed at how much you get done.

Prayer: Lord Jesus, I welcome You into my decluttering project. Thank You for the many blessings You have given me. Please open my heart and hands to be a blessing to others. In Your name I pray. Amen!

DIVERSITY!

For in him all things were created, in heaven and on earth, visible and invisible, whether thrones or dominions or principalities or authorities—all things were created through him and for him. He is before all things, and in him all things hold together.

Colossians 1:16-17, RSV

The Lord created us in His image, yet He beautifully created diversity. So there is commonality and diversity. God shows no partiality (see Acts 10:34), but He loves us all the same.

One country's scenery may differ, but all countries have something in common—night and day, rainfall and sunshine, the moon and sun, etc. The food may be different, but any food serves one purpose—our enjoyment and sustenance of the body. I'm sure some of us enjoy food from a foreign country from time to time. Every country in the world has something unique that another doesn't have. God wants us to share our specialty, for we are not alone on planet Earth.

Human beings have different skin colors, yet we all eat, sleep, laugh, cry and dance. Sometimes, however, we are too broken to recognize the beauty in each other. Some discriminate, thinking God made one inferior to the other. We may not speak the same language, but our body language can communicate a message of joy or discontentment to one another.

While I was in Austria, attending a musical show, many nationalities were in the theater, yet we all clapped in unison of the music. I didn't understand the song's lyrics, but the music was delightful. We must learn to appreciate each other, for we are all God's precious creation.

There are many different flowers on this Earth. Do they compete with or discriminate against each other? Does fruit or meat say that only one group of people can eat it? Does the rain or sun only benefit one group of people?

Unfortunately, many countries are affected by violence, poverty, war, and illnesses. Others have seen prosperity. God gave us authority over all things of the Earth (see Genesis 1:26). Are we good stewards of what God has given us? Do we take care of our lands and people? We must look deeply at ourselves to see how we can help each other and our environment for the betterment of all. Let us ask the Lord for the spiritual light and wisdom to embrace each other wholeheartedly, care for His creation, love His people, serve each other, and be grateful for God's beauty and the gifts of humanity and nature.

Action/Thought for Today: Reflect on these questions.

Prayer: Lord Jesus, give us the grace to love all Your creation and to care for each other. In Your name I pray. Amen!

WHEN WE SAY YES!

For all the promises of God find their Yes in him. That is why we utter the Amen through him, to the glory of God.

2 Corinthian 1:20, RSV

Abraham said yes, and he became the father of many nations. Joseph said yes, used God's gifts to interpret dreams, and God spared the Egyptians from a great famine through this young man's wisdom. Moses said yes, and God used him to deliver the Israelites from bondage. Mary said yes, and our Messiah and Savior was conceived through her.

When we say yes to the Lord, great and marvelous things happen. It may be a significant task or as simple as feeding one homeless person. If you say yes, you can save a person from hunger. It may be to say a prayer for someone. You say yes, and a miracle occurs. It may be to share God's words with a neighbor. You say yes, and the neighbor accepts to follow Christ.

Last year, a woman asked me to pray with her for a specific intention. We prayed daily for several days. A year later, there was a significant answer to that prayer. When we say yes, God blesses others through us. What is stopping you from saying "yes" to the Lord? God does not ask for anything beyond our capacity. He is our Creator, and He knows our strengths and weaknesses. Don't doubt yourself. You are chosen, gifted, and equipped to work in God's vineyard. Don't put God's mission on hold. Say yes now, go forth, and be part of God's plan.

Action/Thought for Today: Whether God calls you for a simple or significant mission, pray for the grace to say yes.

Prayer: Lord Jesus, give me the grace to say, like Mary, "Let it be done according to Your will for me." It is in Your name I pray. Amen!

BE HIS WITNESS!

*But you will receive power when the Holy Spirit has come upon you;
and you will be my witnesses in Jerusalem, in all Judea and Samaria,
and to the ends of the earth.*   Acts 1:8

After Jesus went up to Heaven, the disciples witnessed on His behalf, making His name and good deeds known. They proclaimed His promises of eternal life to all who believed in Him. We must continue the work of the disciples by being Jesus' witnesses in the world. This should be the mission of all Christians.

- Preach the Gospel by following in Christ's footsteps. Our active lives of prayer, charity, love, faith, hope, courage, peace, and joy are examples to our families, friends, coworkers, and those we meet. Our attitudes can bring a change of heart to those who have been far away from God.

- Testify in God's name. We must share with others what the Lord had done for us. When we testify, we glorify the Lord, and we declare the love, goodness, and mercy He bestows upon us.

- Speak on behalf of the Lord wherever you are. We must not be shy about proclaiming God's name. It is through our evangelization that others will know the Lord more deeply.

- Work in God's name to continue His mission in this world. The Spirit of the Lord has anointed all (see Isaiah 61:1-3).

God gave us the power of His Holy Spirit so that we might continue His mighty work of salvation. Through His Spirit, we shall prophesy, see visions, and dream dreams (see Acts 2:17), and *"everyone who calls on the name of the Lord shall be saved"* (Acts 2:21). Therefore, let us ask the Holy Spirit to guide us in what we must do and where we must go, and let us set the world on fire for Him.

Action/Thought for Today: How can we
become Christ's witnesses in the world?

Prayer: Lord Jesus, help us be Your witness in the
world. It is in Your name we pray. Amen!

BLESSED TO BE A BLESSING!

Now the LORD said to Abram, "Go from your country and your kindred and your father's house to the land that I will show you. And I will make of you a great nation, and I will bless you and make your name great, so that you will be a blessing."   Genesis 12:1-4

In this passage, God told Abram to leave his homeland and promised that He would bless him so that he could be a blessing to others. Like Abram, God blesses us so that we can be a blessing. He calls us to be a blessing through our service, resources, spiritual advice, encouragement, etc. Sometimes, it is easier to care only for ourselves, but, as John Donne has said, "No man is an island, entire of itself."[30] God created us to help others and to live together peacefully and joyfully. Have you been a blessing to others? If not, how can you be a blessing to them?

Let me share with you how God once favored me. One day, when cooking for the homeless ministry, as I removed the meat from the oven, the hot water drained from the meat and fell on my thigh and foot. I had a mild burning sensation on my skin, but within minutes, the discomfort was relieved. As I reflected on this incident, I truly saw God's hands sparing me from a severe burn. God showed me favor and protected me so that I could continue to serve His beloved children. Therefore, let us be a blessing by bringing new hope and joy to all in our path.

Action/Thought for Today: Think about how you can be a blessing to others and then take action to make it so.

Prayer: Lord Jesus, teach and show us how to be a blessing to everyone in our life. Thank You, Lord, for all the blessings You have bestowed on us. In Your name I pray. Amen!

WE ALL HAVE ONE FATHER, GOD!

He [John] said, "I am the voice of one crying out in the wilderness, 'Make straight the way of the Lord.'"　　　　John 1:23

One day I was in a meeting with fellow Christian brothers and sisters when someone in the forum mentioned the name of a politician who is a person of color. Another person made an unkind remark, and no one intervened. I felt that I should have said something, but I didn't.

As a Christian, I question myself. Am I reflecting Christ in my words and deeds? I know I am not perfect, but I strongly echo John the Baptist, *"Make straight the way of the Lord."* How can we prepare for the Lord's second coming when we cannot tolerate others because they have different views or a different political agenda? Whether you are a conservative, moderate or liberal, rich or poor, black, white or another race, male or female, God sent Jesus to save all of us and teach us how to love. As the apostle Paul stated: *"There is no longer slave or free, there is no longer male or female, for all of you are one in Jesus Christ"* (Galatians 3:28). Let us pray for the grace to find goodness in everyone and strive for all to see Christ in us.

Action/Thought for Today: When you encounter someone who differs from you, pray that you remember that we all have the same Father, God.

Prayer: Lord Jesus, give me the grace to reflect You in my words, actions, and deeds. Please give me the courage to treat all with respect and for them to see Christ in me. In Your name I pray. Amen!

THE PROMISE!

And your children shall be shepherds in the wilderness for forty years and shall suffer for your faithlessness, until the last of your dead bodies lies in the wilderness.   Numbers 14:33

God told the people of Israel that He would give them the Promised Land. He asked Moses to send out spies to survey Canaan (see Numbers 13:1-3), but they returned with conflicting reports. Caleb wanted to *"go up at once and occupy it, for we are able to overcome it"* (Numbers 13:30), but others engendered fear in the Israelites.

Although Moses reiterated that God would fight their battles, the Israelites rebelled and refused to go (see Numbers 14). Their fear led to disobedience and angered the Lord (see Numbers 14:11-12). He punished them by having them wander in the wilderness for forty years. The Exodus generation died there, and only Caleb and Joshua entered the Promised Land. The Lord fulfilled His promises through the children of the older generation. However, the children suffered for the faithlessness of their parents (see Numbers 14:33).

The Lord wants to free us from slavery to worldly things. Sometimes we don't trust Him or devote ourselves to receiving His promised freedom. These bondages are then passed to our children because of our faithlessness. Sometimes we can diligently work to prepare a future for our children but don't. Our children then suffer the consequences of our unwillingness to fight the good fight. Therefore, let us trust in the Lord, accept His promises, and collaborate with Him in all things so that the next generation will not have to suffer on our behalf.

Action/Thought for Today: What steps would you take to prevent the future generation from suffering?

Prayer: Lord Jesus, help me trust in Your promises. In Your name I pray. Amen!

REMEMBER THESE TRUTHS!

*Guide me in your truth and teach me, for you are God my Savior,
and my hope is in you all day long.*   Psalm 25:5, NIV

Although Jesus suffered a cruel death through crucifixion, His identity and worth did not diminish. He was and is still the Son of God, participating willingly with the Father's plan of salvation. His death and resurrection revealed Him as our Savior and King. Our sufferings also don't change who we are. We are still beloved children of God (see 1 John 3:2). His love for us doesn't change despite our trials and tribulations. Friends, remember these truths about you, regardless of your circumstances:

- You are a child of God (see Romans 8:16-17)
- Don't be afraid. You're not alone.
- God holds you in the palm of His hands (see Isaiah 49:16)
- God loves you (see John 3:16)
- You are wonderfully made (see Psalm 139:14)
- You belong to God.

Know that you are good because you were created out of God's goodness. Don't give up on yourself. God never gives up on you. Continue to pray, plan, aspire, and work toward your purpose for God's greater glory.

Action/Thought for Today: Take some time to
pray and reflect on who you are in Christ.

Prayer: Lord, help me remember the truths about my identity, regardless of my circumstances. In Your name I pray. Amen!

THE DARKEST SATURDAY!

And that He was buried, and that He was raised on the third day in accordance with scripture. 1 Corinthians 15:4

After Jesus was crucified and buried on Good Friday, I imagine that the disciples were lost and afraid. They had lost their Teacher and Master. They must have been thinking, "What will become of us? Will we suffer the same fate?" They resorted to locked doors for fear of the Jews (see John 20:19). Were they praying behind those doors? Did they understand or remember that Jesus had foretold His death more than once? (see Matthew 20:17-19 and Luke 9:21). Did Peter remember that he rebuked Jesus when He predicted His death and that Jesus told him, *"Get behind me, Satan!"* (Matthew 16:23)?

Did the disciples have hope and discuss the upcoming resurrection of the Lord, or were they so broken and saddened by Jesus' death that they didn't recall His teaching? When we face a trial in life, do we suffer from fear or discouragement? Do we recall Jesus' words to us?

- *"I am with you always, to the end of the age"* (Matthew 28:20).
- *"Do not fear, for I am with you, do not be afraid, for I am your God; I will strengthen you, I will help you; I will uphold you with my victorious right hand"* (Isaiah 41:10).

Let us pray not to become despondent during adversity but to hold on to the promises of God: There will be joy after sorrow, sun after the rain, resurrection and eternal life after death. May the peace of God be with you all!

Action/Thought for Today: Spend some time in silence with the Lord.

Prayer: Lord Jesus, thank You for the gift of salvation. I praise and love You. In Your name I pray. Amen!

A BOLD REQUEST!

Declare that these two sons of mine will sit, one at your right hand and one at your left, in your kingdom. Matthew 20:21

The mother of the sons of Zebedee boldly requested a favor from Jesus for her two sons—one to sit with Him at His right hand and the other at His left in His Kingdom. Jesus told her that for them to sit with Him was not for Him to give, but it is for those for whom the Father has prepared it (see Matthew 20:23).

Most mothers dream of their children having a seat of honor, being blessed and successful in all they do. Our requests to the Lord may be the same as the mother of the sons of Zebedee, who probably had good intentions and wanted the best for her sons. But Jesus reminded her of the sacrifice one must make to be a Christian: *"Are you able to drink the cup that I am about to drink?"* (Matthew 20:22).

We must also remember our children's call to discipleship. Have we asked God for our children to love, know, and follow Him, to serve Him for His greater glory, and to align their will with His? Have we asked the Lord to lead them to eternal life? Are our prayers motivated by self-interest or pure love for God and others?

Action/Thought for Today: Let us ask the Holy Spirit to guide our prayers.

Prayer: Lord Jesus, thank You for the gift of motherhood. Teach us how to pray for our children. In Your name I pray. Amen!

JESUS REMEMBERS ME!

Jesus, remember me when you come into your kingdom.
Luke 23:42

Families cherish the last moments and words of their loved ones. The last words one of the criminals crucified next to Jesus were profound, *"Jesus, remember me"* (see Luke 23:42). The other criminal mocked Jesus: *"Are you not the Messiah? Save yourself and us!"* (Luke 23:39). The one criminal confessed His sins by telling the other, *"And we indeed have been condemned justly, for we are getting what we deserve for our deeds, but this man has done nothing wrong"* (Luke 23:41). He then professed his faith as he asked Jesus to save him. Jesus, in His great mercy, promised him that he would be with Him in Paradise that same day (see Luke 23:43). Jesus' mercy is beyond comprehension, too marvelous for our understanding. Whether the first criminal's faith was strong or weak, Jesus washed away his sins, welcomed him, and accepted what he could offer. As I reflect on Jesus' goodness and mercy, I echo the Psalmist in Psalm 116:1-2: *"I love the LORD, because he has heard my voice and my supplications. Because he inclined his ear to me, therefore I will call on him as long as I live"* (RSV).

Action/Thought for Today: If you were dying, what would be your last words to Jesus?

Prayer: Lord Jesus, give me the grace to confess my sins and profess my faith that You are my Lord and Savior. It is in Your name I pray. Amen!

THE GIFT OF SELF!

Do not withhold good from those to whom it is due, when it is in your power to act.   Proverbs 3:27, NIV

Everyone has something to give. Many may think almsgiving only includes giving things such as money, food, shelter, church offerings, and the like. You can provide a spiritual gift or a love donation without money or resources. Almsgiving is also the gift of self and:

- Being Christ's witness by sharing His words with others, increasing faith and hope, and bringing God's light to the world.
- Comforting the sorrowful by sharing their grief and lending a listening heart to the suffering.
- Forgiving and letting go from the generosity of the heart of grudges that set you and the other person free.
- Helping the elderly, such as cutting their grass.
- Mentoring others by giving the gift of time.
- Offering intercessory prayers for others.
- Praying for those who offended you.
- Sharing your talents with others, such as fixing or setting up a computer for the elderly.
- Volunteering in a hospital, nursing home, or prison ministry, providing words of hope and encouragement.
- Volunteering in religious education, youth groups, Bible study, or Sunday School.

Therefore, let us not withhold doing good, but practice charity in deeds and words, as Christ demands.

Action/Thought for Today: Give a gift to someone in need.

Prayer: Lord Jesus, show me who needs my help. Open my eyes and heart to those in need. In Your name I pray. Amen!

SEPTEMBER 21

GROWING IN HOLINESS!

Put on then, as God's chosen ones, holy and beloved, compassion, kindness, lowliness, meekness, and patience. Colossians 3:12, RSV

Growing in holiness is a lifetime process. Have you missed opportunities to grow in holiness? Those opportunities come in different shapes and forms, in the small or substantial events of our lives. God allows us to experience achievements, joys, difficulties, uncertainness, or trials to grow in holiness. For instance:

- Do you display reliance on God when things are going well with you?
- When someone is unkind to you, do you use this opportunity to repay the person with kindness and a smile?
- When one displays impatience with you, do you show patience?
- When someone is a thorn in your side, do you show love anyway?
- When you achieve success in life, do you remain humble and thankful to God?
- When you are in a position of power, do you let go of control?
- Have you given yourself to others, been less self-centered and more present for others?

Everything that happens to us is an opportunity to be more Christlike. We cannot change ourselves, but we can ask for the grace to be an active participant and be willing to let the Holy Spirit work in us and through us. Therefore, we must be ready to die to the flesh and strive to do what is right or just, no matter how painful it may be.

Action/Thought for Today: Take some time to reflect on these questions.

Prayer: Holy Spirit, help me to grow in holiness. Walk with me, lead me, and guide me. In Jesus' name I pray. Amen!

THE SONG OF UNITY!

Behold, how good and pleasant it is when brothers dwell in unity!
Psalm 133:1, RSV

Unity is a love song!
It is a scent of love directed toward one another.
It is the essence of life, for it is a reason to hope and laugh at tomorrow.
Unity is a breeze of fresh air that refreshes the soul.

How beautiful to live in unity, for the sorrowful are readily comforted!
How pleasing it is to the Lord when we love each other!
In unity, heavy burdens are light, for we have more strength.
In unity, we weep and dance with each other.
In unity, we dream and aspire together.
In unity, we pray and praise the Lord better.
In unity, we become one.
There is neither hunger nor thirst in unity, for we share what we have.
There is sweetness in unity!

Unity is a gift!
It is a blessing!
It is a grace!
Let us rejoice in the song of unity!

Action/Thought for Today: Are you living in unity in your community? Pray for this grace.

Prayer: Lord Jesus, teach us to live in unity and love. In Your name I pray. Amen!

THE APPLE OF HIS EYE!

Keep me as the apple of thy eye; hide me in the shadow of thy wings. Psalm 17:8, RSV

Have you ever dreamed of meeting a religious or public celebrity? If you met this person, what would you say or ask? I have heard stories of those who have met a famous person and how fascinating and happy they were. Some said it was a surreal experience. Others cherish photos taken with the celebrity and want the world to see them. Many remember for years what those celebrities said or did.

Do you have the same sentiment about meeting Jesus? What do you think He would say to you? What would you say to Him? With Jesus, no special appointment is needed, or waiting in line for a long time to share a handshake and maybe a photo. All we must do is invite Him, and He will be honored to meet us anywhere and spend as long as we want with Him. The satisfaction of meeting a famous person may last only a few minutes or hours. A celebrity can never meet or satisfy our deepest needs, desires, or the longing of the soul. Jesus can fill our emptiness without limit and with long-lasting effect.

Let us pray that we reflect on our favorite celebrity's virtues, not on their worldly glory. It will serve one well to emulate what is good, just, and pure from that person. Know that we are all famous in God's eyes! You are the apple of His eye!

Action/Thought for Today: What virtues can you imitate from your favorite celebrity?

Prayer: Lord Jesus, thank You for seeing me as the apple of Your eye. Praise the Lord! In Your name I pray. Amen!

JEALOUS OF OTHERS' SPIRITUALITY?

A heart at peace gives life to the body, but envy rots the bones.
Proverbs 14:30, NIV

Just as we can be envious of others' material possessions, we must pay attention to how we respond to others' faith and spirituality. Do we get upset when we see others' faith in action? Have we called anyone a "fanatic" or "holier than thou" or classified them as having "a religious spirit"? If so, let's examine ourselves. Is it because we are jealous of that person's spirituality? Could it be because the person's virtues highlight our defects? Could it be because we want to be like that person but are unwilling to follow Christ's teachings?

God made us among those He created. He could have chosen to create someone else instead, but He chose us, and He wants to establish His covenant with us. He is impartial and has a place in His heart for all of us. God loves you and me! If we ever feel jealous of another person's faith, let us ask the Lord to root out this sin from our hearts and help us establish a purer relationship with Him. He is ready to deepen our faith and spiritual life, and He is able!

Action/Thought for Today: Have you ever been jealous of others' possessions or spiritual life? Ask the Lord to remove envy from your heart.

Prayer: Lord Jesus, forgive us for any thought of jealousy we have ever had. Deepen our faith and love for You. In Your name we pray. Amen!

GRATEFUL FOR THE RAIN!

Yet he has not left himself without testimony: He has shown kindness by giving you rain from heaven and crops in their seasons; he provides you with plenty of food and fills your hearts with joy. Acts 14:17, NIV

When I was a child, I loved playing in the rain. My late grandpa made little paper boats every time it rained, and I remember the joy of running in the rain to catch them as they slowly moved through the stream of the collected water. I remember the fresh air and cleanliness of the Earth after it rained.

While in prayer on a dark and raining day, I suddenly felt the urge to thank God for the rain. The Lord gave me a profound clarity on its importance. It nourishes the Earth and the plants to produce food and flowers and replenishes our water supply. Although I had known the importance of the rain, what I experienced was a heartfelt spiritual awareness and awakening of the soul—a deep knowledge of the goodness and kindness of the Lord who cares for us through nature. Once again, I recalled the sweet memory of playing in the rain with my grandfather.

How often do we have to change our plans because of the rain—an outdoor activity, a day at the beach or park, a neighborhood cookout? Have we taken these opportunities to reflect on the importance of the rain and the goodness of the Lord? The next time it rains, be still and listen to its sound as you embrace this God-given gift. Let God cleanse and purify you as He showers you with blessings and grace upon grace.

Action/Thought for Today: Thank God for the rain.

Prayer: Lord Jesus, I am grateful for the rain.
Give us the grace to appreciate all Your gifts
of nature. I pray in Your name. Amen!

STANDING TALL IN THE GAP!

But Moses implored the LORD, his God, saying, "Why, O LORD, should your anger burn against your people, whom you brought out of the land of Egypt with great power and with a strong hand?"
Exodus 32:11, NABRE

The Lord was angry with the Israelites for their unfaithfulness and disobedience. He said to Moses, *"I have seen this people, how stiff-necked they are. Let me alone, then, that my anger may burn against them to consume them"* (Exodus 32:9-10, NABRE). But Moses pleaded with the Lord to let His anger die down and not punish them (see Exodus 32:11). Intercessory prayers are vital for the salvation of souls. God has given us the same power He gave to Moses to intercede on others' behalf. Just as the Lord relented in the punishment He had threatened to inflict on His people (see Exodus 32:14), through Moses' intercession, He will do the same for us. We need to wake up the Moses within us to "stand in the gap" for our people:

- Mothers, stand in the gap for your troubled sons.
- Fathers, intercede fervently for your daughters who have gone astray.
- Grandparents, plead with the Lord for your grandchildren who have forgotten Him.
- Husbands and wives, intercede for each other daily.
- Children, pray for your family.
- Let us all "stand tall in the gap" on behalf of this chaotic world.

Action/Thought for Today: Who needs prayer in this life? Intercede to God for them like never before.

Prayer: Lord Jesus, thank You for all the intercessors of this world. Give us the spirit of intercession to pray for all. In Your name I pray. Amen!

JUDAH SHALL GO FIRST!

When the Israelites asked, "Who shall go up first for us to do battle with the Benjaminites?" The LORD said: "Judah first."

Judges 20:18, NABRE

The Lord instructed the Israelites to let Judah go first into battle. There were twelve tribes in Israel. Why Judah? Judah means "praise and thanks," so the Lord asked them to give Him praise before engaging in battle. Their praise was an act of worship and trust that they would be victorious in the Lord. Today, the same principle applies to us. Praise should be our first fruit:

- When you wake up in the morning, start your day by praising the Lord, spurning discouragement, disappointment, failures, or self-pity. He will give you the strength to face the ups and downs of the day.
- Before you lie down, let your praise proclaim the goodness of the Lord.
- When facing trials or battles in life, give God praise first and trust that you will have victory with the Lord by your side.
- In all things, let your praise go up like incense and holy sacrifice before the Lord!

Praise God like there is no tomorrow.

Praise Him with every breath and heartbeat.

Praise Him when you are alone.

Praise Him when you are with others.

Praise Him again and again.

Let us never stop praising the Lord and exclaiming His magnificence.

Action/Thought for Today: Write a
prayer of praise to the Lord.

Prayer: Lord Jesus, give us a spirit of authentic worship and praise in all things. In Your name we pray. Amen!

A Prayer of Blind Trust!

O Lord, my heart is not lifted up, my eyes are not raised too high; I do not occupy myself with things too great and too marvelous for me. Psalm 131:1

Lord, sometimes I wish I could understand Your mystery and those of the world, but who am I to hope for these things? The things above and below are inexplicable for me. All I need is to believe in You.

Lord, I know You always existed, even before the creation of this world. You have created me out of Your great love. Give me the grace not to busy myself with the things that are *"too marvelous for me,"* but to trust in You with all my heart.

Let me not be anxious about the mystery of who You are, but rest in You like a baby on its mother's shoulder, knowing that you deeply love me and will provide for my every need.

Help me accept the suspense of Your plans for me, as they slowly unfold like a story of love and patience, and give me a willing spirit to blindly do Your holy will.

O Lord, although I do not understand everything about life, help me act as You wish, go where You will, keep my mind fixed on You, and hope in You now and forever. Lord Jesus, deepen my trust in You.

Action/Thought for Today: Write a prayer of trust to the Lord.

Prayer: *"Let me hear of your steadfast love in the morning, for in you I put my trust. Teach me the way I should go, for to you I lift up my soul"* (Psalm 143:8). In Jesus' name I pray. Amen!

INTO THE DEEP!

He [Jesus] said to Simon, "Put out into deep water and lower your nets for a catch." Simon said in reply, "Master, we have worked hard all night and have caught nothing, but at your command I will lower the nets." Luke 5:4-5, NABRE

As the Lord called Simon to lower his nets into the depths, he is calling you to do the same thing today. Will you obey Him, drop your nets into the depths of His heart, and let Him fill you with good things? Reflect with me.

- Lord Jesus, help me experience the depths of Your love and mercy for me.
- Help me throw my spiritual net deeper into the ocean of Your love.
- Fill my net with Your grace so I can do all things.
- Fill my net with faith so I can move any mountain.
- Fill my net with Your joy so I can share it with the world.
- Fill my net with Your hope so that I can have Your peace beyond understanding.
- Fill my net with wisdom to do Your holy will.
- Most importantly, fill my net with more of You. All I need is my Lord and Savior.

After the disciples had filled their nets, *"They signaled to their partners in the other boat to come to help them. They came and filled both boats"* (Luke 5:7, NABRE). Be sure to bring others to Jesus as the disciples did. Come to the depths of the Father's heart. He is ready to fill your spiritual nets.

Action/Thought for Today: With what do you want the Lord to fill you? Ask Him.

Prayer: Lord Jesus, hold my hand and lead me to the depth of Your heart. Help me to be immersed in Your unfailing love and mercy. In Your name I pray. Amen!

GOD'S MEDICINE!

Do not say to your neighbor, "Come back tomorrow and I'll give it to you"—when you already have it with you. Do not plot harm against your neighbor, who lives trustfully near you. Do not accuse anyone for no reason—when they have done you no harm. Do not envy the violent or choose any of their ways. Proverbs 3:28-31, NIV

The Lord gives us many and specific instructions in the Bible about how to treat our neighbors:

- *"Do to others as you would have them do to you"* (Luke 6:31).
- *"Love your enemy and do good to them, and lend expecting nothing back"* (Luke 6:35, NABRE).
- *"Do not repay anyone evil for evil"* (Romans 12:17).
- *"You shall not take vengeance, nor hold any grudge against the sons of your people, but you shall love your neighbor as yourself; I am the LORD"* (Leviticus 19:18, NASB).

God's rules are like medicine that is good for the soul. If you visit a doctor, you follow his recommendations for your well-being. Likewise, we must adhere to God's rules and respect His commandments. These instructions are often difficult to put into practice, but living according to God's commandments is the true testimony of who we are as Christians, and it is achievable with His grace and mercy.

Action/Thought for Today: Let us pray for the grace to love our neighbors despite their shortcomings.

Prayer: Lord, thank You for giving us neighbors. Give us the grace to love those neighbors as ourselves. We pray in Jesus' name. Amen!

FIGHT THE GOOD FIGHT!

I have fought the good fight, I have finished the race, I have kept the faith.   2 Timothy 4:7

Life presents us with many battles, and we must pick our battles before we engage. Sometimes we fight to succeed in our career, business, and for our family. Other times, we quarrel with others to prove a point, because we disagree or because we are hurt. Oftentimes battles can lead us to discouragement, anxiety, fear, and even to the path of destruction. Before we take part in a battle, we must ask ourselves these questions: What would Jesus do? Are these battles worth it? If indeed a battle is bringing us closer to God, we must resolve to fight the good fight.

- **The Battle for Closeness with Christ:** Life may be difficult or messy. We may be persecuted or ridiculed when we dedicate ourselves to the Lord. Despite it all, love and *"serve the Lord with fear, with trembling kiss his feet"* (Psalm 2:11).
- **The Battle for Courage:** Despite life's misfortunes, failures, or disappointments, we must persevere. With every setback, there is a lesson to learn and a testimony to share.
- **The Battle for Hope and Faith:** Despite the darkness of this present age, we must look forward to tomorrow with expectations of a brighter future in the Lord.
- **The Battle Against Injustice:** We must speak out against discrimination, racism, violence, abuse, etc., but we must always act out of love and for the good of humanity.
- **The Battle for Joy:** Despite our anxieties, fears, and worries, we must rely on God, trust in His divine Providence, and embrace joy. The joy of the Lord is our strength (see Nehemiah 8:10).
- **The Battle for Love:** Despite the pain and sacrifice that come with selfless love, we must love as Jesus taught and commanded us. Love the Lord with all your heart, soul, and spirit, and love your neighbor as yourself (see Matthew 22:36-40).

- **The Battle for Peace:** No matter what is going on in life, we must pray and strive to make peace with God, ourselves, and others.

Action/Thought for Today: Resolve to fight the good fight.

Prayer: Lord Jesus, help us fight the good fight and persevere in our journey with You. In Your name we pray. Amen!

BLESSED IS ANYONE WHO ENDURES TEMPTATION!

No one, when tempted, should say, "I am being tempted by God"; for God cannot be tempted by evil and he himself tempts no one. But one is tempted by one's own desire, being lured and enticed by it; then, when that desire has conceived, it gives birth to sin, and that sin, when it is fully grown, gives birth to death. Do not be deceived, my beloved.　　　　　　　　James 1:13-16

As we strive to be more Christlike, many temptations will come our way. Temptation does not come from God, although He allows it to happen. God does not take pleasure in sins or evil doing; therefore, He does not tempt us. Temptations are the work of the devil to distract us from closeness with God.

Sometimes we allow temptation by willingly doing the wrong thing or adhering to our desires, leading us to sin. We must resist temptation through prayer, meditating on the Scriptures, and focusing our energy on the Lord. When we resist temptation, we grow in virtue and godly character. As James pointed out, *"Blessed is anyone who endures temptation. Such a one has stood the test and will receive the crown of life that the Lord has promised to those who love Him"* (James 1:12). Therefore, let us pray and struggle against evil, sins, our flesh, and the world.

Action/Thought for Today: What is tempting you? What are your plans to resist this temptation?

Prayer: Lord Jesus, give us the grace not to give in to our desires. Teach us how to resist temptations. Purify us, sanctify us, and lead us not into temptation, but deliver us from evil. Thank You, Lord, for Your grace and mercy. In Your holy name we pray. Amen!

DO YOU KNOW WHEN YOU ARE TEMPTED?

No temptation has overtaken you except what is common to mankind. And God is faithful; he will not let you be tempted beyond what you can bear. But when you are tempted, he will also provide a way out so that you can endure it.

1 Corinthians 10:13, NIV

To resist temptations, we must be aware of them. For example, we are tempted when doing the things we should not do, such as overeating, being lazy, overspending, wearing provocative attire, etc. Other forms of temptation come when we go to places we should avoid, watch sinful movies, as well as from lust, pride, power, lies, gossip, and the like.

We must be aware of the enemy of our souls and stay on guard, being vigilant at all times and use our armor of protection—prayer and the Word of God (see Ephesians 6:10-17). The Lord experienced temptation in the desert, yet he resisted (see Matthew 4:1-11). As the Lord resisted temptation, He will not let us be tested beyond our abilities to resist. Therefore, whenever we are faced with the desires of the flesh or worldly passions, let us ask the Lord to help us. He is faithful, and He will help us. *"For we do not have a high priest who is unable to empathize with our weaknesses, but we have one who has been tempted in every way, just as we are—yet, he did not sin"* (Hebrews 4:15, NIV).

Action/Thought for Today: Say an extra prayer that the Lord helps you to resist temptations.

Prayer: Lord Jesus, give me a steadfast spirit and the grace to recognize temptations in my life. Help me to be victorious in this battle. I thank and adore You, O Lord. In Your name we pray. Amen!

YOU ARE A CHILD OF GOD!

And I will be your father, and you shall be my sons and daughters, says the Lord Almighty.   2 Corinthians 6:18, NIV

Are you aware that you are a Child of God? Your life situation may be difficult, but your Father in Heaven will supply everything you need. *"If you then, who are evil, know how to give good gifts to your children, how much more will the heavenly Father give the Holy Spirit to those who ask him"* (Luke 11:13). Therefore, let us remember this truth: God has it all and will provide for us. Let us prayerfully go to Him for our needs.

Do you believe that your Guardian, the Lord, does not sleep and that He watches over you day and night? The Lord will not let your foot be moved; He who keeps you will not slumber nor sleep (see Psalm 121:3-4). He will protect and guide you, and no weapon formed against you will prosper (see Isaiah 54:17). When you face trials, uncertainties, or persecution, don't lose heart. Remember your identity in Christ. YOU ARE A CHILD OF GOD. Run to Him in prayer for help. The more you claim your status in Christ, the more confident you are, and the more deeply you will trust the Lord. Let us always praise and thank Him for His gifts and blessings.

Action/Thought for Today: Decide to accept and believe that you are a child of God and let nothing change your relationship with Him.

Prayer: Dear Father God, I sometimes fret over problems and uncertainties. Give me the grace to claim my identity as Your daughter or son. Help me live my life as a beloved child of yours. In Jesus' name I pray. Amen!

WHAT DEFINES US?

You are a chosen people, a royal priesthood, a holy nation, God's special possession, that you may declare the praises of him who called you out of darkness into his wonderful light.

1 Peter 2:9, NIV

What defines us? Are we defined by what we do, our successes, or our failures? Are we defined by the car we drive, the house in which we live, or the clothes we wear? Are we named after the problems we face, such as loneliness, sadness, fear, depression, illness, etc.? Our possessions and our professions are God's blessings, but they are not who we are. We are God's chosen people, holy and beloved (see Colossians 3:12). God neither loves the rich more than the poor nor those who are rejoicing more than those suffering. God sees our hearts and our whole being, not just our possessions. We are the Body of Christ and individually members of it (see 1 Corinthians 12:27). Therefore, let us pray not to focus on worldly things, but *"Whatever is true, whatever is noble, whatever is right, whatever is pure, whatever is lovely, whatever is admirable—if anything is excellent or praiseworthy—think about such things"* (Philippians 4:8, NIV).

Action/Thought for Today: Take a few minutes and think about what defines you.

Prayer: Lord Jesus, give us the grace not to identify ourselves by what we have or what we do. Help us to remember that we are children of the Most High, chosen and beloved. Lord, thank You for loving and choosing us. In Your name we pray. Amen!

DO YOU CARE WHAT OTHERS THINK OF YOU?

LORD, you have probed me, you know me: you know when I sit and stand; you understand my thoughts from afar. You sift through my travels and my rest; with all my ways you are familiar. Even before a word is on my tongue, LORD, you know it all. Behind and before you encircle me and rest your hand upon me. Such knowledge is too wonderful for me, far too lofty for me to reach.   Psalm 139:1-6, NABRE

Your identity should not depend on what people say about you or think of you. Some may like you despite your flaws and shortcomings, while others may hate you despite your virtuous life. What matters most is what God says about you, for he knows who you are and knows you even better than you know yourself. This is what the Lord says about you: *"Since you are precious and honored in my sight, and because I love you, 'I will give people in exchange for you, nations in exchange for your life'"* (Isaiah 43:4, NIV). There is nothing anyone can say about you that will change God's mind about you, and He will do anything to help you gain eternal life. He created you in His image; therefore, you are His, even if you deny Him. One of the greatest freedoms is living and dying for Christ, worshiping and praising God, not ourselves or others, a life dedicated to knowing, loving, and serving God.

Action/Thought for Today: Do you know who you are in Christ? Do you care about what others think of you?

Prayer: Father God, thank You for creating me in Your image. Mold me, guide me, lead me, and transform me in Your ways. In Jesus' name I pray. Amen!

WHO AM I IN CHRIST?

For God did not give us a spirit of cowardice but rather of power and love and self-control. So do not be ashamed of your testimony to our Lord, nor of me, a prisoner for his sake; but bear your share of hardship for the gospel with the strength that comes from God. 2 Timothy 1:7-8, NABRE

God gives you His Holy Spirit to lead and guide you. In Christ, you are not a slave of fear, shame, guilt, discouragement, and worthlessness. The Lord is always by your side and reminds you often: *"Do not fear: I am with you; do not be anxious: I am your God. I will strengthen you, I will help you, I will uphold you with my victorious right hand"* (Isaiah 41:10, NABRE).

If you are suffering from regret or guilt, remember that, although you cannot change the past, God can restore your life. He said, *"I will repay you for the years that the swarming locust has eaten"* (Joel 2:25, NABRE). Ask the Lord to heal you from past hurts. Ask for His grace, not only to embrace your present life with Him, but to surrender your future to Him.

In Christ, sickness, anxiety, and depression have no hold on you. Therefore, when you face these trials, remember that you can do all things through Christ who strengthens you (see Philippians 4:13). By his stripes, you are healed (see Isaiah 53:5). Let us pray to hold on to God's words, which define our true identity as God's children.

Action/Thought for Today: Are you a slave to fear, shame, guilt, or regrets?

Prayer: Lord Jesus, thank You for delivering us from the fear of sickness, depression, and anxiety. Thank You for giving us Your Spirit of power, love, strength, and self-control. Thank You, Father, for Your kindness and mercy toward us. In Your name we pray. Amen!

You Are Precious in God's Sight!

I praise you, for I am fearfully and wonderfully made. Wonderful are your works; that I know very well.   Psalm 139:14

Are you worried about your looks? Are you too short or too tall? Are you too fat or too skinny? Is there a part of your body that you would like to change? When you feel unhappy about your looks, remember that God created you with great care. Thank Him for loving you enough to make you unique and precious in His eyes. God created man in His image; male and female, he created them (see Genesis 1:27). Then He breathed life into us. *"For the Spirit of God made me, the breath of the Almighty keeps me alive"* (Job 33:4, NABRE). Let us pray to accept and care for ourselves. Never let anyone discourage you about how you look or dress. Worry more about your spiritual life, character, integrity, and conscience than your physical appearance. Always remember that God created you for a purpose and His work in this world.

> **Action/Thought for Today:** Take a look at yourself in the mirror of your heart. See how beautiful God made you. Thank Him for the gift of life.

Prayer: Eternal Father, many times I abuse myself and do not appreciate the gift of life. Forgive me for the times I have not taken care of myself. Thank You because I am wonderfully made. Thank You for loving me. I adore You, my Lord and my God. *"Worthy are you, our Lord and God, to receive glory and honor and power, for you created all things, and by your will they existed and were created. Amen!"* (Revelation 4:11, ESV).

GOD KNOWS YOU!

Before I formed you in the womb I knew you, before you were born I dedicated you; a prophet to the nations I appointed you.
Jeremiah 1:5, NABRE

Have you ever looked at someone and wanted to be in that person's shoes? Have you looked at your neighbor's success and questioned God about yours? Know that God planned for your existence even before He created you. He knows you well and maps your life with great love and care. God ordered things in your life day by day, except for sins. He did not plan for us to sin. Therefore, let us not wish we were someone else, but accept with joy who we are. *"Does not the potter have the right over the clay, to make out of the same lump one vessel for a noble purpose and another for an ignoble one?"* (Romans 9:21, NABRE).

Yes, indeed, as the Creator, God has the right to decide over our lives. We must try to have a deeper trust in God and let Him be God in our lives. He also consecrated us for many different vocations. Therefore, we must try our best to allow Him to fulfill His purpose in us. If we prayerfully seek His guidance, He will guide us. All we have to do is follow His lead.

Action/Thought for Today: If you ever wanted to be someone else, ask for forgiveness and resolve to be yourself.

Prayer: Lord Jesus, You knew me before I was born and You plan my life day by day. Teach me to embrace everything about myself except sin, and help me be at peace with myself. Please grant me the grace to abandon myself to You, remain in Your care, and do Your holy will. In Your name I pray. Amen!

THE FATHER'S BLESSING!

I will proclaim the decree of the Lord, he said to me, "You are my son; today I have begotten you.   Psalm 2:7, NABRE

God the Father declared to Jesus at His baptism, *"This is my beloved Son, with whom I am well pleased"* (Matthew 17:5, NABRE). Just as God blessed and revealed His love for His Son. He invites us to share in the love of Christ as sons and daughters of God, and He blesses us with every spiritual gift. God the Father delights in us, not because we are perfect, but because we are His children.

Jesus conformed to His Father's teachings and ways and taught the disciples what He had learned from His Father. Jesus also expects us to strive to follow His Father's commandment and footsteps. As children of God, we ought to love, expecting nothing in return, forgive those who have offended us, share our blessings and gifts with others, and humbly serve as Jesus did on Earth. Let us pray that Christ dwells in our hearts through faith as we are being rooted and grounded in love (see Ephesians 3:17) and *"to know the love of Christ that surpasses knowledge so that you may be filled with all the fullness of God"* (Ephesians 3:19).

Action/Thought for Today: Are you allowing God to speak those exact words over you, as He did to Jesus—"You are My beloved child"?

Prayer: O God, I thank You for the invitation to share in the love of Christ. Thank You for looking at me with pleasure. Help me to understand how very much You delight in me and help me not to take Your love for granted. Thank You for such a great blessing. I praise and adore You, Lord. In Jesus' name I pray. Amen!

REMAIN IN HIM!

I am the vine, you are the branches. Whoever remains in me and I in him will bear much fruit, because without me you can do nothing. John 15:5, NABRE

Imagine a branch that is not attached to the tree. It would fall in the ground, then be blown away by the wind and die. This branch couldn't produce fruit, for it has no nutrients from the source of life. It is the same for us. If we do not abide in the Lord, we cannot do anything nor produce anything good. Without God, we are empty, lacking the goodness and grace to do good work. We must remain connected in the Lord to bear good fruit through constant prayer and the reading of the Holy Scriptures.

The Lord is a vine grower and takes away every branch that does not bear fruit (see John 15:1-2). He also prunes other branches so that they will bear more fruit (see John 15:2). When God chooses us to do His work, He also purifies and equips us to do so. He removes from our lives whatever is keeping us from doing His work. Any useless branch in us will wither and be thrown into a fire to be burned (see John 15:6). This is a difficult process. Don't get discouraged in the pruning process for it refines and purifies our soul and heart and brings us to new life to partake in God's mighty work in the world.

Action/Thought for Today: What fruit do you want to bear for the Lord?

Prayer: Lord Jesus, give me the grace to remain in You because I am nothing and can do nothing without You. Lord Jesus, I permit You to bear fruit in and through me. In Your name I pray. Amen!

KNOWN BY ITS FRUIT!

Jesus answered, "... The works that I do in my Father's name testify to me; but you do not believe, because you are not among my sheep." John 10:25-26

Does your work testify to God's name as Jesus' did? If you are among the sheep of God, the works that you do and your way of life should speak volumes. One who works through and for the Father will be known by the fruits they bear, for a tree is known by its fruit (see Matthew 12:33). *"The good person brings good things out of a good treasure, and the evil person brings evil things out of an evil treasure"* (Matthew 12:35). Those who labor for the Father will:

- Bring relief to the poor and homeless
- Comfort the suffering
- Evangelize others to lead them closer to God
- Feed the hungry
- Keep a Christian attitude always
- Pray for the healing of the sick
- Pray fervently to bring joy and peace to all.

Therefore, by God's grace, let our deeds speak for us. As St. Basil the Great has said, "A good deed is never lost." [31] God uses our good acts, small or large, to bring healing and prosperity to us and others. Therefore, let's do all things for His glory.

Action/Thought for Today: Does your work testify to God's name?

Prayer: Lord Jesus, help me bear good fruits for Your glory. In Your name I pray. Amen!

FRUIT OF THE SPIRIT!

Abide in me, and I in you. As the branch cannot bear fruit by itself, unless it abides in the vine, neither can you, unless you abide in me. John 15:4, ESV

The fruit of the Spirit is love, joy, peace, patience, kindness, goodness, faithfulness, gentleness, and self-control (see Galatians 5:22-23). They are manifested in us through the Holy Spirit. They are the visible characteristics or attitudes of a Christian. We do not acquire them by our own effort. We must abide in the Lord and pray for the grace to receive them. How do we know that we have received one or more fruits of the Spirit?

- When we respond with charity and kindness to injustice, unfairness, and hatred, the fruit of love is demonstrated in us.
- When we don't fret or get upset and anxious in trials, tribulations, and chaos, the fruits of joy, patience, and peace are manifested in us.
- When we don't get discouraged or despair at what life throws at us, the fruits of faithfulness and patience are present in us.
- When others are unkind to us, but we respond with charity, love, and humility, the fruits of kindness and gentleness are displayed in us.
- When we display integrity and virtue, give the best of ourselves, and perform good acts, especially toward those who persecute us, the fruit of goodness is revealed in us.

Action/Thought for Today: Are the fruits of the Spirit manifested in your life? If not, pray for that grace.

Prayer: Lord Jesus, give me the grace to manifest the fruit of the Spirit. In Your name I pray. Amen!

PRUNE ME, O LORD!

I am the true vine, and my Father is the vine grower. He takes away every branch in me that does not bear fruit, and every one that does he prunes so that it bears more fruit. John 15:1-2

If you want to bear good fruit, you must examine yourself regularly: *"Let us test and examine our ways, and return to the LORD"* (Lamentations 3:40). Through prayers and self-reflection, let us allow the Lord to take away every branch in us that does not bear fruit. It is of the utmost importance that we continue to grow in the Lord and bring forth good fruits for His glory. Therefore, it is helpful to self-reflect and examine ourselves daily in prayer:

- Think of what you are grateful for and thank God for the blessing of the day.
- Ask God to bring to mind your sins or shortcomings. Ask Him for forgiveness.
- Pray for the grace not to repeat the same sins. Decide to do better the next hour or day.
- Let the Lord change you.

As we come to the Lord daily, He gives us more and more grace to see our shortcomings, repent, and get closer to Him. He also allows us to see our improvements—virtues, gifts, and fruits of the Holy Spirit within us. Let us thank the Lord for His mercy and grace.

Action/Thought for Today: Have you taken time to examine yourself? Have you looked back at your week or day?

Prayer: Lord Jesus, sometimes I don't want to look back at my life. Lead me to repentance and prune me to bear good fruits by Your grace. In Your name I pray. Amen!

Chosen and Appointed!

It was not you who chose me, but I who chose you and appointed you to go and bear fruit that will remain, so that whatever you ask the Father in my name he may give you. John 15:16, NABRE

God has chosen us to bear fruit in the world. He calls us on different missions and for various purposes. To bring forth wholehearted fruit with love, we must accept and embrace the work to which God has called us and remain connected to Him. When we abide in Him, we bear fruit that will last, and as He gives us the grace and power to fulfill His purpose. Hence, we must focus on the Lord first for His guidance and leadership, then on the work assigned to us, for He is the source of all things.

What is it that the Lord calls you to do? Do you feel that the work that you do *in* Christ and *for* Christ is insignificant? Do you know that a small ministry of five people serving in the community is as important as someone with a ministry of five hundred people serving worldwide? Regardless of the size of your ministry, God has chosen you for this work at this appointed time. Therefore, let us pray to do His will, work for His glory, and center Him in everything. Let Him help you with all your responsibilities and cares.

> **Action/Thought for Today:** Are you open and ready to bear fruit for the Lord? If not, what is stopping you? Ask the Lord for His help.

Prayer: Lord Jesus, I want to bear good fruit for You. Help me to hear and understand Your calling, obey Your commands, and do Your holy will. I pray in Your holy name. Amen!

NOT ENOUGH LABORERS!

Then he [Jesus] said to his disciples, "The harvest is plentiful, but the laborers are few; therefore, ask the Lord of the harvest to send out laborers into his harvest." Matthew 9:37-38

Do you think that there are already enough ministries or charities in the world? Do you feel that you don't have to proclaim the Gospel of God because there are enough priests, pastors, evangelists, and preachers? Unfortunately, God's harvest does *not* have enough workers, and He is calling us to get out of our comfort zone to work in His harvest because:

Many are searching for peace and need direction and leadership. Many have fallen prey to the enemy and need freedom in Christ. Many do not trust the Lord and are losing hope. Many have not encountered the Lord profoundly. Many need mental, physical, and spiritual healing. Many need to know the Lord and accept Him as their personal and only Savior. Many need to experience God's goodness, kindness, love, and mercy. Many still have not heard the good news of the Gospel.

Therefore, let us pray for the Lord to fill us with His power and grace to labor for Him and produce good fruit. We can do all things in Christ, and if we ask Him, He will supply us with the strength and courage to fulfill His mission in this world.

Action/Thought for Today: Are you determined to labor for the Lord? Ask Him for the grace to partner with Him.

Prayer: Lord Jesus, teach and guide me to work in Your harvest to produce good fruit. It is in Your name that I pray. Amen!

WE ARE CREATED FOR GOOD WORKS!

For we are what he has made us, created in Christ Jesus for good works, which God prepared beforehand to be our way of life.

Ephesians 2:10

What do you consider your most significant contribution in life? Some may feel that they have not contributed to the world because they didn't make the latest discovery in technology, find the cure for cancer, reach the highest rank at work or in society, or participate in considerable ministry work. However, good work is not only achieved through our accomplishments on the world stage; it is also demonstrated in the hidden and small things done with love for our loved ones. This includes such things as cleaning and cooking for the family, doing the laundry or washing the dishes, or food shopping. When we do these things with love, they become extraordinary work in God's eyes. Great work consists of striving to be wonderful parents, amazing sons, daughters, or siblings, great coworkers, faithful family members, and friends.

Good work should be our way of life; therefore, it is of utmost importance that our ministry begin at home, work, or wherever God places us. Let us resolve to do all small, hidden tasks with joy and love for God's glory.

Action/Thought for Today: Pray for the grace to accept the work that God has entrusted to you at this time.

Prayer: Lord Jesus, give me the grace to perform with joy and love all the hidden and small things You entrust to me. In Your name that I pray. Amen!

YOU ARE THE LIGHT!

You are the light of the World.   Matthew 5:14

Many will agree that we live in a dark world. However, Jesus' light has never stopped shining in our hearts and lives. He is forever removing us from the darkness of sin through forgiveness. He has passed on His light to us so that we can shine for others. He calls us to bring His light to others through service, compassion, and love for the greater glory of God, the Father. Our light comes from being an example to God's flock, reflecting the life and characteristics of Christ.

Since we have gifts that differ, let us use them for bringing light in different ways as we work together (see Romans 12:4). Let us be the light by serving others through ministering, contributing to others' needs, and exercising hospitality. Let us be the light by performing acts of mercy, such as sharing a simple word of compassion or scripture, and by our cheerfulness, charity, humility, patience, by praying for one another and sharing others' suffering. Let us be the light by simple Christian behavior, professing our faith in the way we live. Then Christ's light will be made known in this world through us.

Action/Thought for Today: Are you the light of the world? If yes, in what ways? If not, how can you become the light of the world?

Prayer: Lord Jesus, give me the grace to use the gifts You have given me to bring light to others for Your glory. In Your name I pray. Amen!

BE A CANDLE!

No one after lighting a lamp puts it under the bushel basket, but on the lampstand, and it gives light to all in the house. In the same way, let your light shine before others, so that they may see your good works and give glory to your Father in heaven.

Matthew 5:15-16

A sermon that I heard years ago about being the light of the world will remain with me forever. The priest said, "For a candle to bring light, this candle must be consumed. It is okay for us to be a candle in the service of others." We have to sacrifice our all for the sake of the Gospel. The analogy of a candle helps me understand the sacrifices of others that bring the light of Christ to me, to teach me, and to help me grow spiritually. Think about our priests, pastors, and other church leaders, who dedicate their time and talents to bring us closer to Christ.

Furthermore, this sermon reminded me not to be discouraged in the service of others. No matter how physically or emotionally exhausted I am, I must use every opportunity to bring the light of Christ to others through words, deeds, and prayers. Our Lord is the perfect example, for He made the ultimate sacrifice on the cross to give us eternal life. HE WAS CONSUMED for us! Therefore, we must do the same for others. Let us accept being a candle!

Action/Thought for Today: Who in your life needs the light of Christ? Be a candle to them, regardless of the cost.

Prayer: Lord Jesus, thank You for everyone who has shed light on us in our lives. Thank You, Lord, for all our spiritual leaders. Pour Your blessing on all those who have devoted themselves to Your service for the good of humankind. In Your name I pray. Amen!

JESUS IS THE LIGHT!

Jesus spoke to them again, saying, "I am the light of the world. Whoever follows me will not walk in darkness, but will have the light of life." John 8:12, NABRE

Jesus told all of us that we would never walk in darkness if we followed Him (see John 8:12). He is the true light and has shown this to us through His compassion, forgiveness, love, and mercy. He came down from Heaven to teach us how to live. *"If we walk in the light as he is in the light, then we have fellowship with one another, and the blood of his Son Jesus cleanses us from all sin"* (1 John 1:7, NABRE).

We must meditate on the life of Jesus and His words so that we can imitate His characteristics. We must pray for the determination to follow Him with a steadfast heart and spirit. Nothing else will bring us closer to Christ than prayer and meditating on His words. They strengthen our faith. If all Christians follow God's ways, we can light up the world, and darkness will be no more. Our light will be contagious and evident to everyone we meet so that they may depart from darkness and experience the light of Jesus Christ

Action/Thought for Today: Which area in your life does not reflect the life of Christ? Ask the Lord to help you discern and change your ways to be more like Him.

Prayer: Lord Jesus, it is easy to fall into the darkness of this world. Please give us the courage and strength to follow in Your footsteps and walk in Your light. In Your name we pray. Amen!

EXPOSE EVERYTHING TO LIGHT!

Take no part in the fruitless works of darkness; rather expose them, for it is shameful even to mention the things done by them in secret; but everything exposed by the light becomes visible, for everything that becomes visible is light.

Ephesians 5:11-14, NABRE

Do you have unconfessed sins, bad habits, or addiction problems that remain hidden? Are you so accustomed to the darkness of your heart that you avoid the light of Christ? Jesus wants us to bring Him our dirty laundry so that He can cleanse us with His precious blood and bring us to His light. When we expose our sins, we will experience profound freedom in Christ.

The enemy wants us to keep our sins secret. The little voice in our head tell us not to expose these sins to others as they will judge or not love us. That voice is not from God. It is the work of the devil to keep us captive and in darkness. I am not saying you should tell the world about your shortcomings and sins. Those who belong to a sacramental church, resolve to bring your darkest secrets to the confessional as soon as possible. Others, speak to your pastors or spiritual leaders and mentors to help bring light to the darkness of your heart.

Action/Thought for Today: Do you have a dark secret that is holding you captive? Pray for the grace to bring it to the light of Christ.

Prayer: Lord Jesus, I want to bring my sins to the light, but I am afraid that others will judge me. Please give me the grace to confess my sins and walk in Your light. In Your name I pray. Amen!

LET YOUR LIGHT SHINE!

For so the Lord has commanded us, saying, "I have set you to be a light for the Gentiles, so that you may bring salvation to the ends of the earth."   Acts 13:47

Most of you probably have heard the uplifting children's song that says, "This little light of mine, I'm gonna let it shine." It reminds me to let Christ's light shine through me in all I do everywhere I go. Suppose you meet a stranger in the store. As you converse with that person, how can you show your little light? Will that person recognize that you are Christian? Or does your Christianity apply only in church? We must go the extra mile to let our lights shine as Jesus commanded us by being kind, gentle, joyful, loving, peaceful, patient, sympathetic, and open to share the Gospel at every opportunity that arises.

When you walk away from a stranger, they may not know that you are a Christian, but they should at least conclude that there is something good, pure, and sincere about you. *"For the fruit of the light is found in all that is good and right and truth"* (Ephesians 5:9). Therefore, we can know those in the light by their good deeds, pure actions, faith, and truthfulness. Our attitudes evangelize and bring people closer to Christ so that they may obtain eternal life.

Action/Thought for Today: How can you let
the light of Christ shine through you?

Prayer: Lord Jesus, I am sorry for the times I failed
to radiate Your light to others as I should. Grant me
the grace and the courage to let my little light shine
in this dark world. In Your name I pray. Amen!

THE MISSION FIELD!

Go therefore and make disciples of all nations, baptizing them in the name of the Father, and of the Son, and of the Holy Spirit, and teaching them to obey everything that I have commanded you. And remember, I am with you always, to the end of the age. Matthew 28:19-20

Upon leaving church once, a sign spoke to me. It read, "You are now entering the mission field." Indeed, our mission is in this world, and Jesus is with us in this mission field. His light, which shone when He walked on Earth, continues to shine in our hearts and lives. He gives us His light to partner with Him in the work of salvation. But where do we begin?

- Our light must shine in our homes, work, communities, and everywhere else. First, however, we must minister to those closest to us. If we fail to share the light with those around us, we cannot be effective teachers in this world.
- Our behaviors should be consistent. We cannot choose to be Christians only when it is convenient. Be an example everywhere and at all times.
- Don't be ashamed of the Gospel; share your faith with the world.
- Don't conform to this world's darkness; always do what is right.

"If we say that we have fellowship with him while we are walking in darkness, we lie and do not do what is true" (1 John 1:6). Therefore, let us ask the Lord to guide and lead us in this mission field.

Action/Thought for Today: Pray for the grace to be a disciple in your mission field.

Prayer: Lord Jesus, we want to be Your witnesses in the world. Give us the grace to shine Your light on others. We praise You, Lord! In Your name I pray. Amen!

THE FOUNTAIN OF LIGHT!

For with you is the fountain of life; in your light, we see light.
Psalm 36:9

O Lord, my God, you alone are my Light and Salvation (see Psalm 27:1), whom shall I fear? Why should I be afraid? Your light is a blessed fountain that sustains me in my day-to-day living and in times of despair, trials, and tribulations. In the darkness, Your light shines brighter for me and guides me closer to You, so that I will not stumble and fall. When I am lost, You gently remind me: *"Your word is a lamp to my feet and a light to my path"* (Psalm 119:105, ESV). Indeed, Your words counsel me, give me peace, remove my blindness, and open my eyes to see what is right and just.

Lord, it is your light that leads and guides me to continue to walk with you. It strengthens me to bring forth good fruit for Your glory. How awesome You are, Lord, for giving me your light, so that I don't have to rely on my understanding, but can trust in You always (see Proverb 3:5-6). Allow me the grace to always pass Your light on to the world. It is only in You that we see the true light!

Action/Thought for Today: Reflect on God's light in your life.

Prayer: Lord Jesus, thank You for Your light that always shines on us. Help us receive Your divine light so that we may pass it on to the world. In Jesus' name we pray. Amen!

IN TIME OF ILLNESS, SEEK THE LORD!

Come to me, all you that are weary and are carrying heavy burdens, and I will give you rest. Take my yoke upon you, and learn from me; for I am gentle and humble in heart, and you will find rest for your souls. For my yoke is easy, and my burden is light.
Matthew 11:28-30

Sickness can be a path to get us closer to God and purify us of our faults and shortcomings. Once, I was sick and could not do anything about my illness but accept God's will and give Him my heavy burdens. The Lord gave me rest and peace beyond understanding. I am an independent person. This illness humbled me and taught me that I need God to strengthen me, and I need others to care and pray for me.

When ill, we should not despair, but take up our cross and follow the Lord (see Matthew 16:24). Try not to complain, avoid self-pity, accept and obey doctor's orders, and try to the best of our ability to care for yourself so that you can recover. Times of sickness can be frustrating, uncertain, sad, and painful, but if we continue to seek the Lord, bearing the illness is easier. He will supply us with peace, courage, strength, patience, and many graces and blessings.

Action/Thought for Today: Pray for the sick today.

Prayer: O God, wash us from all sins and transgressions and provide us with complete healing of the body, mind, soul, and spirit. Lord, by Your healing power, wash away all our sins, illnesses, and afflictions and make us new again. During our sicknesses, as we are seeking and searching for You, let us find You. Thank You, Lord, for Your healing miracles! We exalt You, O Lord, for Your love and kindness toward us. In the name of Jesus we pray. Amen!

LORD, HEAL ME FROM SPIRITUAL PARALYSIS!

And there people brought to him [Jesus] a paralytic lying on a stretcher. When Jesus saw their faith, he said to the paralytic, "Courage, child, your sins are forgiven." Matthew 9:2, NABRE

Many have spiritual paralysis without being aware of it. It manifests as being lukewarm and indifferent in prayer, family life, or at work. Those who suffer from it continue to live in sin without any regrets, and their speech can be harmful. They lack Christian love, hope, and faith. Those who struggle with spiritual paralysis must go to the Lord in prayer and fasting. They must find Him in the Scriptures, repent, and ask Him for forgiveness and mercy.

Jesus wants to heal us from our defilements. He is saying to every one of us, *"Rise, pick up your stretcher, and go home"* (Matthew 9:6 NABRE). Let us accept God's invitation to renew ourselves in Him, ask for clarity on our weaknesses and paralysis, and implore Him for the healing of our spiritual diseases. Once the paralysis chains are broken, we will become disciples of Christ who only live for and with Him.

Action/Thought for Today: Are you spiritually paralyzed? What is your spiritual paralysis? Ask the Lord to help you see your paralysis and to heal you.

Prayer: Lord Jesus, I surrender my spiritual paralysis to you. Heal my defilements. *"Heal me, O LORD, and I shall be healed; save me, and I shall be saved; for you are my praise,"* (Jeremiah 17:14). In Your name I pray. Amen!

LORD, HEAL ME FROM SPIRITUAL BLINDNESS!

"The man called Jesus made mud, spread it on my eyes, and said to me, 'Go to Siloam and wash'. Then I went and washed and received my sight." John 9:11

One day, we suddenly lost electrical power at work. Everyone screamed because it was very dark, and we could see very little. Within a few minutes, however, the light was restored, and I could feel a sense of relief in everyone. The blind man whose sight Jesus restored would have had an even more profound experience since he had been blind from birth. I am sure he was amazed to see the light, the wondrous works of God's hands, and to receive healing. Therefore, let us pray for healing for those who have physical blindness. Let us be their eyes, hold them by the hand to lead them to Christ, and integrate them into society.

Living in darkness without God's light is infinitely worse. Spiritual blindness, far worse than physical blindness, can cost us eternal life. Spiritual blindness occurs when one does not know or see God. It causes one to ignore the truth of the Gospel of Jesus Christ and to believe in the world's power, fame, and money. When one does not see God, one cannot see others' needs either, such as the suffering of the poor, homeless, sick, and marginalized. One does not see the injustice, racism, and stereotyping that others face. One does not see the face of Christ in one's neighbor. Let us pray for the Lord to shine His light into our darkness.

Action/Thought for Today: Examine yourself. Where are the eyes of your soul and heart? Are you spiritually blind?

Prayer: Lord Jesus, at times I am blind. Heal me from my spiritual blindness so that I can see You in the poor, the homeless, and those suffering. In Your name I pray. Amen!

LORD, DELIVER ME FROM SPIRITUAL BONDAGE!

Jesus then said to those Jews who believed in him, "If you remain in my word, you will truly be my disciples, and you will know the truth, and the truth will set you free."   John 8:31-32, NABRE

Spiritual bondage is the state of being a slave to the things of this world. We are in bondage due to our sinful natures, emotions, desires, and wills. We may tend to repeat the same sin, even when we don't want to sin. As noted by the apostle Paul, *"For I do not do the good I want, but the evil I do not want is what I do"* (Romans 7:19). Sometimes, it is the need to satisfy ourselves and the worldly desires that chain us—fashion, social media, money, power, or fame.

The devil uses our thoughts, emotions, and sins to keep us from God. Therefore, Christians should actively strive to put off the old self (see Ephesians 4:22-24). We should strive to get rid of worldly desires and passions and walk in the freedom that God has given us. We cannot receive His freedom through our own effort, but all is possible with God's grace. *"So if the Son makes you free, you will be free indeed"* (John 8:36). We must submit to God, resist the devil and his schemes, and he will flee from us (see James 4:7). Resist the devil by calling on the Holy Spirit to help you discern what is good, acceptable, and perfect to the Lord (see Romans 12:2). Resist him through humble prayer, fasting, and doing good deeds.

Action/Thought for Today: What is holding you captive? Ask the Lord to help you discern it, and then pray for true freedom in the Lord.

Prayer: Lord Jesus, deliver us from all spiritual bondage, and bring us closer to You. In Your name we pray. Amen!

DAUGHTER, YOUR FAITH HAS SAVED YOU!

"Daughter, your faith has made you well; go in peace."

Luke 8:48

*For the full scripture, see Luke 8:43-48.

Can you imagine bleeding for twelve years with no help or resolution from many doctors? This woman in Luke 8:43-48 must have been desperate, yet she believed that Jesus could heal her if she only could touch the tassel of His cloak. She put her faith into action, and Jesus healed her.

Do you believe that God still performs healing miracles? Yes, indeed. The God who was here yesterday is the same today and will be the same tomorrow. God does not change, even though we do.

From time to time, we walk away from God. Yet, He always offers us His help to bless, heal, restore, save, and love us. All we must do is touch Jesus' garments and let Him touch us back.

Sometimes we don't open our hearts to receive God's blessing; we don't invite Him into our lives. Therefore, God cannot work any miracles in us. Faith helps us receive God's grace and mercy. Today and forever, let us pray to abide in the Lord and open our hearts to accept His love and healing.

Action/Thought for Today: Let's continue to pray
for faith and a healing miracle in our lives.

Prayer: Lord Jesus, we invite You into our lives, to bless, heal, restore, save, and love us. Lord, give us the grace to touch You and be well. Increase our little faith and have Your way with us. We surrender our all to You. In Your name we pray. Amen!

THE PRAYER OF THE FAITHFUL!

Are any among you suffering? They should pray. Are any cheerful? They should sing songs of praise. Are any among you sick? They should call for the elders of the church and have them pray over them, anointing them with oil in the name of the Lord. The prayer of faith will save the sick, and the Lord will raise them up; and anyone who has committed sins will be forgiven. James 5:13-15

James instructed us to pray when we are sick or suffering, and to call the elders (ministers) of the church to anoint us with oil in the Lord's name. James also said the prayer of faith and (intercession) would save, for it will restore health and afford forgiveness of sins. Why? Because sin can be a roadblock to healing. The anointing of the sick is used for both spiritual and physical healing. This is a spiritual weapon the Lord has given us to transform us into a new creation.

Therefore, one who is sick should seek anointing with oil from their minister/priest/ pastor. They should also ask for prayers from friends, family, and religious communities. God works through the intercession of the faithful. Therefore, if we have faith and are living in harmony with the Lord, He will work miracles when we ask in prayer. As He said, *"Everyone who asks receives"* (Luke 11:9, NRSVUE). Sometimes, we may not see an immediate result from prayers, but don't despair. Count on God for healing and salvation. He is the Healer, and He always wants to heal us.

Action/Thought for Today: Drop a note, sharing scriptures and words of encouragement. Visit and/or pray for the sick.

Prayer: Lord Jesus, in Your compassion, forgive our sins and heal us in body, mind, and spirit. We pray for the ministers of the Church and those who are involved in the ministry of healing. In Your name I pray. Amen!

THANKS BE TO GOD!

Jesus said in reply, "Ten were cleansed, were they not? Where are the other nine? Has none but this foreigner returned to give thanks to God?" Then he said to him, "Stand up and go; your faith has saved you."   Luke 17:17-19, NABRE

* For the full scripture, see Luke 17:11-19.

Leprosy is a disease that isolated people and prevented others from touching anyone who had it. As you can see in the Scriptures, the lepers stood at a distance from the Lord, asking for healing, *"Jesus, Master! Have pity on us!"* (Luke 17:13, NABRE). Jesus did not lay hands on them, but in His mercy, He told them to show themselves to the priests. Along the way, they all were healed, yet only the Samaritan returned to glorify and thank Jesus. Nine of them, once healed, forgot about the Healer but accepted the gift of healing. Jesus reproached the nine who did not return to show gratitude; *"Has none but this foreigner returned to give thanks to God?"*

We cannot love the gift more than the Giver. The more grateful we are to God, the more He will bless us. We ought to thank the Lord even if we did not ask for a gift or healing. We should pray for the grace to daily turn our thoughts, words, and actions into praise and worship, and we ought to testify to others for the good the Lord has done for us.

Action/Thought for Today: Have you thanked the Lord after He has healed, blessed, and cared for you? Take a few minutes to thank Him today for His healing, goodness, and mercy.

Prayer: Father, I thank, worship, and praise You for healing, forgiving, loving, and caring for me. I am sorry for all the times I have failed to acknowledge, praise, adore, and worship You. Lord, help me to do better. In Jesus' name I pray. Amen!

WHAT IS GOD'S GLORY?

Look, the LORD Our God has shown us his glory and greatness, and we have heard his voice out of the fire. Deuteronomy 5:24

Although the word *glory* is mentioned frequently in the Bible, it is not easy to describe God's glory. It may have a different meaning for different people, but in scripture, it is God's absolute beauty. It is the beauty of who He is: His character, majesty, holiness, goodness, and the grandeur of the works of His hands. When God spoke in a loud voice and, out of fire, wrote the ten commandments for Moses, He showed Moses His glory (see Deuteronomy 5:22). God's glory is also revealed in His Son, Jesus Christ, in His public ministry, death, and resurrection.

If one knows the Son, one knows the Father (see John 7:29). We see who God is through Jesus. In thanksgiving for God's glory, we must do all things for Him, live and die for Him, and submit our all to Him. We must praise, worship, and sing to Him: *"Holy, holy, holy is the Lord of hosts; the whole earth is full of his glory"* (Isaiah 6:3).

Action/Thought for Today: Talk to a friend today about God's glory. Pray for the Lord to direct you to the right person.

Prayer: Father, we praise You for Your infinite beauty. We glorify You in our daily lives and in all that we do. We pray in Jesus' name. Amen!

WHEN YOU EAT OR DRINK, GIVE GLORY TO GOD!

So whether you eat or drink, or whatever you do, do everything for the glory of God. 1 Corinthian 10:31

Often, we eat and drink without thinking of God. We habitually say our routine prayer before a meal, without really paying attention to God's blessing. If you do not eat or drink for God's glory, talk to someone who is sick and cannot eat or someone on tube feeding. Think about someone living in poverty who doesn't have any food. That will give you a better perspective of God's daily blessing upon your life.

Do you use food or sweets for comfort when life is upside down? Do you have a habit of overindulging in food or eating unhealthily? If you do, think of God with every meal. It will make a difference. Remember that food cannot solve life's problems, and we must turn to Jesus, who always wants to help us with everything. With Jesus, let's establish boundaries on our food choices and consumption. That will require sacrifice, but it will be an incredible blessing.

Action/Thought for Today: Try to fast one day this week or skip a snack. Thank God for your daily bread.

Prayer: Lord Jesus, give us the grace to glorify You every time we eat or drink. Thank You for our daily bread. I praise and exalt You, O Lord. In Your name we pray. Amen!

WHEN YOU WORK, GIVE GLORY TO GOD!

Whatever your task, put yourselves into it, as done for the Lord and not for your masters, since you know that from the Lord you will receive the inheritance as your reward; you serve the Lord Christ. Colossians 3:23-24

In my daily work life, I pray for the people I serve and my co-workers. I may have a stressful and exhausting day at work, but God always rescues me, and my weariness never lasts for long. When those hard days come, I usually see and feel the presence of the Lord at work in me. We can use our problems or difficult days to seek God in all we do by turning our work into prayer and thanksgiving.

In your workplace, strive to be the light of Christ by truly living your faith. This requires having a positive attitude, being cheerful in your daily duty, and being a source of comfort to your colleagues and clients. Proverb 16: 3 teaches us: *"Commit your work to the LORD, and your plans will be established."* In other words, when you work for God's glory, you will succeed in whatever work you do. Always ask the Holy Spirit to be present with you in the workplace, and you will be satisfied and content despite any hardship, for you are serving your Lord and Master.

Action/Thought for Today: Say a prayer at work today and daily. Let us thank God for our work.

Prayer: Lord Jesus, thank You for my work. Teach me to serve my clients with Your hands, love them with Your heart, and see them as You do. Give me the grace to be a source of Christ's light to my co-workers. I commit my work to You for Your greater glory. In Your name I pray. Amen!

IN DEEDS OR WORDS: GIVE GLORY AND THANKS TO GOD!

And whatever you do, in word or deed, do everything in the name of the Lord Jesus, giving thanks to God the Father through him.
Colossians 3:17

To bring glory to God in words and deeds requires the right attitude. Be joyful and patient in all you do and in your conversation with others. Be kind and compassionate toward others. Serve, speak with your heart, and share the love of God in your daily actions. When we do good deeds for others, it helps them journey through life with peace, confidence, and serenity. Such acts may be small, but if done well and from the heart, they may change someone's life forever. *"Let your light shine before others, so that they may see your good works and give glory to your Father in heaven"* (Matthew 5:16).

When you do good for someone, they may say: "May God bless you." That's giving glory to God and being grateful for the good deed. Your right action is from God, directed back toward Him for His blessing, glory, and honor. Therefore, let that light of yours always shine while continuing to do good.

Action/Thought for Today: Plan to do a good deed today for God's glory.

Prayer: Lord Jesus, teach me to give You glory in words and deeds. I glorify Your name at all times. In Your name I pray. Amen!

IN YOUR BODY, GIVE GLORY TO GOD!

Do you not know that your body is a temple of the Holy Spirit within you, whom you have from God, and that you are not your own? For you have been purchased at a price. Therefore, glorify God in your body. 1 Corinthians 6:19

We are faithfully and wonderfully made by the Lord (see Psalm 139:14), and He requires that we take care of the bodies that He has given us.

- The world may demand that we adhere to the latest fashion, a particular brand, or style of clothing. We may dress to impress others, but our bodies are the temples of the Holy Spirit. Therefore, we should be mindful of what we wear.
- God gave us a tongue to proclaim and give glory to His name. Therefore, we must be mindful of how we speak to others. We must strive to speak with love and kindness.
- God gave us eyes to see Him; let us be mindful of what we watch.
- God gave us ears to listen to Him; let us be mindful of that to which we listen.
- God gave us a heart to love; let us pray that He opens our hearts to love Him and others more and more.
- God gave us hands to serve; let us serve all with love for His greater glory.
- God gave us feet to run to Him; let us be careful where they go. Do they run to evil?
- God is the Author of our lives; be careful how your body behaves.

Action/Thought for Today: Pay special attention to your body today based on this reflection.

Prayer: Lord Jesus, clothe us and teach us to behave with compassion, kindness, humility, meekness, and patience. In Your name we pray. Amen!

WHEN YOU CELEBRATE, GIVE GLORY TO GOD!

Go, eat your food with gladness, and drink your wine with a joyful heart, for God has already approved what you do.

Ecclesiastes 9: 7, NIV

In my family, it is customary to celebrate almost every occasion. Sometimes, while planning a celebration, we may forget to include God in the plan. However, I have realized that life's greatest satisfaction is achieved when we do everything for His glory. Any milestone in life reflects God's blessing and favor. As we celebrate, we ought to be grateful and bring honor to God. This requires that we focus our hearts, thoughts, words, and actions toward Him.

We should invite God to all celebrations, parties, and gatherings. Make God's name known by beginning with prayer and thanksgiving, whether it is a birthday, anniversary, graduation, retirement, or family gathering, etc. By proclaiming God's name at every celebration, you allow family and friends to witness the incredible work of God in your life. As Isaiah 63:7 reminds us, *"I will tell of the kindness of the LORD, the deeds for which he is to be praised, according to all the LORD has done for us"* (NIV).

Action/Thought for Today: At your next gathering, be sure to make God's name known and pray for your guests before the event.

Prayer: Lord Jesus, I bless and glorify Your name in all that I do. Let me think of You often so that I always remember to bring glory to You. Let all my thoughts, words, and actions be for You, with You, through You, and for Your greater glory. Lord, I glorify You, and I bless Your name! In Your name I pray. Amen!

TO GOD BE THE GLORY!

And my God will fully satisfy every need of yours according to his riches in glory in Christ Jesus. To our God and Father be glory forever and ever. Amen.   Philippians 4:19-20

Are you working and serving others for your glory or for God's glory? Many tend to seek their own glory. In professional life, one may be looking for affirmation from others or the desire to stand out. One may sacrifice the family and spiritual life to climb the ladder of success. In the Christian life, one may be very involved in the church community simply to feel good about oneself or to show one's piety and holiness to others.

People who are not seeking their own glory carry their faith at work in a humble way and provide an exemplary attitude to others. They devote time to God and family. They take time for spiritual and human formation. They fulfill their professional and family obligations in such a way that it reflects God's light to others. They offer God their duty at home to reflect a Christian environment. They dedicate their professional and volunteer work or ministry to God, serving with kindness and friendliness, knowing they are serving Christ.

Action/Thought for Today: Strive to glorify
God in your actions at work and home.

Prayer: Lord Jesus, I pray that You remove every
tendency that makes me want to seek glory. Teach me
humility, O Lord, and grant me the grace to seek You
in my daily actions. In Your name I pray. Amen!

God Is Good All the Time!

Not to us, Lord, not to us but to your name be the glory, because of your love and faithfulness. Psalm 115:1

I will glorify and praise the Lord, not because life is good to me, not because people are always good to me, but because God is good to me all the time. No matter what is going on in my life, I know that God is by my side. In life and death, He promises to be with me. When I walk in the valley of the shadow of death, I fear no evil, for God is with me (see Psalm 23:4 NABRE). When I fall, God picks me up, and leads me in His ways. The Lord carries me through the storms of life, calms the winds of my life, and never abandons me. Therefore, I will glorify the Lord every day of my life. *"O give thanks to the Lord, for he is good; for his steadfast love endures forever"* (Psalm 107:1)

Action/Thought for Today: Take a few minutes to reflect on God's goodness in your life. Then thank Him for His goodness.

Prayer: Lord Jesus, You are good. You are so good to me. Please give me the grace to depend on You and glorify You in all things. I praise and adore You, Lord. In Your name I pray! Amen!

GIVE GLORY TO GOD IN ILLNESS AND SUFFERING!

But he was wounded for our transgressions, he was bruised for our iniquities; the chastisement of our peace was upon him; and with his stripes we are healed. Isaiah 53:5, ASV

I will glorify the Lord, not because I am well or sick, but because I am healed and cleansed by Christ's precious blood shed for me. When I am physically or spiritually sick, God gives me peace. He forgives me, and by His stripes, I have been healed. When my heart hurts from injustice, discrimination, and unfair treatment, God whispers His love into my ears and brings a joyful song to my mouth. He heals me from my shame, guilt, and fear and makes me whole again.

When you are ill or hurt, take the time to thank and glorify God. Know that, from every experience, there is a lesson to learn, a testimony to share, and a blessing from above. Open the eyes of your heart to see the many gifts acquired through your suffering. We have every reason to give glory to God in our illness and our pain. Let us shout together, "GLORY TO GOD!"

Action/Thought for Today: Do you glorify the Lord just because you are well or at all times?

Prayer: Lord Jesus, thank You for healing my body, soul, and mind. Thank You for giving me a joyful song in my suffering. Thank You for Your mercy and kindness toward me. I praise and adore You. In Your name I pray. Amen!

GLORY TO GOD IN THE MORNING!

For to you I will pray, LORD; in the morning you will hear my voice; in the morning I will plead before you and wait.

Psalm 5:3-4, NABRE

I will give praise and glory because God has blessed me with a new day. He wakes me up in the morning, not because I am good, but because He shows me His great mercy. The Lord watches me through the night and comforts me when I cannot sleep. He wakes me up each morning with a new song in my heart, a song of hope, love, and faith to carry on and to bring His light to others.

"In the morning let me hear of your mercy, for in you I trust. Show me the path I should walk, for I entrust my life to you" (Psalm 143:8 NABRE). When you wake up every morning, ask the Lord for your daily assignment, the path you must take, and trust in His loving and divine providence. *"Trust in the LORD with all your heart, and do not rely on your insight. In all your ways acknowledge him, and he will make straight your paths"* (Proverbs 3:5).

Action/Thought for Today: In what areas of your life have you failed to glorify God? Thank Him for every day!

Prayer: Lord Jesus, we praise You, we bless You, we adore You, we glorify You, we give You thanks for Your great glory. We thank You for each new day. In Your name we pray. Amen!

GRACE UPON GRACE!

Blessed be the God and Father of our Lord Jesus Christ, who has blessed us in Christ with every spiritual blessing in the heavenly places, just as he chose us in Christ before the foundation of the world to be holy and blameless before him in love. He destined us for adoption as his children through Jesus Christ, according to the good pleasure of his will, to the praise of his glorious grace that he freely bestowed on us in the Beloved. Ephesians 1:3-6

I will glorify the Lord with all of you, because, despite our weaknesses, failures, doubts, regrets, and shame, we are still children of God, children wonderfully made and redeemed by His love and mercy. I will glorify Him because, despite being a sinner, we have received His grace upon grace: *"Out of his fullness we have all received grace in place of grace already given"* (John 1:16, NIV).

I will give praise to God because He looks toward his lowly servants and fills us daily with spiritual gifts and blessings to do His work in the world. *"For it is God who works in you to will and to act in order to fulfill his good purpose"* (Philippians 2:13, NIV). He continues to mold us to look, love, and serve more like Him. Let us claim and use our gifts and blessings for the greater glory of God.

Action/Thought for Today: What barriers prevent you from accepting to be molded by the Lord? Thank God for the many graces upon graces He has given us.

Prayer: Lord Jesus, for the many graces that You are pouring on us daily, we thank You. For the blessings that are obvious, we praise You. For the blessings that we cannot see, we bless Your holy name. For the blessings that come with joy, hope, love, faith, and peace, we worship You. For the blessings that come with grief, pain, and discomfort, we glorify You. For the challenges that bring us closer to You, we adore You. In Your name we pray. Amen!

WE ARE GOD'S FAMILY!

For the one who sanctifies and those who are sanctified all have one Father. For this reason Jesus is not ashamed to call them his brothers and sisters, saying, "I will proclaim your name to my brothers and sisters, in the midst of the congregation, I will praise you."
Hebrews 2:11-12

I will give God glory because He gave us Jesus, our only Savior, our only Way, Truth, and Life (see John 14:6). I will give thanks to God, for He gave us Jesus to teach us how to love, live, serve others, and be one family. He wants us to be one family on this Earth. As family, He asks us to follow Jesus' footsteps—caring for the marginalized, poor, sick, and those in need. The Lord wants us to encourage others in their daily lives, encourage them with prayers, and build up each other (see Hebrews 3:13). By doing so, we give God love, praise, and glory. *"so we, though many, are one body in Christ and individually parts of one another"* (Romans 12:5, NABRE).

I will glorify God because we belong to Jesus' family. We do not belong to the world but to the Most High, Jesus Christ. Our ideas, inspirations, and beliefs are from God's truth; hence, we praise the Lord, reject the world's ideas, and do not care what the world thinks of us. We bless the Lord for choosing us to be part of His family.

Action/Thought for Today: Who is God to you? Take a moment to reflect. Then be thankful for who He is!

Prayer: Heavenly Father, thank You for making us a member of Your family. In all circumstances, help us remember that we are one family, and we ought to encourage, love, and serve each other. In Your name we pray. Amen!

I BELONG TO CHRIST!

[The LORD God said], "Behold, all souls are Mine; the soul of the father as well as the soul of the son is Mine. The soul who sins shall die."   Ezekiel 18:4, ESV

St. John Eudes said, "I ask you to consider that our Lord Jesus Christ is your true head and that you are a member of his body. He belongs to you as the head belongs to the body. All that is his is yours: breath, heart, body, soul, and all his faculties. All of these you must use as if they belonged to you, so that in serving him, you may give him praise, love and glory."[32] I give glory to God because, although I do not always act or behave as part of the Body of Christ, He does not chastise me. He is still there to bring me back gently, that I may be restored and made whole again, for He is the Lord, my God (see Jeremiah 31:18). I glorify the Lord for in the many times I turn away from Him, He helps me repent, and gives me back the joy of His salvation. Indeed, I give praise for belonging to the Lord God.

Action/Thought for Today: What steps will you take to be one with Christ in your words and deeds?

Prayer: Heavenly Father, often I do not act as if I belong to You. I let the world put me down. I thank You, for You are always there to rescue me. Please help me remember that I am forever Yours, and I give You all the glory, praise, and honor. In Your name I pray. Amen!

I WILL BLESS THE LORD AT ALL TIMES!

I will bless the LORD at all times, his praise shall continually be in my mouth. My soul makes its boast in the LORD, let the humble hear and be glad.   Psalm 34:1-2

Lord, I will give You glory today, tomorrow, and forever!

I will glorify You because You love me personally with zeal and passion. Even when life is challenging, and I may not feel Your love, I know that You love me.

I will glorify You, Lord, for calling me Your daughter even when I "mess up" in the worst way possible. You do not judge or criticize me, but You gently show me the way and give me the grace to start over.

I will praise You, Lord, for You never give up on me even when I give up on myself.

I will adore You because I know You hear my voice, even when I do not see a solution to a problem or an answer to my prayers.

I will not stop worshiping You, even when I am weary and faint, for I know I can always trust You.

I will glorify You for Your daily provision, which sustains me in every way.

I will bless Your name for holding my hand and walking with me, which is the safest walk of life.

I thank You, Lord, for showing me Your way when I am lost.

"O, magnify the LORD with me, and let us exalt his name together" (Psalm 34:3).

Action/Thought for Today: Take a few minutes in prayer to glorify the Lord.

Prayer: Lord, forgive me for not taking the time to praise and glorify You in everything. Please give me the grace to bless Your name at all times. In Your name I pray. Amen!

WHAT A GOOD MEDICINE!

A cheerful heart is good medicine, but a crushed spirit dries up the bones.   Proverbs 17:22, NIV

I was being interviewed once, and I was very nervous, to the point my heart was racing. One of the interviewers made a simple, humorous joke, and everyone in the room laughed. At that moment, my heart felt better. The tension in the room was gone. This was the effect of laughter. Have you laughed lately?

We live in a world that is so busy, difficult, troubled, fast-paced, and goal-oriented that we sometimes forget to laugh or have a sense of humor. Laughter is good medicine. It breaks down the heaviness of the heart and brings out the joy within us. It relaxes the soul. God would not have created laughter if it were not good for us. Healthy and pure laughter is a gift from God.

As Christians, we must also be careful not to make crude jokes or make fun of others just to make someone laugh. These are times when laughter may wound the heart and rejoicing may end in grief (see Proverbs 14:13). Otherwise, let our mouths be filled with laughter as our tongues sing praise to the Lord (see Psalm 126:2). Let us laugh without fear of the future (see Proverbs 31:25) because we trust in God. Never be afraid to laugh at yourself and laugh in gratitude to God for this great blessing.

Action/Though for Today: Do you take the gift of laughter for granted? Pray for the Lord to put laughter in your mouth.

Prayer: Lord Jesus, thank You for the gift of laughter. Please give us the courage to laugh despite the pain and uncertainty of life. We rejoice in You always. In Your name we pray. Amen!

GRATEFULNESS AND THANKFULNESS!

Give thanks to the Lord, invoke his name; make known among the peoples his deeds!   Psalm 105:1, NABRE

We sometimes take for granted many of our blessings. Gratitude has many benefits in our lives:

- Gratitude opens the door to God's heart and helps us glorify Him in a deeper way.
- Gratitude allows us to accept that everything we have is because of God's grace, which is sufficient for us.
- Gratitude helps us see God's goodness amid the trials and tribulations.
- Gratitude helps us be content with what we have, which is important for a life of joy, peace, and satisfaction.
- Gratitude increases our faith as we remember God's deeds in our lives, and blindly trust Him for the future.
- Gratitude makes us recognize God's blessings.
- Gratitude brings forth generosity.
- Gratitude helps us better appreciate God's gifts in our lives, His daily sustenance and presence.

There are not enough words or songs to magnify the Lord, but with our limited words, let us open our hearts and praise the Lord today and always. Let us thank God for the gift of our family, friends, and all the blessings in our lives. Let us be content with God's blessing and appreciate His goodness.

Action/Thought for Today: Start a gratitude journal or share a testimony of God's goodness in your life on a regular basis.

Prayer: Father, give us a spirit of gratitude in all circumstances. Give us the grace not to take for granted the blessings of this life. We thank You and praise You for Your goodness and mercy. In Your name we pray. Amen!

THE GIFT OF WATER

I will sprinkle clean water on you, and you will be clean; I will cleanse you from all your impurities and from all your idols.

Ezekiel 36:25, NIV

I didn't care for water when I was younger, avoiding any activities that involved it. Over the years, I learned to appreciate the gift of water, especially coming from a third-world country where clean water is a luxury. Many may take this gift for granted because it is so readily available. However, there is a lack of water in many parts of the world. Let us reflect on some facts about this life-saving grace:

- God created water at the beginning of creation (see Genesis 1:20).
- Jesus was baptized in the River Jordan (see Matthew 3:13). We, too, are baptized in water. It purifies the soul and brings us into Christian faith.
- Jesus' first miracle involved water. He turned water into wine (see John 2:1-11).
- Jesus offered water to the Samaritan woman as a spiritual drink to renew her heart and soul (see John 4:4-42). God also places this spiritual drink at our disposal.
- Water is essential for life. It protects the baby in the womb and hydrates our body to promote health.
- Water is necessary; we bathe, clean, cook, and wash our clothes with it.
- The sound of water can be used as music to relax the mind and body.

Let us pray to be grateful for this God-given spiritual and physical blessing.

Action/Thought for Today: Make every effort to not waste water.

Prayer: Lord Jesus, thank You for pure and clean water.
Give us the grace to preserve it and bless all the third-world
countries with pure water. In Your name we pray. Amen!

TASTE AND SEE!

Taste and see that the LORD is good; blessed is the stalwart one who takes refuge in him.   Psalm 34:9, NABRE

When I tell people that I had my share of symptoms from covid-19, one question often comes up, "Did you lose your sense of taste and smell?" Thankfully, I did not. Having been asked these questions so many times made me realize the importance of the gift of taste and smell. It was a wake-up call not to take this great gift for granted. When we eat, we are better satisfied when savoring the full flavor of our food.

God is so good to us that He places at our disposal the gift of taste for our pleasure and benefit. Our taste can also prevent us from eating spoiled food. It can help us compare different flavors to choose what is best for us. We cannot deny the importance and life-saving protections of all the human senses—sight, hearing, smell, taste, and touch. Let us not take any of them for granted.

We see in the Bible that people often break bread together as a sign of love, peace, and solidarity. When we come to the table of the Lord, in the Holy Eucharist, we experience the body of Christ given to us through His love for us (see Luke 22:19-20). The Psalmist, indeed, tasted the goodness of the Lord through his encounter with Him. We, also, can taste the goodness of God when we experience Him to the fullest, acknowledging Him in everything.

Action/Thought for Today: Have you tasted the goodness of the Lord? Thank Him for His blessings.

Prayer: Lord Jesus, thank You for the five senses given to me because of Your goodness. Give me the grace not to take any of Your blessings for granted. In Your name I pray. Amen!

GIVE WHAT YOU HAVE!

What shall I return to the LORD for all his bounty to me? I will lift up the cup of salvation and call on the name of the LORD.
Psalm 116:12-13

Everything we have is from God, and He continues to sustain us. His blessings are as vast as the sea and cannot be measured. The gift of salvation alone is beyond price. How can we repay the Lord? He does not need anything from us. However, He has done so much for us that we must manifest our gratitude toward Him however we can.

In the book of Leviticus, when someone brought a guilt offering to the Lord for a sin he had committed, he would bring a lamb or a goat. If he could not afford a goat, he would provide two turtledoves or young pigeons, and if he could not afford two pigeons or turtle doves, he would bring a tenth of an ephah of fine flour (see Leviticus 5:1-13). As you can see, God accepts what we have. He never obliges us to give more than we can, but He wants us to give our best.

"Give back to Caesar what is Caesar's and to God what is God's" (Mark 12:17, NIV). The essential gift to God is an undivided heart, one that honors, loves, and worships Him. We can pay homage to God by trusting in His name for our future needs. And when we share our resources with others, we give back to God a small portion of what He has given us.

Action/Thought for Today: Have you shown gratitude to the Lord by sharing your resources with Him and others?

Prayer: Lord Jesus, thank You for all Your bounty. I praise and worship You. In Your name I pray. Amen!

FOR OUR ENJOYMENT!

As for those who in the present age are rich, command them not to be haughty, or to set their hopes on the uncertainty of riches, but rather on God who richly provides us with everything for our enjoyment.   1 Timothy 6:17

Private and public transportation were a privilege when I grew up in Haiti. Most people used bicycles, horses, donkeys, or their feet as their primary mode of transportation. My family didn't have a car, but my parents managed well, without complaining. Transportation does play a significant role in life:

- Families can easily visit each other, especially loved ones in need.
- Paramedics can transport someone to the hospital quickly, saving many lives through this service.
- School bus drivers take our kids to school, giving parents more flexibility to work or stay with little ones at home.
- Senior citizens can still go to church or community activities. Without transportation, they are cloistered in their homes, isolated from others, which can cause discouragement and depression.
- Truckers deliver our food, medicine, and other life essentials to the stores.

The list is endless. We must not take reliable transportation for granted. Are you grateful to God for it? The next time you feel like complaining about your car, think of those in third-world countries who don't have access to one or to public transportation.

Action/Thought for Today: Help someone who does not have reliable transportation.

Prayer: Lord Jesus, thank You for the many gifts You have given me for my enjoyment. In Your name I pray. Amen!

GRATITUDE IN THE MIDST OF TRIALS AND UNCERTAINTIES!

O give thanks to the LORD, for he is good, for his steadfast love endures forever. Psalm 136:1

When your world seems to be falling apart, pray that you don't focus on the problems, but, instead, count the Lord's blessings and grace. Place them in your heart, focus on the big and small miracles, and you will see the goodness of the Lord in your life.

It is vital to thank God in all things—in joys and trials, and in the many gifts He has bestowed on us. Gratefulness brings us closer to God and others. The apostle Paul reminded us: *"Always giving thanks to God the Father for everything, in the name of our Lord Jesus Christ"* (Ephesians 5:20, NIV).

Gratitude increases endurance and determination to persevere in your spiritual growth and overcome life's difficulties with peace and patience. The more grateful you are, the happier you will be. The more you appreciate God's gifts and blessings, the more God will bless you. Let us unite our voices and praise the Lord for His many benefits: *"Praise the LORD, all you, nations! Extol him, all you peoples! For great is his steadfast love toward us, and the faithfulness of the LORD endures forever. Praise the Lord!"* (Psalm 117:1-2).

Action/Thought for Today: Start a gratitude journal and thank God for His blessings daily.

Prayer: Lord Jesus, so many times I have forgotten the many blessings You bestow on me. Please forgive my ingratitude, and give me the grace to be grateful in all circumstances. Thank You, Lord, for Your goodness and kindness. It is in Your name I pray. Amen!

I SHALL SEE THE GOODNESS OF THE LORD!

I believe that I shall see the goodness of the LORD in the land of the living. Wait for the LORD; be strong, and let your heart take courage: Wait for the LORD! Psalm 27:13-14

I am writing this reflection at the time of the Covid-19 Pandemic. The coronavirus affects people differently. Some suffer from illness, job loss, or the death of a loved one. Others must deal with children home from school or social distancing and isolation. Others have their faith challenged, patience tested, plans put on hold, and lack of control comes to light. Amid these challenges, the Lord wants to transform us into His likeness. He wants us to grow in faith, rest in Him, look to Him for answers, and surrender our all to Him.

Our Father does not sleep (see Psalm 121:4); He is watching us from above with profound mercy and love. God says to all of us: *"Be still and know that I am God"* (Psalm 46:10). Trust in Me with all your heart (see Proverb 3:5), for I care for you (see Psalm 55:22), and I will never leave or forsake you (see Hebrew 13:5). I invite you to pray for a deeper trust and faith in the Lord. Abide in God with all your heart and let Him transform you into the best version of yourself as you face these trying times.

Action/Thought for Today: Pray for those who are affected by the coronavirus.

Prayer: Father God, help me trust and believe that You care and will always provide for me. Lord Jesus, I pray especially today for those who have lost their jobs, those in social isolation and those deeply affected by this virus. Father, I know that nothing is impossible with You. Therefore, I place all into Your precious hands. In Jesus' name I pray. Amen!

NOVEMBER 23

PRAISE THE LORD!

Praise the LORD! Praise the LORD, O my soul! I will praise the LORD as long as I live; I will sing praises to my God all my life long. Psalm 146:1-2

Praise the Lord today, tomorrow, and at all times. He is worthy to be exalted, for He is faithful amid adversities, turmoil, disappointments, illness, and heartache. Praise the Lord, for He is delivering us from sickness and death. Glorify the Lord, for He is opening doors of opportunity and blessing in our lives. Sing to the Lord, for He is breaking all that chains us and giving us a new life in Him. Praise the Lord again and again because He is restoring this broken world, protecting us from all evil, and sustaining us in our daily needs.

How can we stop singing and praising our God, who is so good to us all the time? When we praise the Lord, He brings light and peace to our confused world and the darkest moments of our lives. Let us praise and worship the Lord with our souls and adore Him in place of those who do not know Him or/and refuse to accept Him.

Action/Thought for Today: No matter what is going on in your life, take a few minutes to pray with one or more of the Hallelujah Psalms today (Psalms 146-150).

Prayer: Lord Jesus, we praise and worship You with all our hearts. Please give us the courage to praise You in adversity, the joy to worship You as long as we live, and the grace to help others adore and love You more and more. In Your name I pray. Amen!

HALLELUJAH TO THE KING!

My soul proclaims the greatness of the Lord, my spirit rejoices in God my Savior for he has looked upon his handmaid's lowliness; behold, from now on will all ages call me blessed.

Luke 1:46-48, NABRE

What has come to be called The Magnificat is the canticle of Mary. As noted in the Gospel of Luke, it is the hymn of praise to the Lord that she sang when she met her cousin Elizabeth. She sang this hymn to magnify God for choosing her to bear His Son. When I see the goodness of the Lord, I cannot help but sing Hallelujah to the Lord. My Hallelujah is serving the homeless, especially this time of year. My Hallelujah is praying with and for those who are sick. My Hallelujah is comforting those who are suffering. My Hallelujah is testifying of the goodness and kindness of the Lord to others. My Hallelujah is offering myself to the Lord as a living sacrifice. It is pleasing to the Lord to praise Him through the eyes and hearts of the poor, rejected, marginalized, exploited, ill, and those who suffer from racism and injustice. How do you praise the Lord for what He has done for you? What is your song of praise?

Action/Thought for Today: Write your hymn of praise to the Lord or help someone as a means of glorifying the Lord.

Prayer: Lord, I sing Hallelujah to You, for You are compassionate, kind, and full of love. Thank You for raising Your lowly servants to proclaim Your holy name. Thank You for the good deeds You have done in our lives. We praise and glorify You! We magnify You, and we sing Hallelujah to You! In Jesus' name we pray. Amen!

A CHRISTMAS CENTERED ON CHRIST!

Thanks be to God for his indescribable gift! 2 Corinthians 9:15

Right after Thanksgiving, the Christmas season begins. It is called Advent in the religious community. The stores are already filled with Christmas decorations, radio and television advertisements are well on the way, and calendars are busy with Christmas party invitations. Some already feel the busyness of the season. However, there are ways to have a Christmas centered on Christ and a stress-free holiday season. Some suggestions:

- Pray every day. Don't compromise your spiritual life.
- Read Advent meditations with your family daily.
- Do charitable projects for those who are lonely or need help, such as visiting the sick, feeding the homeless, giving a gift to a child in need, etc.
- Keep your Christmas decorations simple.
- Keep your gift list simple. Try to finish your Christmas shopping by Thanksgiving to avoid the stress of the holiday season.
- Do a little every day to leave room for prayers and family time.
- Send your Christmas cards by early December to avoid the stress of rushing at the last minute.
- Be realistic. Don't feel obligated to attend all the parties. Get together with some friends after the holiday.

Action/Thought for Today: Spend some time in prayer and ask the Lord for guidance and help.

Prayer: Lord Jesus, guide and lead me in Your way. In Your name I pray. Amen!

Choose Him!

Another said, "I will follow you, Lord, but first let me say farewell to my family at home." To him Jesus said, "No one who sets a hand to the plow and looks to what was left behind is fit for the kingdom of God." Luke 9:61-62, NABRE

For the full scripture reference, see Luke 9:57-62.

How often do we say, "I will follow You, Lord, but let me get married, finish school, or get a better job first" or, "Lord, I will serve You when my kids get older, or I retire. Then I will have more time." These things are all important, but we cannot put off following Jesus. The time to follow the Lord is now. Time will not wait for the moment when we're ready.

Are we compromising worshiping the Lord for a job or our family's needs? Are we compromising attending church because we are too busy or feel that we're not ready? Are we compromising our spiritual life for social media or TV?

Jesus is telling us to put Him first. He wants to walk with us at every stage of life, whether we have small children or are retired or busy. Jesus wants to establish our plans with us. Let us pray to seek God in every season of life.

Action/Thought for Today: Let us reflect on these words from Joshua: *"Choose today whom you will serve, but as for me and my household, we will serve the Lord"* (Joshua 24:15, NABRE).

Prayer: Lord Jesus, help me follow You without fear, hesitation, reservation, or looking back. Please help me give my all to You. In Your name I pray. Amen!

INCREASE MY CAPACITY!

Your will be done, on earth as it is in heaven. Matthew 6:10

One day, facing a dilemma and not knowing how to react or even pray on this issue, I asked the Lord to "step into the situation." The Spirit of God joined me, and my prayer changed:

Lord, increase my capacity to give without counting the cost and love beyond measure.

Increase my capacity to be joyful in all circumstances.

Increase my capacity to be still in Your presence and find peace.

Increase my capacity to forgive beyond seventy-seven times.

Increase my capacity to go where You send me without fear or hesitation.

Increase my capacity to have faith that can move mountains.

Increase my capacity to run after You without being faint or weary.

Increase my capacity to serve You and others beyond measure.

Lord, increase my thirst for You and satisfy my desire to be one with You.

Strengthen my trust and hope in You and lead me to the heart of the Father.

Friends, the Lord smoothly resolved the dilemma within a few weeks, while teaching me to love and trust Him more. It is imperative to pray, even when we don't know what to say in prayer, don't have a desire to pray, or are emotionally bruised or disturbed. God will work wonders through our prayers.

Action/Thought for Today: Pray the prayer above with me.

Prayer: Lord Jesus, thank You for Your Spirit
who prays within us and rescues us in times
of need. In Your name we pray. Amen!

ALL IS VANITY!

Vanity of vanities, says the Preacher, vanity of vanities! All is vanity. What does man gain by all the toil at which he toils under the sun?   Ecclesiastes 1:2-3, RSV

Everything is vanity and passing—our good or bad name, legacy, title, fortune or poverty, accomplishments, and everything else. This does not mean we should not do anything in life. It means we should always be mindful of God in our daily dealings. *"The world and its desires pass away, but whoever does the will of God lives forever"* (1 John 2:17, NIV). I encourage everyone to reflect and base their lives on this scripture: *"From Him [God], through Him, and to Him are all things"* (Romans 11:36).

- Everything we do should be through God. When we adopt this model, life may be challenging, but we can accept His will.

- Everything should be done for God's greater glory. If we do that, we will do His will. Even if we don't know His will, He will help us align our will with His.

- Everything should be done with God. If we walk and work with Him, we will receive the crown of life at the end of our journey.

Therefore, it is of utmost importance to pray for the grace to live a life in Christ and seek eternal life.

Action/Thought for Today: Reflect on Romans 11:36.

Prayer: Lord Jesus, walk with me, work through me, be with me, and let me do all things for Your greater glory. In Your name I pray. Amen!

SPIRITUAL INHERITANCE!

A good person leaves an inheritance for their children's children, but a sinner's wealth is stored up for the righteous. Proverbs 13:22, NIV

My parents gave me a priceless heritage—a life centered on Christ. Without realizing it, I follow in their footsteps, and my faith is a product of their spirituality. We can never know how much our children learn from us. Therefore, with God's grace, it is worth trying to be a model to our family. When my children ask me to pray for their friends, I usually say, "Let's pray together for them." I hope, by these efforts, they will learn the power of God and come to believe in Him more and more.

There is nothing wrong with accumulating wealth for our children. However, spiritual inheritance is far more valuable than wealth. *"How much better to get wisdom than gold! To get understanding is to be chosen rather than silver"* (Proverb 16:16). A wealthy person with the knowledge and wisdom of God may be more inclined to help those in need, instead of living a lavish lifestyle. Hence, they will use their inheritance for the greater glory of God.

We can pass on a spiritual inheritance through prayers and by:

- Abiding in the Lord
- Being an example of God's forgiveness, goodness, kindness, love, and mercy
- Practicing courage, humility, patience, peace, perseverance, etc.
- Using our gifts, talents, and resources wholeheartedly for God's glory.

Action/Thought for Today: What kind of inheritance will you leave for your children?

Prayer: Lord Jesus, keep me firm in the faith to pass it on from generation to generation. In Your name I pray. Amen!

THE JOY OF CHRISTMAS!

May the God of hope fill you with all joy and peace in believing, so that you may abound in hope by the power of the Holy Spirit.   Romans 15:13

Everything about Christmas is joyful. We cannot deny this fact. Homes are brightly decorated, and the colors in the streets are beautiful. We can imagine the laughter of family and friends at gatherings. Secular music echoes "Tis the season to be jolly," or "It's the most wonderful time of the year." The churches sing, "Joy to the world, the Lord has come."

Why is Christmas so joyful? This joy comes from the goodness of the Lord. He came as a baby to save humanity and give us abundant life. God is present in our sadness, trials, and tribulations. Therefore, let us pray to experience His everlasting joy and peace. Despite our difficulties, we must embrace the joy of the Lord, share it with others, and fight to remain joyful.

Action/Thought for today: Are you willing to accept the joy of the Lord despite life's misfortunes and uncertainties? Ask the Lord for His grace.

Prayer: Lord Jesus, help us experience the joy of Your salvation in our sadness, trials, and tribulation. It is in Your name I pray. Amen!

CHRISTMAS DECORATIONS!

And you will have joy and gladness, and many will rejoice at his birth.   Luke 1:14-16, RSV

As we joyfully decorate our homes for Christmas, let us turn our hearts to Jesus in gratitude for the gift of Himself.

- As you hang your ornaments on the Christmas tree, turn your heart into a tree and decorate it with joy, love, humility, kindness, and peace. Ask the Lord to help you maintain these spiritual ornaments.
- Let the ribbon on your tree or wreath be a cord of unity in your family, workplace, and community.
- Let the treetop star be your guiding light so that others can follow your footsteps, just as the magi followed the star that led them to Jesus.
- As you place gifts under your tree, offer the gift of yourself to God as a living sacrifice. He continues to give Himself daily to save us. Ask Him to help you be a gift of encouragement, loyalty, and prayer to others.
- Fill your Christmas stockings with a spiritual message bringing hope and good tidings to family and friends.
- Carry the Christmas spirit in your heart as you serve those who are in need this season.
- As you arrange the nativity set in your home, let Christ's love be reborn in you.

Action/Thought for Today: Turn your Christmas decorating activities into a prayer.

Prayer: Lord Jesus, let me see You in all things. Help me bring You into all the activities of my daily life. In Your name I pray. Amen!

ANOINTED FOR GOD'S WORK!

Rejoice with those who rejoice, weep with those who weep.

Romans 12:15

I see so many Christmas ornaments and decorations everywhere this season, but do you see Jesus? I see Jesus in the brokenhearted. I see Jesus in the poor in spirit. I find Jesus in the heart of the homeless, sick, poor, rejected, and lonely. *"The Lord is near to the brokenhearted and saves the crushed in spirit"* (Psalm 34:18). Let us make an effort to look for Jesus in others. Let us open our hearts to all during the holiday season and at all times.

Christmas must not be a one-day-per-year event; we can make it daily ... if we love each other, share our talents and goods, and support those in need. We ought to pray and strive to have the Christmas attitude every day, participating in Jesus' mission as noted in Isaiah 61:1: *"To proclaim good news to the poor, to bind up the brokenhearted, to proclaim freedom to the captives, and release from darkness the prisoners"* (NIV). We are all anointed to build up God's people.

Action/Thought for Today: How can you be Jesus for someone this week?

Prayer: Lord Jesus, give me the grace to bring You to the homeless, sick, poor, rejected, and lonely. Give me a compassionate heart and help me to rejoice with those who rejoice and weep with those who weep. Teach me to bind up the brokenhearted and be Jesus to those I encounter daily. In Your name I pray. Amen!

LORD, GIVE ME EARS TO HEAR YOU!

The seed sown on rocky ground is the one who hears the word and receives it at once with joy. Matthew 13:20, NABRE

Christmas music, movies, and stories are everywhere, on the radio, TV, etc. There is no dispute that Christmas entertainments are joyful and uplifting; however, we can get carried away by them. What are we listening to, the multiple festivities of the world or the voice of Jesus? The devil wants to distract us with the noise of the secular world during this holy season so that we fail to listen to the voice of God. Let us stand firm in the faith, steadfast in prayer, and defeat the evil one by fixing our minds, thoughts, eyes, ears, and hearts on Jesus to receive His love and words with joy. Ask the Lord for the grace to have ears to hear His gentle voice and guidance. Take courage, and know that although our prayers are imperfect, God never fails to listen to us because He loves us so much. Therefore, let us pay attention to His voice as well.

Action/Thought for Today: In your prayer today, take five minutes of silence to listen to the whisper of God's voice.

Prayer: Lord Jesus, speak, for Your servants are listening (see 1 Samuel 3:10). Please give us the grace to hear with our hearts and ears and receive Your Word with joy. Help us fix our minds, thoughts, eyes, ears, and hearts on You only. In Your name I pray. Amen!

GO TELL IT!

*Today in the town of David a Savior has been born to you; he is
the Messiah, the Lord.*   Luke 2:11, NIV

One of my favorite Christmas songs goes, "Go, tell it on the
mountain, over the hills and everywhere; go, tell it on the mountain that Jesus Christ is born." Are you telling the message of
Christmas to your family, at work, in casual conversation, and
everywhere else? Or are you debating with others on the latest
gifts available or what they want for Christmas? Is Christmas
"business as usual," going to the traditional festivities and buy-
ing gifts?

I've heard many say, "It doesn't feel like Christmas this year," or
"Something is missing this Christmas." What is missing is the
turning of our hearts into a cradle to receive Jesus. It doesn't feel
like Christmas because we're searching for Christ in the wrong
places, instead of looking deeply into our own souls and opening our hearts in prayer and thanksgiving to appreciate the gift
of Jesus. Therefore, let's go tell everyone that the Good News of
Christmas is still alive in the hearts of the faithful. Tell everyone
that we are celebrating because we believe that our Savior was
born to live among us, to teach us how to live and love, and to
dwell in our hearts. What is your reason for celebrating this
season?

Action/Thought for Today: As you gather with family and
friends this Christmas, please take some time to testify. Tell
them what Christmas means to you. Pray that they will learn
something special from your experience with the Lord.

Prayer: Lord Jesus, give me the grace to proclaim the message
of Christmas wherever I go. In Your name I pray. Amen!

THE FIRST NOEL

But when the fullness of time had come, God sent his Son, born of a woman, born under the law, in order to redeem those who were under the law, so that we might receive adoption as children.
Galatians 4:4-5

I first learned the Christmas carol, "The First Noel," in high school, and it has impacted my life. I imagine the shepherds who saw the star and followed it to see Jesus. I imagine what the angels and poor shepherds working in the field experienced when they found the King of kings. Their joy must have been beyond understanding, and they had the privilege of worshiping the Lord. It is also an honor for us to experience the birth of Jesus in our hearts and through the eyes of our ancestors.

- Since the first Noel, Christmas has come yearly, but the traditions and message of Christmas have never changed.
- Different parts of the world and different families celebrate Christmas differently, but it is still a message of LOVE.
- If we each take a different day and call it Christmas, the message will be the same LOVE was born on Christmas Day.

Love came down to save humanity. For God so loved the world, that He sent His only Son to save us (see John 3:16). When we celebrate with friends and family this year, let us put the gifts and festivities aside and take some time to reflect on the true meaning of the love of Christmas.

Action/Thought for Today: What are some steps you can take to make Jesus the reason for Christmas?

Prayer: Lord Jesus, give me the spirit of Christmas so that I can welcome You in my heart and home. In Your name I pray. Amen!

December 6

I Need Your Grace!

I trust in your mercy. Grant my heart joy in your salvation, I will sing to the Lord, for he has dealt bountifully with me!

Psalm 13:6, NABRE

I am writing this reflection during the Covid-19 Pandemic in December 2020. Although it is the Christmas season, we are going into the second wave of this virus. Many states have mandated that people not gather with others, only their own households. Many may say, "How can I be joyful this Christmas? How can I enjoy this special holiday with friends and family?" As Christians, we must make the best of life, be radiant, and bring joy to our environment regardless of the situation. We were created to bring the light and joy of Christ to others; therefore, our attitude must reflect Christ at all times. We ought to strive not to let the disappointments of life, our misfortunes, or others' shortcomings change our mood and bring desolation or discouragement. Let us look upon the Lord to fill us with everlasting joy and blessing. His grace is always sufficient for us, and His power is made perfect in weakness (see 2 Corinthians 12:9).

Action/Thought for Today: No matter what happens today, let us strive to keep our hearts joyful through God's grace.

Prayer: Lord Jesus, give us the fruit of the Holy Spirit—JOY. Thank You for this precious gift. Help us always to remember that the *"joy of the Lord is our strength"* (Nehemiah 8:10). In Your name we pray! Amen!

December 7

Spiritual Alertness!

Beware, keep alert; for you do not know when that time will come.   Mark 13:33

*For the full scripture reference, see Mark 13:32-37.

Advent reminds us that we must be alert and awake at all times and ready for the Second Coming of the Lord. We do not know His timing. Preparation for the Lord's return is a difficult undertaking, but it must be part of our daily lives, regardless of our struggles. This constant effort requires God's grace, for we cannot save ourselves. However, our willingness to respond to His grace is crucial. We sometimes fall short in partnering with God for our salvation, so we must pray for the grace to recognize our faults and begin again.

Let us ask the Lord to give us a new strength to stay firm in the faith despite life's many problems. Let us also pray for the courage to wait with hope for His final coming. At the end of times or of our lives, let us pray to be able to echo the apostle Paul, *"I have competed well; I have finished the race, I have kept the faith. From now on the crown of righteousness awaits me, which the Lord, the just judge, will award to me on that day, and not only to me, but to all who have longed for his appearance"* (2 Timothy 4:7-8, NABRE).

Action/Thought for Today: Take one step today to prepare for the Lord's Second Coming.

Prayer: Lord Jesus, give me the grace to be alert, awake, and ready as I wait for Your Second Coming. Please give me the wisdom to know what to do to be prepared for You always. Guide me in Your way, dear Lord. In Your name I pray. Amen!

READY FOR THE LORD?

Rejoice in hope, be patient in suffering, persevere in prayer.

Romans 12:12

Preparation, discipline, and planning are essential for success in everything in life. Whether it is your spiritual, family, social, or professional life, every aspect requires some level of discipline and planning. A few years ago, for my mom's 75th birthday, we organized a special celebration with family and friends. We planned the event for six months, and it was a success. As I reflect on this, it reminds me that I must make the same effort to prepare for the Lord's coming.

Where am I in my spiritual journey with the Lord? Am I spending time in prayer, or am I too busy with the world and Christmas activities during this holiday season? Am I serving those in need, or am I too preoccupied in my own world? Am I rejoicing in the hope of the Lord or too worried about my tomorrow?

Let us make a conscious effort to make God the center of our lives as we wait patiently for His coming. With a prayer of praise, intercession, and thanksgiving to the Lord, let us prepare our hearts more deeply, so we can fully rejoice at Christmas and always.

Action/Thought for Today: Let us take a few minutes to reflect on the questions above.

Prayer: Lord Jesus, give me the grace to rejoice in Your name, the wisdom to plan for Your final coming, and the discipline to pray and worship You always. Thank You for Your love, kindness, and mercy. In Your name I pray. Amen!

CHRIST'S LIGHT!

For so the Lord has commanded us, saying, "I have set you to be a light for the Gentiles, so that you may bring salvation to the ends of the earth." Acts 13:47

I see so many Christmas lights everywhere—in the streets, businesses, and homes. These lights may be beautiful, but what the world needs right now is Jesus—the true and everlasting Light. The light of Christ points us in the right direction, frees us from bondage, and gives us clarity to do the right thing.

This Advent, are you being guided by the lights in the streets or the light of Christ? Are you lighting up someone's life or only your home? Christ calls us to live in His light and be the light of the world by bringing good tidings to others, touching the less fortunate, and encouraging everyone with hope and love. Rejoice always, for the Lord has chosen you to be the light in this world. I encourage you to sit at the feet of Jesus, fervently praying to experience His light and to make a difference in someone's life, by showing the light of Christ to them.

Action/Thought for Today: How can you bring the light of Christ to others? Make a plan, pray about it, and go for it.

Prayer: Lord Jesus, give me the grace to bring Your light to others for Your glory. Give me the grace to use the gift You have given me and be an instrument of peace, joy, and love. I pray in the holy name of Jesus. May He be glorified in Heaven and on Earth. Amen!

READY TO RECEIVE THE KING?

Happy the one who listens to me, attending daily at my gates, keeping watch at my doorposts; for whoever finds me finds life, and wins favor from the LORD. Proverbs 8:34-35, NABRE

We are a few days away from Christmas, and the King is coming in majesty! Are you finished with your home decorating? Have you completed your Christmas shopping, your gift wrapping, and festivity planning? There is nothing wrong with all these preparations and the gatherings of friends and family. But how are you preparing your heart to celebrate the birth of our King once again? Are you ready to receive the King?

- Now is the right time to prepare your heart for the Second Coming of the Lord.
- Now is the right time to spend more time praying and worshiping the Lord.
- It is never too late to be ready and to offer the King your heart, mind, soul, and all that you are and have.
- It is never too late to ask the Lord for forgiveness to repent from wrongdoing and resolve to live for God.

Indeed, it is time to deepen our relationship with God. Let us keep Christ in our hearts as we approach Christmas and for the rest of our lives. This season will then be more meaningful to us.

Action/Thought for Today: How are you preparing your heart to receive the King?

Prayer: Heavenly Father, help us prepare our hearts for the Second Coming of Your Son, Jesus, who will come once again to judge the living and the dead. Thank You, Lord, for the gift of salvation. It is in Jesus' name I pray. Amen!

GOD REJOICES OVER YOU!

Or suppose a woman has ten silver coins and loses one. Doesn't she light a lamp, sweep the house and search carefully until she finds it? And when she finds it, she calls her friends and neighbors together and says, "Rejoice with me; I have found my lost coin." Luke 15:8-9, NIV

Will you be home for Christmas? When a family member or friend calls and says: "I'll be home for Christmas," or, "I'm spending Christmas with you," I rejoice as I prepare my home, the best meal, and plan fun times together. Jesus also rejoices when we return to Him and spend time with Him in prayer. He sings for joy every time we repent after sinning and resolve to do better. He also rejoices with us when we praise and worship Him.

Will you be spending time with Jesus this Christmas? Will you return to Him without reservation? Will you prepare your heart and rid yourself of bitterness, anxiety, anger, unforgiveness, as well as the world's affairs? Go home to Jesus, and take Him all your burdens and concerns, as well as your joys, achievements, and successes. He is ready to welcome you, help you, and give you peace and joy this Christmas and always. God is speaking to you today and saying: "I delight in you" (see Psalm 149:4). He desires for you to be saved (see 1 Timothy 2:4), so that one day you can be with Him forever in Heaven, your final home.

Action/Thought for Today: Reflect on the above questions and make or review your plan to go to Jesus.

Prayer: Lord Jesus, thank You for rejoicing over us every time we return to You. In Your name I pray. Amen!

REJOICE IN GOD'S PEACE AND HOPE!

The angel said to them [the Shepherds], "Do not be afraid; for behold, I proclaim to you good news of great joy that will be for all the people. For today in the city of David a savior has been born for you who is the Messiah and Lord.

Luke 2:10-11, NABRE

*For the full scripture reference, see Luke 2:8-20.

"Do not be afraid!" In the Scriptures, Jesus repeated this phrase many times. He came to this troubled world to give us peace, and He does not want us to live in fear. Fear is an enemy of our soul; it keeps us captivated and takes away our joy. Fear also takes away our hope and peace, and disturbs us in the walk of faith, preventing us from receiving God's blessings. It is the tactic of the enemy to distract us from God's presence in our lives.

Most of the things we are afraid of never happen. Yet, some of us are afraid of the future and the unknown. Through prayers of praise, thanksgiving, and invoking Jesus' mighty name and power, let us take our joy and peace back from the enemy and live according to God's will. Let us pray to stand firm in our decision that fear is no longer welcome and has no place in our lives, for we are covered under God's mantle of grace. I say again: Rejoice in God's peace and hope!

Action/Thought for Today: Pray for the grace to not let fear control your life.

Prayer: Glory and praise to You, Lord Jesus, for You have come to bring us peace, joy, and love. Thank You for delivering us from fear, Lord. You are worthy to be praised. At the name of Jesus, may all knees bend in Heaven and on Earth. In Jesus' name I pray. Amen!

WISH LIST!

Elijah was a human being like us, and he prayed fervently that it might not rain and for three years and six months it did not rain on earth. Then he prayed again, and the heaven gave rain and the earth yielded its harvest. James 5:17-18

As a child, if I asked for something special for Christmas, my parents always tried to please me. As an adult, I do the same for my family members. We are all longing for something special for Christmas and in life. What do you want this Christmas? Are you hoping for spiritual gifts or financial, physical, and personal blessings? Perhaps for a wish to come true? Just as the Lord answered Elijah's prayer, He will do the same for you. Therefore, don't lose hope. Continue to pray fervently. Jesus will bless you with your heart's desire.

In this troubling and uncertain life, all I want for Christmas is to rejoice in Jesus, my Savior. All I want for Christmas is for my friends, family, and everyone else around me to be well and sit with me at the feet of Jesus to contemplate His majesty. There is no better place to be than in the heart of Jesus. Having Jesus as Friend is my greatest treasure and Christmas gift.

Action/Thought for Today: Just like Jesus, be a gift to someone today. Let them know that you care. Help your family and friends rejoice in the Lord.

Prayer: Thank You, Lord Jesus, for being my Best Friend! Thank You for answered prayers. Please give me the grace to sit at Your feet all the days of my life. Praise You, O Lord! I rejoice in Your goodness and mercy. In Jesus' name I pray! Amen!

CHRISTMAS IS A GIFT OF LOVE!

Although you have not seen him you love him; even though you do not see him now yet believe in him, you rejoice with an indescribable and glorious joy, as you attain the goal of [your] faith, the salvation of your souls.　　　　1 Peter 1:8-9, NABRE

As we prepare for Christmas, the focus must be on Jesus, for He is the reason for this special time. There would no Christmas without Jesus, our Savior. His birth reminds us of the ultimate sacrifice He made, coming to Earth in the likeness of man, to save us through the cross and give us peace and joy. He did it all for our future joy, a priceless gift. We should be *"Looking to Jesus the pioneer and the perfecter of our faith, who for the sake of the joy that was set before him endured the cross, disregarding its shame, and has taken his seat at the right hand of the throne of God"* (Hebrew 12:2). Jesus has given His life for you. Have you given your heart to Him without limit? Do you love God and your neighbor without reservation? The Lord teaches us to *"Love the Lord, your God, with all your heart, with all your being, with all your strength, and with all your mind, and your neighbor as yourself"* (Luke 10:27, NABRE). Christmas is a gift of love!

Action/Thought for Today: God is challenging you to love Him and your neighbors. Do you truly love Him and them?

Prayer: Lord Jesus, give us the grace to give You our hearts. Fill us with inexpressible and glorious joy as we surrender our all to You. Give us the grace to love You and our neighbors. In Your name we pray. Amen!

LESSONS FROM ANNA!

She [Anna] never left the temple, but worshiped night and day with fasting and prayer. And coming forward at that very time, she gave thanks to God and spoke about the child to all who were awaiting the redemption of Jerusalem. Luke 2:37-38, NABRE

Mary and Joseph took Jesus to Jerusalem to present Him to the Lord: *"As it is written in the law of the Lord, every firstborn male shall be designated as holy to the Lord"* (Luke 2:23). At that time, the prophetess Anna, an elderly widow, spoke wisely about the child. Anna was filled with the Holy Spirit who revealed to her the true essence of the Child Jesus. She spoke to all who had been waiting for the coming of a Savior.

We can learn from Anna's prayer life. She lived quietly, never left the temple, and worshiped day and night with fasting and prayer (see Luke 2:37). Her connection with the Holy Spirit grew with prayer. We may not be like Anna, but we can devote ourselves to prayer (see Colossians 4:2) and make it our top priority. By putting God first in our lives, our relationship with Him will deepen. Jesus is also our model, for prayer was a significant part of His life. The Scriptures teach us that He often prayed as a means of communicating with His Father.

No one has enough time. When we are busy and preoccupied in our worlds, the first thing to go is our prayer time. Anna taught us to sit at the feet of Jesus and that His presence will be evident in us through the power of the Holy Spirit.

Action/Thought for Today: How can we model Anna's life of prayer?

Prayer: Lord Jesus, increase my love for prayer so that I can worship You without ceasing. It is in Your name I pray. Amen!

REJOICE, PRAY, AND GIVE THANKS!

Rejoice always, pray without ceasing, give thanks in all circumstances; for this is the will of God in Christ Jesus for you.
1 Thessalonian 5:16-18

To rejoice, pray, and give thanks are some of the instructions given to us by the apostle Paul, as we wait patiently for the Second Coming of the Lord. We must imitate the attitude of the disciples and rejoice despite persecutions or trials. We ought to pray frequently, raising our hearts and minds to the Lord often, and He will make a way for us in everything. The Lord never said we would be free of troubles; instead, He said, *"I am with you always, to the end of the age"* (Matthew 28:20). Therefore, pray and be thankful for his interventions. We should strive to give thanks at all times for God is with us in joy and success, as well as sorrow, failures, and disappointments. When we practice those teachings from the apostle Paul, the Holy Spirit fills us with joy and transforms our lives from negative to positive. Furthermore, our lives are more meaningful, joyful, grateful, and filled with God's grace and blessings.

Action/Thought for Today: Examine yourself. Are you joyful, prayerful, and grateful at all times?

Prayer: Lord Jesus, bless us with the gift of joy amid trials and persecutions. Teach us to pray always and to have a grateful heart. In Your name we pray. Amen!

WHO DO YOU SAY THAT I AM?

When John heard in prison what the Messiah was doing, he sent word by his disciples and said to him, "Are you the one who is to come, or are we to wait for another?" Matthew 11:2-3

While John was in prison, facing death, and with no hope of deliverance, perhaps he may have been disappointed in Jesus for not rescuing him. We can see that he was uncertain about whether or not Jesus was the Messiah. He sent the disciples to inquire about Jesus' true identity. But Jesus told the disciples to tell John what they had heard and seen, so they could assure him that Jesus was indeed the Christ. Jesus was bringing joy and peace to those who were suffering through healing, restoration, and comfort.

When you look at the chaos in this world, do you sometimes question the presence of the Lord? In your suffering and disappointment, do you wonder where Jesus is? The Lord continues to send His messengers to proclaim the Good News and reassure us that He is the Messiah. Jesus works miracles every day, in ways we sometimes cannot see. He continues to perform wondrous deeds in our time. We must trust Him through the ups and downs of life and expect that all will be well. God's plan may not be what we have hoped for, but it will always be the best for us, according to His wisdom. Therefore, rejoice and trust in the Lord!

Action/Thought for Today: Reflect on this question from the Lord: *"Who do you say that I am?"* (Matthew 16:15).

Prayer: Lord, so many times I doubt who You are. Please give me the grace to recognize Your wondrous deeds in my life and to trust You in all things. In Your name I pray. Amen!

RESPONDING TO THE KING WITH FAITHFULNESS!

Now this is how the birth of Jesus Christ came about. When his mother Mary was betrothed to Joseph, but before they lived together, she was found with child through the Holy Spirit. Matthew 1:18

*For the full scripture, see Matthew 1:18-25.

Mary was engaged to Joseph, but before they were married, he discovered that she was pregnant. Because it was unclear to him how that happened, Joseph decided to divorce her quietly and not expose her to public embarrassment. But then an angel of the Lord appeared to him in a dream and said: *"Joseph, son of David, do not be afraid to take Mary your wife into your home. For it is through the Holy Spirit that this child has been conceived in her"* (Matthew 18:20, NABRE).

When God revealed to Joseph His plans that Jesus would save the world, Joseph did not ask any more questions. He did what the angel had commanded him. Joseph's actions demonstrated his faithfulness to the Lord and that he had entrusted himself entirely to His Creator.

We must follow the footsteps of Joseph and surrender our all to the Lord. This surrendering to God is well expressed in the prayer of St. Ignatius of Loyola: *"Take, Lord and receive all my liberty, my memory, my understanding, and my entire will. All I have and call my own, you have given to me; to you, Lord, I return it. Everything is yours; do with it what you will. Give me only your love and your grace. That is enough for me"* (Paraphrased by David L. Fleming, S.J.).[33]

Action/Thought for Today: Will you let the Lord take control of your life? Will you trust Him?

Prayer: Lord Jesus, bless us with the grace to respond to You with the faithfulness and wisdom of Joseph, so that You can work extraordinary things through us. In Your name we pray. Amen!

WOULD YOU TRUST THE KING?

But the angel said to him, "Do not be afraid, Zechariah, for your prayer has been heard. Your wife Elizabeth will bear you a son, and you will name him John." Luke 1:13

*For the full scripture, see Luke 1:5-25.

Elizabeth and Zechariah were righteous before God, but they had no children. Elizabeth was barren, and both were advanced in age (see Luke 1:7). The angel Gabriel appeared and revealed to Zechariah that his wife would have a son, and he should be called John (see Luke 1:8-13). His mission would be to prepare people for the coming of the Lord. Zechariah was skeptical of the angel's message and questioned him, *"How will I know that this is so?"* (Luke 8:18).

Joseph and Zechariah were both righteous men, but when God revealed His plans to them, they responded differently. Joseph answered with faithfulness; Zechariah doubted. How do you react when the Lord chooses you to carry out His mission? We tend to be more ready to answer God with love and faithfulness when we can understand His plan for us. However, when things are not going as expected or the Lord surprises us with a mission, we may respond with fear, disbelief, and doubt. In both instances, God said, "Do not be afraid; I am about to work wonders in your life through the Holy Spirit. Will you trust Me?"

Action/Thought for Today: When God surprises you with a mission, do you react like Joseph or Zechariah?

Prayer: Lord Jesus, so many times You choose to work miracles in our lives, but our disbelief prevents us from cooperating with You. Please help us trust You in all circumstances. In Your name we pray. Amen!

YES, TO THE KING!

The angel said to her, "Do not be afraid, Mary, for you have found favor with God. And now, you will conceive in your womb and bear a son, and you will name him Jesus."   Luke 1: 30-31

*For the full scripture, see Luke 1:26-38

Mary was a poor, very young, Jewish girl, but God chose her to be the mother of Jesus. I wonder how much Mary understood when the angel Gabriel told her that she would conceive a child named Jesus, He would be great, and His Kingdom would have no end (see Luke 1:32-33). Knowing that she had no relationship with a man, Mary must have been confused and afraid, but she accepted without hesitation because she loved and trusted the Lord. Mary must have known that her mission was not a simple task. Nevertheless, she said yes and became part of salvation history.

God uses ordinary people like Mary to do extraordinary work in this world. They usually start with a simple yes to the Lord, letting go of themselves, trusting in the work of God, and allowing Him to use them to the fullest for His glory. Sometimes, God does not reveal His plan at the beginning of their mission. However, their faith and obedience to the Lord empower them for His calling in their lives.

Today, God chooses us to continue His work of salvation. He asks all of us to grow in faith and obedience so that He can fulfill His purpose through us.

Action/Thought for Today: Do you want to do extraordinary work for the Lord but feel that you cannot serve Him because you are an ordinary person? Just say yes, and God will use you!

Prayer: Father God, I give You full permission. Have Your way with me and use me for Your purpose and mission. I pray in Jesus' name. Amen!

BEHOLD, THE KING IS COMING TO YOU!

Exult greatly, O daughter of Zion! Shout for joy, O daughter of Jerusalem! Behold: your king is coming to you, a just savior is he, humble, and riding on a donkey, on a colt, the foal of a donkey.
Zechariah 9:9, NABRE

When a king, president, or world leader is traveling or coming to a city, he or she is protected by police and security, and city officials clear the streets to ensure the dignitary's safety. Jesus, the true King, and the Kings of kings, came humbly, riding on a donkey in the streets of Jerusalem. He did not need any security or any barriers from the people in the streets, for He came to save us. He came to forgive our sins, heal the sick, set the prisoners free, deliver us from all evils, and give us everlasting joy and peace.

What a glorious sight it must have been for the crowd to welcome the promised Messiah in Jerusalem! We, too, must accept Him and rejoice greatly, for the Lord comes to us in our daily struggles, our joys, and our pain. As we are getting ready for Christmas, let us remember the first coming of the Lord and prepare for and patiently wait for His Second Coming. Are you prepared to receive the King?

Action/Thought for Today: Pray for the grace to receive the King in your heart and life.

Prayer: Lord Jesus, I am not worthy to receive You in my heart, soul, and spirit, but I offer You myself as a living sacrifice. I present to You my prayers of thanksgiving, petition, praise, and adoration. I offer You my joys, works, and sufferings. I give You my talents, time, and service. Please accept all that I am and all that I have. In Your name I pray. Amen!

SEEK CHRIST AT CHRISTMAS AND ALWAYS!

But let all who take refuge in you rejoice; let them ever sing for joy. Spread your protection over them, so that those who love your name may exult in you. Psalm 5:11

Christmas is just a few days away. Some people feel the typical holiday stress. They worry they do not have enough time to get things done before Christmas: gift wrapping, Christmas shopping, etc. Some are sad, upset, feeling isolated due to their situations. Where is Jesus in all of this? Have you missed your prayer routine during this time because of all the things you have to do?

In my prayer, the Lord asked me to focus on Him, for He is the Source of all good things. He is, indeed, the Source of my joy, hope, and peace. The Lord extends the same message to you. He asks you to let go of the distractions of the season and bring your heart closer to Him.

Therefore, family in Christ, do not search for joy and peace in the wrong places. Search for Christ in your heart, and He will give you peace. Remember to keep Christ in Christmas, seek Him at Christmas and all times, and let Him find you. Let us continue to open our hearts to receive the King, to take refuge in Him, and to *"let the light of his face shine on us"* (Psalm 4:6).

Action/Thought for Today: As we continue our Advent journey, examine yourself to see where your heart is.

Prayer: Lord Jesus, You are the Source of all good things. Help us not to be consumed with the typical holiday stress and distraction. Give us the grace to take refuge in You and to seek You in all that we do. We pray in Your name. Amen!

EMMANUEL! EMMANUEL!

Look, the virgin shall conceive and bear a son, and they shall name him, "Emmanuel," which means "God is with us."

Matthew 1:23

Rejoice! Rejoice! Jesus came to this Earth to be with us and He lives in our hearts. We do not have to search for Him in specific signs or wonders. The Kingdom of God is in our midst. He also lives in the hearts of our family members and friends, as well as in strangers in the street. He is in the small details, as well as in the significant events of our lives.

I know some people have difficulty believing in things they cannot see, but *"The kingdom of God is not coming with things that can be observed; nor will they say, "Look here it is! or "There it is!" For, in fact, the kingdom of God is among you"* (Luke 17:20-21). Sometimes, we do not recognize God in our lives, but if we pay closer attention to His movement, we will see Him and how He arranges things for us and others. Even when God is silent, we must strive to remember that He is with us and within us. He wants to dwell in us and bring us everlasting joy. Therefore, let us be mindful to look for the Lord in our day-to-day living; He is always with us.

Action/Thought for Today: Spend some quiet time with the Lord today and let Him rest in your heart.

Prayer: Lord Jesus, help us to remain in You and You in us. O come, Emmanuel, and live in our heart forever. In Your name we pray. Amen!

O COME, LET US ADORE HIM!

Jesus was born two thousand years ago. His birth remains the most famous in world history. His birth changes our lives forever, for He blesses us with the gift of salvation. Let us reflect on some life lessons from the story of Jesus' birth:

Joy in Our Trials!

And Joseph too went up from Galilee from the town of Nazareth to Judea, to the city of David that is called Bethlehem, because he was of the house and family of David, to be enrolled with Mary, his betrothed, who was with child. While they were there, the time came for her to have her child. Luke 2:4-6, NABRE

Joseph and Mary arrived in Bethlehem and could not find a room in the inn to spend the night. Imagine Mary and Joseph finding joy amid their trials because Jesus was with them. We, too, can find joy in the ups and downs of life if we know Jesus.

Humility!

And she gave birth to her firstborn son. She wrapped him in swaddling clothes and laid him in a manger because there was no room for them in the inn. Luke 2:7, NABRE

Mary gave birth in a stable and placed Jesus in a manger. It was hardly the best accommodation to deliver a baby, yet Jesus, our King, was born there. Mary and Joseph accepted their modest lodging. Do you complain when things don't go your way? Let us pray to accept the will of God.

Jesus taught us humility by his birth. He came as a baby, depending on His parents to care for Him. Do you rely on Jesus for everything? Do you accept help from others?

Jesus came as a poor person, visited by the shepherds. Do you see Jesus in the poor or do you look away?

Glorify God!

The angel said to them [the shepherds], "Do not be afraid; for behold, I proclaim to you good news of great joy that will be for all the people. For today in the city of David, a savior has been born for you who is Messiah and Lord." Luke 2:10-11, NABRE

The shepherds received the message of the birth of Jesus and were filled with joy. They went to worship the Lord. Do you accept the news of the gospel joyfully? Do you adore Jesus in good and bad times?

Action/Thought for Today: Let us adore and glorify Christ with humility and sincerity of heart.

Prayer: Lord Jesus, we adore You in the manger of our hearts. *"Glory to God in the highest and on earth peace to those on whom his favor rests"* (Luke 2:14, NABRE). In Your name we pray. Amen!

THE GREATNESS OF HIS GOVERNMENT!

For unto us a child is born, unto us a son is given; and the government shall be upon his shoulder: and his name shall be called Wonderful, Counsellor, Mighty God, Everlasting Father, Prince of Peace.
Isaiah 9:6, ERV

In this day and age, most people have little to no confidence in our world and national leaders. But we can find comfort that the everlasting government is resting on Jesus' shoulder, for He is our mighty God and Father. With Jesus' government, we don't have to worry about partiality, where one group is better off than another. We can take comfort knowing that our King, Jesus, will govern with dignity, kindness, love, and fairness. This news should fill us with joy, hope, and peace.

Furthermore, Jesus will make all things right, restore His creation, and there will be eternal joy in His Kingdom. As noted in Psalm 146:7-9, "The LORD executes justice for the oppressed; who gives food to the hungry. The LORD sets the prisoners free; the LORD opens the eyes of the blind. The LORD lifts up those who are bowed down; the LORD loves the righteous. The LORD watches over the strangers; he upholds the orphan and the widow, but the way of the wicked he brings to ruin." Therefore, let us rejoice in Jesus and glorify Him. Let us bring the Good News of the Gospel to all people, especially those losing hope and trust in the Lord.

Action/Thought for Today: How can you help others believe in the Good News of the Gospel?

Prayer: Lord Jesus, thank You for filling us with hope, joy, and peace. Please give us the grace to believe in the Good News of the Gospel. In Your name we pray. Amen!

December 26

Our Treasure Chests!

On entering the house, they [the wise men] saw the child with Mary, his mother; and they knelt down and paid homage. Then, opening their treasure chests, they offered him gifts of gold, frankincense, and myrrh. Matthew 2:11

*For the full scripture, see Matthew 2:1-12.

The story of the three wise men calls us to bow down, worship, and offer the King our all. What have you given to Jesus lately? Are you ready to lay down your all for His glory? Let us reflect on some of the gifts in our treasure chests that we can offer to Him.

Our Heart: Have you given your heart to the Lord without limit? God will always accept the hearts of those who seek Him.

Our Time: Do you sometimes forget to spend time with Jesus in prayer? Let's try to spend more quiet time with Jesus every day. He reminds us: *"Be still and know that I am God"* (Psalm 46:10).

Our Talent: Have you used your talents to serve the Lord? He has given you many spiritual gifts and blessings to enrich you (see 1 Corinthians 12:1-11).

Our Service: When you serve others humbly, you serve Jesus.

Our Tithes: Have you given God His fair portion? Have you helped others in need? *"Give, and it will be given to you. A good measure, pressed down"* (Luke 6:38.)

Action/Thought for Today: What do you want to offer to Jesus?

Prayer: Lord Jesus, we worship and praise You with our hearts, and we offer our all to You. It is in Your name we pray. Amen!

THROUGH JESUS, HIS SON!

Long ago God spoke to our ancestors in many and various ways by the prophets, but in these last days he has spoken to us by a Son whom he appointed heir of all things, through whom he also created the worlds.   Hebrews 1:1-2

In the past, God, the Father, communicated to our ancestors through His prophets, through dreams, visions, and visits from angels, etc. Most recently, He has been speaking to us through Jesus Christ, His Son. Through Jesus, we can see and talk to the Father, for Jesus is "the exact imprint of God's very being" (Hebrews 1:3). *"He is the image of the invisible God, the firstborn over all creation"* (Colossians 1:15). If we want to know what God is like or how He thinks, we must know Jesus, His character, teachings, and actions, etc.

How well do you know the Son of God? To know Jesus, we must read His words, meditate on His life, listen to His voice, and most importantly, spend time in prayer with Him. The more time we devote to know Jesus, the more we will know the Father. God sent Jesus to this world for us to have full knowledge of Him and have a personal relationship with Him. For, *"No one comes to the Father except through me,"* said Jesus (John 14:6). Therefore, let us abide in Jesus, and through Him, we can hear and see God, the Father.

Action/Thought for Today: How well do you know Jesus? How might you know Him better?

Prayer: Father God, thank You for giving us Jesus as our Savior and, through Him, allowing us to know You better. Please give us the grace to have a more profound knowledge of You. In Your name we pray. Amen!

His Father's Will!

[Jesus said], "I came down from heaven not to do my own will but the will of the one who sent me." John 6:38, NABRE

Jesus came down from Heaven as a baby to do his Father's will. Despite many trials, and enduring the cross for our salvation, Jesus accepted His Father's will and persevered until the very end. Jesus can teach us how to do the Father's will. All we have to do is ask. He does not turn away those who sincerely seek His help.

We don't always know God's will. How do you know that you are doing God's will? We can only hope that we are through prayers, steadfast faith, spiritual guidance, discernment of the Spirit, and putting forth our best effort. We should examine our motives in doing His will by questioning ourselves: Am I doing this for my benefit or for God's?

Submitting to God's will may not be easy at times, but as the apostle Paul stated, *"Do not be conformed to this world, but be transformed by the renewing of your minds, so that you may discern what is the will of God—what is good and acceptable and perfect"* (Romans 12:2). Therefore, let us pray to make a resolution to submit to God's will in our daily life and in a manner pleasing to Him as we call to the Son: "Jesus, we need Your help!"

Action/Thought for Today: How do you know that you are doing God's will?

Prayer: Lord Jesus, show me the way. Tell me what You want me to do. Hold my hand every step of the way and help me do Your will. In Your name I pray. Amen!

EXTEND HOSPITALITY TO ALL!

The angel of the Lord appeared to Joseph in a dream and said, "Rise, take the child and his mother, flee to Egypt, and stay there until I tell you. Herod is going to search for the child to destroy him." Joseph rose and took the child and his mother by night and departed for Egypt. Matthew 2:13-14, NABRE

Joseph had to flee to Egypt with Mary and Jesus to protect Jesus from being killed by Herod. Imagine that you were an Egyptian not knowing the holy family's story, and they were seeking refuge in your land. Would you look down on them because they were foreigners? Would you judge them, thinking that they had come to exploit your land? Or would you welcome them into your life and show them hospitality?

The book of Hebrews teaches us, *"Let mutual love continue. Do not neglect to show hospitality to strangers, for by doing that some have entertained angels without knowing it"* (Hebrews 13:1-2). Hospitality is welcoming others to your life, sharing their burdens, listening to their stories, and giving them a helping hand. It is also opening your doors to others, sharing a meal, and giving and receiving love without counting the price. When we offer our services and resources to others, we are using the gifts that God has entrusted to us. God has given us many gifts, not for ourselves, but to build up each other. Let us accept, welcome, and serve Jesus in others, especially those in need.

Action/Thought for Today: How will you show hospitality to others? Will you use your God-given gifts to lift others up?

Prayer: Lord Jesus, help me not to neglect hospitality to strangers. I offer You myself and all the gifts You have given me. Use them all for Your greater glory. In Your name I pray. Amen!

THE FULLNESS OF HIS GRACE!

From his fullness we have all received, grace upon grace. The law indeed was given through Moses; grace and truth came through Jesus Christ. John 1:16-17

What a year! Has it been challenging? Was it a successful year? For many, the world is upside down, and so much has been stripped away, lives lost, social isolation, loss of employment, life's uncertainties, social and political disharmony, etc. For some, it may have been a year of tranquility, reflection, and setting priorities in order. Regardless of our situation, we are always hoping for a better year.

Despite the trials and tribulations, God has poured His grace on us. His grace is an unmerited favor and blessing that we have received because of God's mercy, love, and kindness. We can agree that it is the fullness of Jesus' grace that helped us through life.

We wake up every morning because of God's grace. We continue with our daily lives because of our hope in the Lord. As the apostle Paul stated, God's grace is sufficient for us, and His power is made perfect in our weakness (see 2 Corinthians 12:9). Indeed, nothing is impossible with God's grace. As we close this year, let us raise our hearts and minds to Heaven, thank God for His grace and mercy, and renew ourselves in the Lord.

Action/Thought for Today: Do we deserve God's grace? Think of a moment of grace you experienced this year and thank God for it.

Prayer: Lord Jesus, thank You for Your grace. When life is difficult, please help us to remember that Your grace is sufficient for us. In Your name we pray. Amen!

AMEN, AND AMEN!

"Blessed be the LORD, the God of Israel, from everlasting to everlasting." Then all the people said "Amen!" and praised the LORD.
1 Chronicles 16:36

The word amen is widely used by many religions. We so routinely say "amen" that we may not take the time to savor its true meaning. At every mass, worship service, prayer meeting, and at the end of our prayers, we exclaim, "Amen!" This is also the last word in the Bible: *"The grace of the Lord Jesus be with all the saints. Amen"* (Revelation 22:21). But the meaning of *amen* is so profound in that it implies more than a closing statement.

What does *amen* mean? *Amen* in Hebrews means "So be it, or truly, or verily." In other words, it is used "to confirm, support, or uphold." Jesus used this *amen* word many times in His teachings (*"Amen, Amen, I say to you…"*) to emphasize His messages. *Amen* implies that we can trust in God's words and promises, and our lives depend on them. It affirms that we accept the truth of the Gospel and plan to live it out day by day.

Now, as you attend church services, mass, or during your prayer times, pay attention to the power of these four little letters: AMEN! Let your *amen* be a word of hope and belief amid trials, tribulations, and life's uncertainties. Let your *amen* be a word of acknowledgment and acceptance of God's grace, love, and mercy. May *amen* have a more profound meaning to you as you express this powerful word of trust in the Lord.

Action/Thought for Today: What does *amen* mean to you?

Prayer: Lord Jesus, thank You for giving us Your words to confirm Your love for us. In Your name we pray. AMEN!

ENDNOTES

1. https://www.azquotes.com/quote/1056831
2. *Catechism of the Catholic Church*, Second Edition. (Washington, D.C., United States Catholic Conference, Inc.:1994) pg. 613
3. http://www.websters1913.com/words/Faith
4. Fernandez-Carvajal, Francis, *Through Wind and Waves* (Strongsville, OH, Scepter Publishing: 2012) pg. 66
5. https://www.goodreads.com/quotes/353530-i-know-now-that-true-charity-consists-in-bearing-all
6. https://www.brainyquote.com/quotes/saint_augustine_384153#:~:text=Saint%20Augustine%20Quotes&text
7. Burt, Donald X., *Day By Day with Saint Augustine* (Collegeville, MN. Liturgical Press: 2006)
8. https://www.catholic365.com/article/2595/five-quotes-by-st-teresa-of-avila-on-prayer.html
9. https://www.houmatimes.com/opinion/godly-giants-shed-light-on-deeper-spiritual-life-2/
10. https://tamilovesvintage.com/2018/03/06/i-alone-cannot-change-the-world-but-i-can-cast-a-stone-across-the-water-to-create-many-ripples/
11. https://www.merriam-webster.com/dictionary/ambassador#:~:text=d%C8%AF(%C9%99)r-,1,an%20official%20representative%20or%20messenger
12. A saying I heard from my friend, Dr. Johanne Belizaire-Francois
13. *Catechism of the Catholic Church*, pg. 989
14. Kirby, Fr. Jeffrey, *Lord, Teach Us to Pray: A Guide to the Spiritual Life and Christian Discipleship* (Charlotte, NC. St. Benedict Press: 2014) p. 78
15. *La Fontaine Fables* (Paris, France. Garnier-Flammarion: 1966) p. 39
16. https://www.littlewithgreatlove.com/st-pio-pray-hope-and-dont-worry/
17. This reflection was inspired by my reading of *The Gaze of Mercy* by Raniero Cantalamessa (Frederick, MD, The Word Among Us Press: 2015)
18. Ibid
19. Ibid
20. For more on this story, see *The Gaze of Mercy* by Raniero Cantalamessa (Frederick, MD, The Word Among Us Press: 2015) pgs. 178-179
21. This reflection was inspired by my reading of *The Gaze of Mercy*

by Raniero Cantalamessa (Frederick, MD, The Word Among Us Press: 2015)

22. Ibid
23. https://www.oed.com/clutter
24. https://www.merriam-webster.com/dictionary/freedom
25. https://www.ewtn.com/catholicism/devotions/prayer-of-saint-teresa-of-avila-364
26. https://www.oed.com/vigilance"
27. https://www.merriam-webster.com/dictionary/courage
28. https://www.vocabulary.com/dictionary/pilgrimage
29. https://saginaw.org/a-helpful-prayer-before-and-during-your-pilgrimage
30. https://web.cs.dal.ca/~johnston/poetry/island.html
31. https://www.goodreads.com/quotes/48030-a-good-deed-is-never-lost-he-who-sows-courtesy
32. https://www.liturgies.net/saints/johneudes/readings.htm
33. https://www.pcusa.org/site_media/media/uploads/oga/pdf/prayers-of-ignatius-of-loyola.pdf

Author Contact Page

You may contact Rhode Jean-Aleger directly in the following ways:

Email: Jaxprayerclub@gmail.com

Website: www.Jaxprayerclub.com

Printed in the USA
CPSIA information can be obtained
at www.ICGtesting.com
LVHW012319240923
759175LV00015B/920